T0161141

"*Assuming Boycott* is **an essential contribution** to an ongoing, urgent conversation about how artists, writers, and thinkers have time and again created subtle, meaningful, powerful, and vibrant ways to engage the political sphere. This book is a valuable guide to cultural boycotts from South Africa to Palestine." —Walid Raad, artist, professor, Cooper Union

"The **brilliant writers and debaters** assembled here come at the issue from different angles, all from the central belief that art is never not political. In the end, they are less interested in arguing for or against tactics than they are in advocating an art of political thinking." —Holland Cotter, co-chief art critic, *The New York Times*

"The use of boycotts has long inspired passionate debate, not least in the arts. Should artists float above the unseemly stuff of politics, or should they leverage their work as a form of strategic protest? A recent spike in the use of boycotts, or withdrawal of one sort or another, makes these questions more pressing than ever. The essays assembled in this volume engage a broad spectrum of provocations and positions—drawn from the past and the present—offering us a window onto an **endlessly fascinating** subject." —Negar Azimi, writer and senior editor, *Bidoun* Magazine

"An **informative and clarifying** collection that helps us understand what we gain when we work together, in context." —Sarah Schulman, activist, professor, writer of *The Cosmopolitans*

"*Assuming Boycott* defiantly holds the best arguments regarding boycott. It shows that boycott is not only a form of sanctions but also an invitation to dialogue. This collection of essays offers a historical perspective with comparative case studies, making it **the ultimate resource** to help decide where to draw the ethical line." —Galit Eilat, writer and curator, co-curator of 31st São Paulo Biennial

"Without a trace of left-wing melancholy, the authors offer us **an essential guide** to the terrain of cultural politics today. With colleagues and comrades like these, one feels not only bolstered but downright emboldened." —Hal Foster, Townsend Martin Professor of Art and Archeology, Princeton; editor, *The Anti-Aesthetic: Essays on Postmodern Culture*

"Artistic resistance has seldom proven so socially useful, or as complicated. This **intellectually engaging** study targets the paradoxes, limitations, and media spectacle of organized cultural boycotts and state-sponsored censorship from South African apartheid in the 1980s, to present day Israel-Palestine, Cuba, the Gulf States, the United Kingdom, and the United States among other geopolitical zones of conflict." —Gregory Sholette, artist and author of *Delirium and Resistance: Activist Art and the Crisis of Capitalism*

Assuming Boycott

ASSUMING BOYCOTT

RESISTANCE, AGENCY, AND
CULTURAL PRODUCTION

Edited by
Kareem Estefan,
Carin Kuoni,
and Laura Raicovich

OR Books
New York · London

© 2017 Kareem Estefan, Carin Kuoni, and Laura Raicovich

Published for the book trade by OR Books in partnership with Counterpoint Press. Distributed to the trade by Publishers Group West.

All rights information: rights@orbooks.com

All rights reserved. No part of this book may be reproduced or transmitted in any form or by any means, electronic or mechanical, including photocopy, recording, or any information storage retrieval system, without permission in writing from the publisher, except brief passages for review purposes.

First printing 2017

Cataloging-in-Publication data is available from the Library of Congress. A catalog record for this book is available from the British Library.

ISBN 978-1-944869-43-4 paperback
ISBN 978-1-944869-44-1 e-book

Text design by Under|Over. Typeset by AarkMany Media, Chennai, India.

10 9 8 7 6 5 4 3 2 1

TABLE OF CONTENTS

FOREWORD

Carin Kuoni and Laura Raicovich

Boycott is a tool of our time, a political and cultural strategy that
has rarely been more prominent than now. Examples abound of
contemporary artists holding institutions accountable for the ethical
standards enacted in them. By addressing labor issues in the United Arab
Emirates, the funding structures and political entanglements of biennials
from Sydney and Saint Petersburg to São Paulo and New York, and calls
to join a cultural boycott of Israel, artists are leveraging their power to
shift the ways culture is produced on individual, civic, institutional,
and educational levels. Indeed, art institutions and universities, cities,
and entire countries have been affected by positions that pose as
"withdrawal" or "disengagement" and in fact often result in various
actions and pointed engagement around specific ethical questions.

  In our roles as cultural producers, we recognized implementation
of boycott as a distinctly political tactic, one that generated a parallel
uptick in calls for accountability in artistic endeavors. In 2014 we began
planning a series of seminars and programs at the Vera List Center
for Art and Politics at The New School to engage students, artists,
thinkers, and general audiences in a deep consideration of the multiple

trajectories of these particular contemporary conditions in which we are all implicated. Presented under the Vera List Center's curatorial focus theme Alignment, the resulting seminars and the many conversations that they spurred, as well as the culminating colloquium that took place in the spring of 2015, revealed an extensive world of ideas we felt required a publication. Fortunately, the publisher of this volume, OR Books, agreed.

This book is the result of an ongoing effort to contend with the meanings of boycott and withdrawal as significant cultural practices of our time. It focuses on key texts developed during specific campaigns as well as essays retrospectively reflecting on and synthesizing the often heated debates that accompanied particular acts of boycotts or refusal. In so doing, we hope this book not only reveals in-the-moment realities, but also tracks shifts in language and implementation of principles over the course of debate and dialogue. Above all, this gathering of texts seeks to explore how strategies, alliances, lead actors, and guidelines have responded and adapted to a changing cultural, political, and economic environment.

The seminars, and now this publication, center on the notion that cultural production opens avenues for new ways of thinking. How productive or conducive can the methods of withdrawal and boycott be for politically oriented artistic practices? What are the conditions under which decisions on forms of engagement are made? How does distance, physical, experiential, or intellectual, impact artists' engagement or disengagement? How effective are these strategies and what are the long-term impacts? What are the significant historical referents for this kind of work? What is the relationship between boycott, censorship, self-censorship, and freedom of expression? And how do these practices shape an entire field, regardless of whether one endorses a boycott or not?

To address these inquiries, the essays are grouped in four interconnected sections: an exploration of the cultural boycott of South

Africa during the apartheid regime; a deep dive into the call for a
cultural and academic boycott of Israel from Palestinian civil society;
multiple discussions of who speaks (for whom) and who is silenced in
the debates and campaigns surrounding contemporary boycotts; and
finally, an assessment of the meanings and realities of engagement and
disengagement from afar in a period of proliferating biennials and global
cultural events. The texts have grown out of papers and discussions
delivered at the seminars and the colloquium, augmented by key texts
reprinted for their special relevance to these topics. The authors, who
are artists, scholars, curators, and activists, each consider the ways in
which withdrawal and boycott have impacted the conditions for engaged
discourse and/or art making. Taken together, the essays shed light on
boycotts as cultural work and unpack their motivations (why a boycott),
practices (how a boycott), and consequences (what effects does a boycott
create).

    We both operate from a deep commitment to the expanded
role culture and art can and must play in imagining a more just world,
particularly in light of recent developments in the U.S. Questions of
the agency of artists in social and political spheres, and how culture can
enact change through a politics of (dis)engagement are central at both
the Vera List Center and the Queens Museum. We hope that in the
drive to make meaning in our times, we are able to open ourselves both
individually and collectively to imagine wholly different power structures
that center on equity and care. This book represents one element of these
efforts, complemented by ongoing programs, exhibitions, and educational
initiatives at the Vera List Center and the Queens Museum.

    Such an endeavor is not accomplished without the significant
contributions of many. The authors of the essays featured in this anthology
have shown extraordinary brilliance and dedication to making a book
that truly contributes to urgent contemporary discourse. We are grateful

to all of them, our wise and compassionate companions and guides: Nasser Abourahme, Haig Aivazian, Ariella Azoulay, Tania Bruguera, Noura Erakat, Mariam Ghani, Nathan Gray, Chelsea Haines, Sean Jacobs, Yazan Khalili, Hlonipha Mokoena, Svetlana Mintcheva, Naeem Mohaiemen, Ahmed Öğüt, John Peffer, Joshua Simon, Ann Stoler, Radhika Subramaniam, Eyal Weizman, and Frank Wilderson.

Kareem Estefan, our collaborating editor, deserves enormous thanks and kudos for his intelligence, research, and diligence in editing this book. Truly, we could not have assembled such an ambitious project without his dedication and it is evident in every page of the book. Kareem joins us in thanking for their invaluable advice Omar Berrada, Marisa Mazria Katz, Sina Najafi, Molly Oringer, Georgia Phillips-Amos, Walid Raad, and Nitin Sawhney.

The entire team of the Vera List Center has contributed to the book their expertise and rare dedication: Zoe Carey, editorial assistant; Emily Donnelly, manager of programs and administration; Amanda Parmer, curatorial assistant since 2016 and, before her, Johanna Taylor, programs associate. The work of the center is sustained and nurtured by the Vera List Center Advisory Committee, and Carin would like to acknowledge the committee's unfailing support and encouragement and the leadership of its chair, James-Keith Brown. She would also like to single out Mary Watson, executive dean, The Schools of Public Engagement at The New School.

In OR Books, we've found the dynamic publisher and political context this book demands. We're grateful to publishers Colin Robinson and John Oakes, and thank John in particular for his astute editorial guidance.

INTRODUCTION: BOYCOTTS AS OPENINGS

Kareem Estefan

The figure of the artist, once praised as a solitary genius endowed with the privilege of aesthetic autonomy, has been assigned and reassigned a series of protean roles in the decades since the decline of high modernism. In a perennial riff on Walter Benjamin's politicized conception of the "author as producer," contemporary art discourse has posited the artist as ethnographer, as activist, archivist, historian, witness, critic, educator, and organizer. Such a list could be extended further, but the common thread is clear enough: today all but the most blue-chip contemporary artists are lauded, and critiqued, largely on the basis of their social research and political engagement. At the same time, politically engaged artists are already challenging the role of self-consciously political art at a moment when institutional critique, as the artist Andrea Fraser put it, has become an institution of its own.[1]

In an incisive essay titled "Good Intentions," the art critic and *Bidoun* senior editor Negar Azimi asks, "What is the difference between representing politics and actually enacting it?...And what is the good of engaged art—whether it takes the form of governmental critique or institutional critique or otherwise—when it is subsumed back into the system?"[2] Azimi's text, published too early in 2011 to reflect that year's radical political upheavals, now reads less as a critique than a premonition. A rising wave of artists are today ensuring that their activism exceeds the bounds of their artistic production by disrupting the system—the funding structures and institutional frameworks—that both facilitates and circumscribes its circulation.

In the past several years, there has been a remarkable surge in protest actions—especially boycotts—targeting art institutions and events that receive corporate or government support tied to politics that exhibiting artists find objectionable.[3] This has been a particularly visible development at biennials, at least four of which faced boycotts in the year 2014 alone: the 19th Sydney Biennale, because of its financial ties to notorious migrant detention centers off the coast of Australia; the 10th Gwangju Biennale, after an exhibiting artist's painting was pulled from the show due to political pressure; the 31st São Paulo Biennial, which received funding from the Israeli Consulate in violation of an ongoing cultural boycott of the state; and Manifesta 10, hosted at a Russian state institution in St. Petersburg shortly after Vladimir Putin's anti-LGBTQ laws and aggression against Ukraine made global headlines.[4] But the trend has not been limited to one-off global events. In 2011 the Gulf Labor Coalition—a group of artists that had been privately negotiating with the Guggenheim Museum to improve labor conditions for the workers that would build its new branch in Abu Dhabi—went public with a list of demands and announced a boycott, collectively refusing to have their artworks collected for the Emirati institution until such conditions were met. That same year, which saw uprisings spread from Tunisia and Egypt to Spain, the United States, and many other countries, also witnessed the emergence of Occupy Wall Street–affiliated collectives (such as Occupy Museums and Arts & Labor) that advocated on behalf of unpaid interns in the arts and exerted pressure on Sotheby's and the Frieze Art Fair for their use of non-unionized labor.[5]

In my view there are at least three reasons for the uptick in acts of protest, refusal, withdrawal, and boycott among artists. First, as suggested above, artists have been inspired by the revolutions and occupations of 2011, as well as the many social movements presently responding to enduring conditions of injustice and inequality, from #BlackLivesMatter to #NoDAPL.[6] Second, as arts institutions have increasingly embraced politically engaged art, the conflict between artists' social commitments and the often troubling financial ties and complicities of the institutions supporting them has at times become untenable. Fairly or not, an artist who makes video installations about climate change will face more public pressure than an abstract painter to ensure the museum exhibiting her work does not have climate-deniers like the Koch Brothers on its board, or rely on donations from BP or Exxon-Mobil. Third, the internet and particularly social media not only facilitate and publicize such pressure, but also connect distant localities imbricated in the same global networks of art and politics, making visible the commonality of struggles "here and elsewhere" and giving artists tools to raise awareness and organize campaigns transnationally.

These recent catalysts notwithstanding, it is important to note certain precedents for today's boycotts. The 1968 Venice Biennale, for example, was overwhelmed by anti-capitalist protests that forced its sales office to close.[7] In 1969 the São Paulo Biennial faced a boycott campaign that left the exhibition with substantially less art on display, and affected numerous São Paulo biennials to come, as artists around the world protested the relentless persecution of Brazilian artists under a U.S.-backed military dictatorship.[8] In the 1970s, as the Iranian Shah's repression of dissidents became more widely known, artists including

John Cage and Merce Cunningham boycotted the royal family's annual Shiraz Festival of the Arts.[9]

The most famous example of a cultural boycott undoubtedly remains the campaign waged against apartheid South Africa that acquired international prominence in the 1980s (though it was initiated decades prior). *Assuming Boycott* thus begins with a section on the legacy of this boycott movement, reassessing its aims, tactics, and implications for cultural production. It is essential to understand the history of the South African boycott for many reasons, but particularly, in our context, because of its direct relation to a present campaign: the Palestinian-led Boycott, Divestment, and Sanctions (BDS) movement against Israel, which takes the anti-apartheid movement as its model and, like it, includes a cultural and academic boycott.[10]

Initiated in 2005, BDS and in particular the cultural boycott of Israel—the subject of this volume's second section—represents the most sustained ongoing campaign examined here. The movement, which targets institutions that invest in or are supported by the State of Israel, and not Israeli individuals, calls for an end to the military occupation of Arab lands, full equality for Palestinian citizens of Israel, and the right of Palestinian refugees to return to their homes.[11] Because its demands entail not only an end to the fifty-year-old occupation, but a thoroughgoing transformation of Israel's demographic makeup and status as a "Jewish state," BDS has proved controversial not only among Israel's hardline supporters but also for some liberals critical of the occupation.[12] It has nonetheless become prominent in the cultural sphere through the support of scores of public intellectuals, including Judith Butler, Naomi Klein, Gayatri Spivak, and the late John Berger, as well as the votes of organizations such as the American Studies Association to boycott Israeli academic institutions.[13] And it has been hotly debated in the realm of the visual arts, where the idea that culture represents an

14

ideal space for dialogue beyond the dividing lines of politics is especially strong.[14]

Assuming Boycott takes a critical detour from the pro/con axis of debates surrounding cultural boycotts. The title of this anthology signals a new starting point; we begin with the assumption that art does not transcend the political conditions under which it is exhibited, and that artists are increasingly assuming the agency to demand that their art be shown and circulated in accordance with their ethics and solidarities. We recognize that boycotts are a condition of our time and that our work as cultural practitioners is affected by them regardless of whether or not we endorse a particular campaign. In this context, we wish to suggest that acts of boycott are often beginnings and not ends, that they frequently generate challenging and productive discussions rather than shutting down dialogue.

The capacity of arts boycotts to yield further and richer debate has been recognized, at times, even by those working for targeted institutions. Curator Joanna Warsza, who organized the public program for Manifesta 10 in St. Petersburg, personally supported a strategy of challenging Russian state policies as well as the biennial's host institution from within, but also defended the boycott, arguing, "Boycotts make institutions more sensitive, more vulnerable and more apt to change. And institutions should not suppress them but consider the claims. So I would consider the boycotts as a form of mobilization, not a form of quitting."[15] Likewise, the curatorial team for the 31st São Paulo Biennial, regardless of their individual positions on BDS, supported the exhibiting artists' right to demand that the biennial reject Israeli funds, writing in a collective statement that the boycott should serve as "a trigger to think about the funding sources of major cultural events."[16] While similar respect is typically granted to artists' freedom of speech by most curators and arts institutions targeted by boycott, the above two responses are uncommonly supportive of the premise that cultural boycotts give rise to important debates. More often than not, cultural institutions—from global mega-museums like the Guggenheim to advocacy organizations such as the National Coalition Against Censorship to socially engaged arts nonprofits like Creative Time—stand against cultural boycotts as limitations on expression—forms of censorship, even.[17]

The third section of *Assuming Boycott* therefore takes up questions of freedom of speech and (self-)censorship as they relate to cultural production and boycott. Do boycotts inhibit free expression and dialogue, or do they instead shift the terms of debate, setting new conditions for the relations among artists, institutions, and the publics impacted by their cultural production? When are boycotts techniques of censorship, and when are they essential tools for those who have not been politically or materially empowered to speak? Is it sufficient, or responsible, to defend the value of free speech, without critiquing various forms of social inequality that bestow prominent platforms for political expression upon some while systematically marginalizing others? Such questions spill into this volume's fourth and final section, which examines the dynamics of political (dis)engagement as it unfolds at a distance. As much as campaigns that see citizens of the United States and Europe advocating for the rights of imprisoned asylum seekers or exploited construction workers across the world are celebrated as evidence of transnational solidarity, participating activists face charges that they should stay out of complex local situations they don't understand, refrain from enforcing their values on different cultures, and attend to political problems in their own countries. Here, the question—at a global scale—remains, who speaks (for whom)? And who is silenced?

The contributors to this anthology do not find consensus regarding the value of (dis)engagement from afar, or the ways in which boycotts may curtail, foster, or redirect expression. Several of them have been directly involved in organizing withdrawals from biennials or other cultural events (locally or at a distance), but many have also applied political pressure by other means, rejecting the tactic of boycott. Some dispute the notion that a boycott represents total disengagement, pointing to the proliferation of high-stakes conversations engendered by a threat of (publicized) withdrawal from a prominent event. Others argue, however, that boycotts foreclose more nuanced conversations and relinquish the mediating role of art as a bridge, sacrificing the possibility of critically intervening in situations of injustice with the aim of changing minds.

Cultural boycotts remain unpalatable in part because art is seen as intrinsically aligned with liberal tenets including freedom of expression, cross-cultural dialogue, and social uplift through education.[18] Artists who undertake boycotts can harness this assumption by revealing the gap between the politics of their own work and the politics of its exhibition and circulation, thereby using the progressive rhetoric of art institutions as leverage to enact political change. But they may also wish to bypass such institutions entirely, as the artist Ahmet Öğüt suggests by asking, "Are biennials still pedagogic sites with transformative aims that can have a lasting effect on civil society? Or are they part of the neoliberal capitalist idea of 'festivalism,' which is more concerned with scale, budget, number of visitors, and branding?"[19] If artists increasingly decide to forgo global biennials, they may consider boycotts a starting point for cultivating more ethical institutions. As Eyal Weizman suggests in this volume, referring to BDS, boycotts can be "part of a wider spectrum of political actions that *block* non-democratic and unequal platforms and *open* democratic platforms for co-resistance." This hopeful proposition captures the spirit of the diverse contributions to *Assuming Boycott*, a series of critical inquiries that consider the ways cultural boycotts move beyond disengagement or withdrawal to posit imaginative forms of engagement and solidarity, and open new avenues for effecting change at the evolving conjuncture of art and politics.

THE CULTURAL BOYCOTT OF APARTHEID SOUTH AFRICA

In historical assessments of the most effective boycotts, the international movement to boycott, divest from, and place sanctions on apartheid South Africa is typically given pride of place, with only the Montgomery bus boycott held in comparably high regard for its pivotal role in sparking the U.S. civil rights movement. But as with so many historical processes and figures that were once controversial and are today almost universally hailed, the legacy of the anti-apartheid boycott often appears as little more than an image of victory. Just as Nelson Mandela, upon his death, was distilled into an icon stamped with the words "justice" and "reconciliation"—as if he had never been branded a terrorist by the Reaganite Right or critiqued as insufficiently revolutionary by elements of the Left—there is a danger that the boycott of South Africa may become historically sealed, remembered only as a foregone conclusion. The essays included in this section critically examine the cultural boycott in particular, and in relation to the broader anti-apartheid movement, revisiting some of the central dilemmas that artists faced as they navigated their roles as cultural producers as well as activists dedicated to bringing about the end of apartheid.

In his essay on the legacy of the cultural boycott, the scholar and Africa Is a Country *founder Sean Jacobs traces a history of international solidarity* that began in the 1940s and '50s, when select American and British unions representing theater artists and musicians encouraged their members not to perform in South Africa, and reached a peak with the "Sun City" campaign launched by prominent American musicians in 1985. Jacobs highlights several successes as well as limitations of the cultural boycott. He credits it for isolating South Africa and compelling its white citizens to confront their illusory cosmopolitan self-image, and further notes how media coverage of boycott violations "provided prominent forums for opponents of the apartheid regime to articulate their struggle, where they may have experienced media blackouts before." At the same time, he underscores the problems of applying a boycott to as unwieldy a target as culture, arguing that the sports boycott was most effective because its target was precise and nationally significant. Despite the cultural boycott's defects, however, Jacobs claims that it "cemented the idea of culture as an agent of politics, and not just a reflection of politics," thereby paving the way for the cultural boycott of Israel and other solidarity actions undertaken by artists in the present.

Drawing from his book Art and the End of Apartheid, the art historian John Peffer addresses the distinct ways that politically engaged South African artists conceived of the role of art at a time of escalating struggle. He distinguishes between two approaches: the "committed art" of the Medu Ensemble, with its direct, social realist aesthetics, and the more abstract, experimental spirit embodied by the Thupelo workshops. While Medu articulated a militant belief that art must be a weapon in the fight against apartheid, the Thupelo group cultivated a unique environment in which artistic expression was central to "the making of a new community that was opposed to the racially separatist, culturally isolating, and developmentally demeaning status quo." However, both approaches garnered at least tacit approval from the ANC leadership, despite Thupelo's international ties, which likely violated the terms of the cultural boycott. And despite the two groups' evident differences, Peffer presents their visions as complementary, in that both believed "creative communities were a means to seek a culture of the future, a future beyond authoritarian racialism."

In her essay on popular music in South Africa, the anthropologist Hlonipha Mokoena similarly observes that confusion about who and what to boycott was widespread throughout the struggle against apartheid. Often, too, the cultural boycott backfired against black South African musicians subject to international isolation and domestic censorship. However, Mokoena argues, these conditions also led to the development of a robust local music scene. Mokoena focuses on the career of Brenda Fassie, a "bubblegum" singer who rose to fame from a Cape Town township, becoming the rare black musician popular among black and white South African audiences alike. Interestingly, due to the far-reaching censorship within South Africa, Fassie remained ignorant of the cultural boycott until she teamed up with Harry Belafonte to record an album rebuking Paul Simon's Graceland (the most notorious violation of the boycott). In this context, Mokoena stresses that "the cultural boycott was an ambiguous tool of struggle, especially from a local South African perspective," but also credits it as the seed for a wide range of countercultural forms that would come to define post-apartheid popular music.

Offering a trenchant perspective on the tense political realities and debates of the final years of apartheid, the writer and film scholar Frank B. Wilderson III presents an excerpt from Incognegro: A Memoir of Exile and Apartheid, his lyrical, penetrating account of the years he spent in Johannesburg as a professor by day and militant ANC activist by night (as well as his subsequent return to the quieter racism of his native United States). In this passage, Wilderson and a South African law student named Khanya, who would later become his wife, find themselves in a potentially lethal face-off with two gangsters displeased by this outspoken woman's incisive appraisals of strikes and boycotts, and her partner's provocative criticism of Nelson Mandela and the ANC's accommodationist elements. Wilderson mobilizes his teaching of Frantz Fanon to argue that Mandela will only clear the way for neoliberal *multiculturalism to replace the authoritarian racism of the apartheid state, angering his interlocutors but winning their attention and forcing them to contemplate the prospect of a facially tolerant, "laissez-faire White supremacy" to come.*

Varied in their form, focus, and conclusions, these texts are joined by their close engagement with and critical reevaluation of the cultural elements of the anti-apartheid struggle as it unfolded. Far from merely celebrating the achievements of the boycott movement, they revitalize urgent debates of the time and pose pressing questions about the boycott's legacy, ensuring that theories and tactics of cultural production and distribution developed during the apartheid era can inform present artistic actions against injustice wherever it exists in the world.

THE LEGACY OF THE CULTURAL BOYCOTT AGAINST SOUTH AFRICA[1]

Sean Jacobs

South African apartheid became an international issue for the first time when the interim Indian government in 1946 requested that the inaugural session of the United Nations General Assembly include discrimination against Indians in South Africa on its agenda.[2] Six years later, in 1952, the UN General Assembly declared that "a policy of 'racial segregation' (apartheid) is necessarily based on doctrines of racial discrimination."[3] Then in 1963, the UN Security Council called on member states to halt the sale and shipment of arms, ammunition, and military vehicles to South Africa.[4] The exiled African National Congress (ANC), which dominated resistance politics outside South Africa from 1960 to 1990, spearheaded this boycott strategy against South Africa, initially focusing on economic and military sanctions.[5] Gradually, the resistance movements became convinced of the power of culture as a "terrain of struggle." For example, the ANC started its own choir, founded a radio station, and worked with South African musicians like Hugh Masekela, Miriam Makeba, and Abdullah Ibrahim to raise awareness of South Africa and build mass solidarity for its struggle back home.[6] As literary scholar Rob Nixon notes, "The historic attempts to vindicate apartheid by way of cultural argument made [culture] a symbolically crucial sphere for disruption."[7]

Cultural boycotts have a long history as a solidarity tactic of South Africa's liberation struggle (especially in the United Kingdom and United States), dating back to the beginning of the 1960s and paralleling, as well as complementing, economic and military sanctions. Nixon traces the first public resolution in support of the cultural boycott to 1946, when the Actors' Equity Association, an American labor union representing theater artists, discouraged its members from performing in South Africa. In 1954, Trevor Huddleston, an English priest close to the ANC, made an appeal for "a cultural boycott of South Africa" in a leading British newspaper.[8] A few years later, in 1956 and 1957 respectively, Equity (the British Actors' Union) and the British Musicians' Union banned its members from performing in South Africa. Then in 1963, dozens of British playwrights followed their actor counterparts and signed a declaration that prevented agents from touring their shows to theaters "where discrimination is made among audiences on grounds of colour." British filmmakers joined the declaration in 1964. That same year, Irish filmmakers (encouraged by the Irish Anti-Apartheid Movement) followed suit, as did the British Screenwriters Guild in 1965. Over the next decade and a half, a range of British television and film unions added their voices to a boycott call.

Meanwhile, in the United States in 1965, more than sixty artists and musicians, including a number of leading stars, signed a declaration sponsored by the American Committee on Africa barring them from performing in apartheid South Africa.[9] By the mid to late 1970s, anti-apartheid protests forced the closure of South African performances, such as the popular musical *Ipi Ntombi*, in New York City. Later, in 1981, the largest federation of performing artists' unions, the Associated

Actors and Artistes of America, decided its nearly 250,000 members could not perform in South Africa.[10]

But a number of prominent American and British entertainers, including black American musicians and actors, still traveled to South Africa, sometimes even performing for segregated audiences. Many artists defied declarations from their trade unions, which could not effectively enforce resolutions. Compounding this predicament, the South African government and its allies in the local entertainment industry offered inducements that these artists, some of whose careers were in decline at the time, found hard to refuse. This continued well into the 1980s, when the cultural boycott had been mainstreamed in the West.

The cultural boycott against South Africa received an early boost, however, when in December 1968 the United Nations adopted a resolution "to suspend cultural, educational, sporting and other exchanges with the racist regime and with organizations or institutions in South Africa which practice apartheid."[11] The real turn came more than a decade later, in December 1980, when the UN General Assembly passed a tougher resolution urging member states to take direct steps to adopt the boycott. The vote was mostly supported by Third World countries, while the United States and Canada voted against the resolution, and Western European countries abstained. As a consequence, the UN Special Committee Against Apartheid began compiling names (a "blacklist") of performers and entertainers who had traveled to South Africa. The intention was to shame artists who defied the boycott, make them targets of protests, and even affect their bottom line. Initially, the blacklist had little public traction. Then in 1985, a group of prominent American musicians, including Bob Dylan, Bruce Springsteen, George Clinton, and Lou Reed, organized by guitarist Stevie van Zandt (of Bruce Springsteen's E Street Band), made a music video highlighting apartheid conditions in South Africa, "Sun City."[12] The song's title referenced the holiday and gambling resort in a South African Bantustan—one of many ersatz "independent homelands" set up to exclude blacks from desirable land, urban areas, and political representation—where most visiting artists, who broke the boycott, went to perform. In the wake of the song's release and popularity, the campaign appeared to discourage a number of artists from performing in South Africa.[13]

The cultural boycott was successful to the degree that it was largely because, by the late 1970s, there was widespread popular consensus about "the evil of apartheid," especially in the United States and Britain. The movements for economic and military sanctions against South Africa were already well established and the strategy to "isolate" South Africa had already succeeded in effecting an arms and oil embargo as well as a sports boycott.

Secondly, the boycott succeeded because white South Africans suffered culturally. For many white South Africans, the country was an outpost of "Western civilization" in Africa and their cultural universe was oriented toward the United States and Europe. Sanctions cut them off from those worlds. South Africa's pariah status as a racist, authoritarian state also clashed with the false view that white South Africans had of themselves as cosmopolitan and open-minded.

Thirdly, when official sanctions and industry-led boycott efforts dating back to the 1960s and 1970s failed to deter artists from traveling to South Africa, peer pressure or shaming served as a more effective form of community regulation among performers (especially American performers). Campaigns like "Sun City" were successful largely because performers were appealing directly and emotionally, in song, rather than a UN committee or a trade union making an explicitly political, and often formulaic, statement.

After the popularity of the campaign, when artists disregarded the boycott and traveled to South Africa, public showdowns between the artist and supporters of the boycott attracted widespread media attention. Paul Simon, most famously, faced public scrutiny even before he traveled to South Africa in 1986 to record his album *Graceland*. Such showdowns became major media events that often dominated the news cycle for days. In the process, they focused attention back on apartheid as a form of systematic oppression and provided prominent forums for opponents of the apartheid regime to articulate their struggle, where they may have experienced media blackouts before.

However, the boycott faced a number of obstacles and challenges. For one, the question over whether to maintain a "blanket boycott" or to selectively target artists who broke the boycott was never resolved. A related critique, leveled from the right and from liberals, both in Europe and South Africa, revolved around whether a political institution—the UN—and a political movement—the ANC, which created a "cultural desk" for this purpose—should have the right to police the behavior of artists. Some South African artists with close ties to the ANC also objected to either the UN or the ANC (which was then operating at a distance outside South Africa) deciding where and with whom they could perform, countering that art should be produced "for art's sake" and not subjected to political interference.[14] Other local artists who openly opposed apartheid, and suffered for it, also took exception to the boycott because it negatively impacted their long-term career prospects, as artists who were in their prime then and whose visibility and potential revenue streams were limited to South Africa because of the boycott.[15] As Nixon notes, "It often proved difficult to back the ban's symbolic importance with strategic precision, not least because it was the most exacting boycott to define, monitor and coordinate." Nixon continues:

> Culture is pervasive, ordinary and conflictual;
> this makes it an exasperatingly baggy and diffuse

political target. Even if one considers culture in
the limited sense of the arts, each artistic medium
has distinctive forms of creation, distribution, and
reception which from the boycotters' standpoint,
demand discrete strategies in response.[16]

Second, while artists were barred from traveling to South Africa, their
music—and the same was true of books and some television programs—
was still available in South Africa. Record companies continued to
operate there, sometimes through local subsidiaries, or the music of
affected artists continued to be distributed there by other means.

In addition, there was the well-funded lobbying and propaganda
of the South African state and its business allies, which undermined the
boycott. Their tactics included luring prominent entertainers to South
Africa despite the threat of shaming or isolation of artists who broke the
boycott (which often turned out to be brief). For example, the American
singer Linda Ronstadt was paid $500,000 when she traveled to Sun City
in 1983, to play only six concerts, and Frank Sinatra "earned a reported
$1.5 to $2 million for a brief visit in 1981."[17]

The boycott has a complicated legacy, especially in terms of how
it affected South African music. This is most obvious in the case of
Paul Simon's *Graceland* album. Even though Simon broke the boycott,
and despite what we make of him—he comes across as naïve and
priggish[18]—the South African artists who worked with him received
a considerable boost in international visibility, and so did popular
attitudes against apartheid. That said, the career-ending effects of
the boycott were probably more profoundly felt among South African
athletes, who had no chance at an international career if they remained
in South Africa, or whose careers ended abruptly after they broke the
boycott.

In terms of the long-term results of the boycott, probably its most far-reaching legacy is the widely accepted idea that culture and politics *are* interconnected. Furthermore, the cultural boycott emphasized that, rather than merely responding to political situations, culture could be politics. In other words, it cemented the idea of culture as an agent of politics, and not just a reflection of politics.[19]

Second, the cultural boycott contributed to the moral isolation of apartheid and, more directly, exposed the systematic workings of apartheid to a popular audience, beyond the racist violence that surfaced in the news now and then. For example, the "Sun City" song had a tremendous impact in raising awareness of the apartheid regime's Bantustan or "homeland" policy among young people in Reagan's America.

Finally, and crucially, the Palestinian-led Boycott, Divestment, and Sanctions movement (BDS), which includes a cultural and academic boycott, is another obvious legacy of the South African cultural boycott. BDS leaders and their allies have emphasized these connections in publicity materials and campaigns.[20] For example, Desmond Tutu, a leading ally of BDS, in 2010 used this logic when discouraging the Cape Town Opera from performing in Israel: "Just as we said during apartheid that it was inappropriate for international artists to perform in South Africa in a society founded on discriminatory laws and racial exclusivity, so it would be wrong for Cape Town Opera to perform in Israel."[21] Similarly, more than one hundred artists based in the United Kingdom, including Roger Waters and John Berger, explicitly connected BDS to the South African cultural boycott when they announced their intention to boycott Israel in a 2015 letter sent to *The Guardian*:

> During South African apartheid, musicians announced they weren't going to "play Sun City." Now we are saying, in Tel Aviv, Netanya, Ashkelon, or Ariel, we

> won't play music, accept awards, attend exhibitions,
> festivals, or conferences, run masterclasses or
> workshops, until Israel respects international law and
> ends its colonial oppression of the Palestinians.[22]

As the success—or possible shortcomings—of cultural boycotts continue to be debated, the South African case points to another form of boycott and its impact on political attitudes and reform. Possibly more decisive than economic, military, and cultural sanctions, which apartheid regularly bypassed, was in fact the sports boycott.

Apart from "the narrow focus and strategic clarity"[23] enjoyed by sports protesters, one reason that sports boycotts seem to work particularly well—when international diplomacy and common sense have failed—is the perceived gravity of the threat of withdrawing a rogue nation from the community of sport.[24] The Israeli government and sports associations' indignant responses to recent threats of Israeli expulsion from the European (UEFA) and worldwide (FIFA) associations that govern soccer, for example, are particularly instructive. People have strong feelings about sports, which are, of course, closely tied to national achievement and nationalism. Furthermore, the causes and effects of sports sanctions may be more palpable than those related to economic sanctions; for many citizens, being denied access to certain commodities is less painful than being excluded from the international community of sports. Up to now BDS has paid less attention to a sports boycott, so it remains hard to gauge what the effects of a sports boycott would be. The South African experience, however, has shown that sports boycotts can be very powerful tools for international solidarity groups, and if BDS is to learn from its antecedent in the anti-apartheid movement, it would do well to place more emphasis on the arenas—the soccer stadiums—where apartheid came into global focus decades ago.

ART, RESISTANCE, AND COMMUNITY IN 1980S SOUTH AFRICA[1]

John Peffer

During the 1950s and 1960s, while the rest of Africa was gaining independence from European colonialism and the civil rights movement was gaining ground in the United States, South Africa was subject to the entrenchment of apartheid laws. During the first decade of National Party rule, successive legislative acts classified the population according to race, forbade interracial sexual relations, mandated separate facilities for citizens according to color (including music halls and exhibition spaces), created a separate and inferior "Bantu Education" system for black students, forced all non-white adults to carry a *dompas* (pass book) that itemized their employment history and their movements, and made opposition politics punishable as "communist" treason. Mixed-race urban areas such as Sophiatown, Johannesburg's famed hotbed of progressive art and jazz, were declared "whites only," bulldozed, and its residents further segregated into what would become Soweto. Black opposition parties were banned and their leaders were either imprisoned or fled into exile. In response, Father Trevor Huddleston, a leading philanthropic figure

in Sophiatown, and a patron of black artists, initiated the cultural
boycott against South Africa that would later be adopted, in 1969,
as United Nations Resolution 2396, whose Article 12 *"Requests* all
States and organizations to suspend cultural, educational, sporting
and other exchanges with the racist régime and with organizations
or institutions in South Africa which practice *apartheid*."[2] The
boycott was promoted by leaders in exile of the banned African
National Congress (ANC), and was only fully rescinded as South
Africa prepared for its first democratic elections in 1994.[3]

In the following excerpts, adapted from my book *Art and
the End of Apartheid*, I discuss two approaches to the culture
question within the anti-apartheid movement of the 1980s, a
period of particular intensification of the struggle for democracy
in South Africa. They are the "committed art" approach advocated
by activists in exile in Botswana, and the community-building
approach practiced by a small group mostly based in Johannesburg
that experimented with abstract painting. Though appearing at first
to be in opposition, the two groups were in fact closely linked, in
terms of specific personalities and in terms of an understanding that
creative communities were a means to seek a culture of the future, a
future beyond authoritarian racialism. The Medu Art Ensemble in
Gaborone, Botswana was composed of mostly South African activists
and artists in exile who were working closely with the ANC. From
their position just over the border from South Africa they produced
posters and various communiqués that were smuggled back into the
country. Medu was a clearinghouse and a leading advocate for the
concept that art should be used as a "weapon" of the anti-apartheid
struggle, and especially forcefully so in the directness of its imagery.
Medu was not itself subject to the boycott. It was not located within
South Africa, but also its membership included those who both

stridently promoted the boycott and were in a position to decide who should be given a pass, at least by the ANC. Medu is important because it served as a role model for those within South Africa, and it inspired (and enflamed) debates on what should constitute a "relevant" culture within South Africa during the 1980s. On the other hand there was Thupelo, a "group" we should call them, though "Thupelo" itself was the name of a series of art workshops in Johannesburg, linked loosely to an international artist workshop in New York called Triangle, that were attended by roughly the same cohort of South African artists over several years. While developing a creative (and nonracial) community with international aspirations against the grain of the apartheid ideology—something the Medu group also strove for—Thupelo also experimented with forms of nonfigurative abstract painting that the "committed art" advocates found deeply unsettling. At the height of the anti-apartheid struggle and at a time when the cultural boycott was one of its strident weapons, Thupelo invited international guest artists each year whose work, at least its abstract appearance, seemed to be the farthest thing from "committed art."

I. Art Versus the Total Strategy

In the wake of the 1976 Soweto student uprising, and the subsequent rise to national power of former minister of defense P. W. Botha as prime minister after 1979, the South African government devised what it called the "total strategy." This was a counterinsurgency plan designed to push back the rise of Black Power, using military, psychological, political, and economic means. The Botha government's strategy was meant to combat what they perceived was a Communist-backed total onslaught on a mixed terrain. This idea was based on the exaggerated fear that South Africa was a central concern of the Russians and the Americans in

their Cold War conflicts and proxy wars in Africa. According to South
African historian Gavin Cawthra, the total strategy included aspects
of both reform and repression, in line with American political scientist
Samuel Huntington's theory on how to rout a popular revolution.[4] A slow
and partial repeal of petty apartheid laws (those related to segregation
in public spaces) was enacted, black trade unions were tolerated, and
a new tricameral parliament was created that offered limited national
representation for "Coloured" and "Indian" populations, but not for black
South Africans. These partial efforts at reform resulted, in 1983, in a
revitalization of the popular insurgency that had begun in 1976 after
the student uprising in Soweto, but had lost much of its momentum by
the end of the decade. The resurgence of protest actions and political
violence in the early 1980s was followed by police crackdowns, increased
censorship, and the declaration of a State of Emergency in 1985 that was
renewed each year until the end of the decade. Also in 1983 the United
Democratic Front (UDF), an alliance of progressive and grassroots
organizations, was formed to counter the state's repressive tactics and
to demand total eradication of the apartheid system. UDF affiliates
broadly supported the aims of nonracialism and democracy outlined
in the Freedom Charter, and their activities were loosely coordinated
with those of the African National Congress leadership in exile.[5] As
part of the lead-up to the creation of the United Democratic Front,
the Medu Art Ensemble organized an art festival in 1982 to promote
a culture of "commitment" toward a future democratic South Africa.

The Medu Art Ensemble was a multiracial collective of visual
artists, writers, and performers formed in 1978 in Gaborone, Botswana.
Medu was made up of mostly South African artists and activists
living in exile, and included several participants from Botswana as
well as European and American expatriates. Contributors to Medu
publications and projects over the next seven years included Mongane

Serote, Thamsanqa Mnyele, Mike Hamlyn, Albio and Theresa Gonzales, Patrick Fitzgerald, Gordon Metz, American poet and artist Judy Seidman, James Matthews, Tim Williams, Bachana Mokoena, Marius Schoon, Mafika Gwala, Kenyan writer Ngugi wa Thiong'o, Keorapetse Kgositsile, Mandla Langa, Miles Pelo, Heinz Klug, Muff Anderson, James van Wyk, Mike Kahn, and others.[6] Medu members shared a common determination to fight apartheid using the tools of culture. They established links with progressive cultural organizations and magazines within South Africa, such as the Junction Avenue Theatre Company and *Staffrider* magazine in Johannesburg, and the Community Arts Project in Cape Town.[7]

Medu Art Ensemble comrades, especially Mnyele and Serote, argued for a "peoples' culture." For them a true culture of the people would be one that was not exclusive to the elite world of art galleries, but was seen in the streets, on t-shirts and posters, and in political songs and poems performed at political rallies. Medu was a think tank for cultural revolution. Its mission was to debate and develop ways to use art that would give voice and vision to the growing popular struggle back home. Medu produced posters and a newsletter that were smuggled across the border, and were reproduced and disseminated inside South Africa to UDF-affiliated organizations. Their *MEDU Art Ensemble Newsletter* promoted the idea that South African art needed to be relevant to the anti-apartheid struggle if it was to be relevant at all. This was also the message of the event hosted by Medu during July 1982, titled "Culture and Resistance."

Several hundred South African visual artists, writers, musicians, and actors, many of them living in exile in Europe and America, attended the Culture and Resistance festival. They convened for a week of talks, art exhibitions, and performances. Many had never met before, though they may have previously known each other's work. Others were able to see old friends from across the country or from exile. For most of the festival's attendees, especially for black South Africans living under apartheid pass laws and urban areas restrictions, the opportunity to connect socially with other colleagues at this scale was a rare occasion. By most accounts it was an exhilarating week filled with intense discussion about how to steer the trajectory of culture in South Africa in a progressive direction. Each day there were papers on fine arts, film, photography, music, dance, writing, and theater. An accompanying exhibition titled "Art Towards Social Development" was held at the Botswana National Gallery and Museum. A range of visual artists' works were shown, including those by David Koloane (who also acted as co-organizer), Sydney Kumalo, Dumile Feni, David Mogano, Bongiwe Dhlomo, Peter Clarke, Keith Deitrich, Kim Berman, and Charles Sokhaya Nkosi, as well as a documentary photography section with Paul Weinberg, Cedric Nunn, Myron Peters, Lesley Lawson, Jimi Matthews, Ben Maclennan, Omar Badsha, Paul Alberts, Joe Alphers, Bee Berman, Paul Konings, and David Goldblatt.

The stated purpose of the festival was to examine and propose suggestions for the role of art in the pursuit of a future democratic South Africa. "Political struggle is an unavoidable part of life in South Africa, and it must therefore infuse our art and culture" and "art is a weapon of the struggle," were the slogans proclaimed by Medu at the conference section of the festival.[8] Speakers debated the relevance of the arts to the intensification of the struggle after 1976. In preparation for the launch of the UDF movement the following year, and twelve years before the first democratic elections would be held in South Africa, ideas about what culture could look like in a future South Africa were discussed at Gaborone. Strategies for resisting the status quo were also debated. The keynote speaker was the writer Keorapetse Kgositsile, and his passionately partisan speech set the politicized tone for the rest of the festival. Kgositsile underscored the importance of the gathering using socialist rhetoric, and he emphasized the central role of the ANC at the head of the revolution:

> A few years ago a fellow South African writer asked me
> to explain to him how people like [Alex] la Guma and
> I could be in the Movement but still manage to write
> poems and novels. And I replied, with a bit of acid on
> my tongue, that I had always wondered how a South
> African writer could be outside the Movement but hope
> to write anything of value or significance...I hope that
> in discussing "Culture and Resistance in South Africa,"
> I will make a contribution towards clarifying a few
> things about what time this is in our life; what tasks
> are facing us; what writers and other artists worth their
> salt are doing in living up to their responsibilities...In
> declaring 1982 the Year of Unity in Action, the year in
> which to move forward to a democratic South Africa,
> we must act in unity and unite, in action. Comrade
> O. R. Tambo, President of the ANC, points out that:
> "The comradeship that we have formed in the trenches
> of freedom, transcending the barriers that the enemy
> sought to create, is a guarantee and a precondition
> of our victory. But we still need to build on this
> achievement. All of us—workers, peasants, students,
> priests, chiefs, traders, teachers, civil servants, poets,
> writers, men, women and youth, black and white—
> must take our common destiny in our own hands."[9]

Following a brief history of struggle-oriented poetry, Kgositsile concluded his talk with an art-inflected echo of Marx's definition of the social species-life of mankind, from *The Communist Manifesto*: "[T]here is no such creature as a revolutionary soloist. We are all involved. The artist is both participant and explorer in life. Outside of social life there is no culture, there is no art; and that is one of the major differences between man and beast."[10] With these words, Kgositsile urged collectivity as a core practice in the arts, a form of practice that would bring into being new communities for a new South Africa. Visual art, though not mentioned directly by Kgositsile (or by ANC leader Oliver Tambo) would nevertheless become one of the most potent vehicles for this revolutionary idea of community, and the social world of artist groups like Medu was a harbinger of a nonracial political future in South Africa. Though the existence of such "grey areas" in art preceded the Medu Art Ensemble by many years, the festival Medu organized in 1982 should be recognized as one of the most important flash points in the history of South African art. "Grey Areas" was an official apartheid government designation (and de facto acknowledgment) during the late 1980s that certain urban neighborhoods could not be completely racially segregated. These were often the same places where artists opened studios and created a convivial social scene across the color bar, a sort of bohemian space with multiple and hybrid possibilities. The term may be applied in a metaphorical sense to those cultural phenomena that could never be accurately classified according to apartheid criteria.[11] One takeaway from the Medu conference was that during the early 1980s the social life of art would become an even more crucial site for the struggle against apartheid.

II. Art as a Liberated Zone

Today, art students learn that Abstract Expressionism was born in America in the context of the Cold War, but few are aware that this aesthetic had another life, in another place and time, or that the endgame of abstract painting was played again by proxy in Africa during the final decade before the fall of the Berlin Wall. This was a pivotal moment in South African history, when the struggle for political representation was intensified by the gathering of a mass democratic movement against apartheid. The corresponding struggle over aesthetic representation became increasingly disputatious during this period. During the 1980s, black artists' experiments with nonfigurative abstract art took place at the same time that pressure was mounting, in the wake of the historic Culture and Resistance festival in Gaborone, for all "cultural workers" to conform to a critical, realist, committed art. One effect of the transnational translation of an art style was the creation of a new idea of art-as-community, against the grain of the social separateness of apartheid. What in the West was considered a "formalist art exercise" became, in Africa, a "community art movement." The story of this transition is part of the history of the often overlooked dispersal of international modernism beyond the borders of the United States and Europe. It has profound significance for the deeper understanding of the tension between "Western" and other modernities, and for the interpretation of the politics of culture in South Africa.

In 1985, the UDF was two years old, and organized mass protests took place across South Africa on a scale not seen before. In June, South African commandos crossed the border into Botswana and raided houses associated with Medu and ANC members, killing twelve in their homes, including activist and artist Thami Mnyele and Medu treasurer Mike Hamlyn. A State of Emergency was declared to pacify selected "hot spots." During successive States of Emergency from 1986 to 1990, South Africa experienced an escalation in mass resistance, state-sponsored violence, and internecine warfare. By 1986, approximately 40,000 people had been detained without trial, hundreds were killed during police attacks in the black townships or during interrogation, and leaders of

UDF affiliate organizations were targeted for assassination by the State. One of the strategies of the resistance movement was for grassroots street committees to make the black townships ungovernable, and thus to deny the regime legitimacy by creating "liberated zones" within South Africa. The intensification of the insurrection also led to a rise in vigilantism, often with police backing, as well as street battles between rival anti-apartheid groups. At the height of this civil conflict, the throwing of firebombs and the placing of gasoline-filled tire "necklaces" on victims' heads often followed accusations of collaboration against the struggle. By 1987, casualties from fratricide exceeded those from the war against the government.[12]

Efforts were also made during the 1980s to make art less easily labeled as "black" or "white." In the midst of the political turmoil, a group of fifteen artists and selected guests gathered at a holiday resort at Hunter's Rest during August 1985, in the scenic Magaliesburg Mountains near Rustenberg, an hour and a half outside Johannesburg.[13] For two weeks they worked nonstop, made large-scale paintings and mixed media work, and experimented with sculptural forms constructed from found materials. They paused only for meals and for critique sessions led by Bill Ainslie from the Johannesburg Art Foundation and Peter Bradley, a visiting artist from the United States. The artists at Hunter's Rest were participating in the first of several annual workshops that were organized by Ainslie and David Koloane along with Anthusa Sotiriades (and with an initial impetus from British artist Anthony Caro and philanthropist Robert Loder) and were supported by the United States–South Africa Leadership Exchange Program (USSALEP), the Federated Union of Black Artists (FUBA) and donations from local businesses. The intention of the project (initially called the FUBA-USSALEP Workshop) was to create a temporary respite for black artists who lived in isolation from other artists, had limited access to the kinds of art facilities available to white artists, and worked in a representational mode on a limited scale. In the idyllic setting of the workshop, these artists were encouraged to explore the freedom of color and nonobjective painting associated with Abstract Expressionist or Color Field art. At Hunter's Rest, they poured, splattered, scraped, and stained paint over yards and yards of canvas. Most participants had previously had limited and conservative schooling in art, and were accustomed to making do with "studios" in cramped township rooms, where by necessity they worked on small drawings, linocut prints, or watercolors. For them the new experiences of technique, medium, and scale, and of camaraderie, were a kind of communal liberation. The FUBA-USSALEP Workshop was an eye-opening adventure, one that altered the direction of black artists' work in subsequent years.

As a result, most of the art produced during the subsequent annual workshops also appeared to follow Abstract Expressionism in look and technique. For instance, in an untitled work from 1986 by Dumisani Mabaso (which was used as the cover of a fundraising brochure for the workshop), a series of swooping arrows made of twisted cord traverses a field of vertical lines of colored paint that have been hurled onto the canvas.[14] In the same brochure Durant Sihlali's *Blue Haze* (1985) featured a ghostly figure with arms held up, emerging from a tangle of dripped filaments of blue and red pigment. The workshop was a welcome rest from the everyday violence of the occupied townships during the States of Emergency. It was also a luxury, a zone for aesthetic free play during a time when the call for literal political content in art had become mainstream in progressive circles in South Africa. The free-form spirit of the first workshop was epitomized by Cape Town artist Garth Erasmus in his mixed-media painting titled *Playground* (1985), in which gobs of paint, glyph-like marks, and tubes of artist colors are embedded in the surface. These objects look as if they have been tossed into the air, and frozen in mid-flight. *Playground*, as its title suggests, evoked both a liberation from the daily concern for survival, and a search for novel methods for aesthetic expression through the addition of the element of chance.

The 1985 FUBA-USSALEP Workshop was so inspirational for the artists who attended that it was repeated annually until 1991, each time with a slightly different group.[15] During its second year the workshop moved to the conference hotel at the Alpha Training Centre in Broederstroom, and its name was changed to "Thupelo," a South Sotho word meaning "to teach by example."[16] The choice of the name Thupelo mirrored other slogans popular within the progressive movement at the time, including the Congress of South African Students' motto "each one teach one" and the title of the literacy magazine *Learn and Teach*. The name indicated the project's initial aim as an enrichment program for black artists: a small group of professional artists would be brought together to learn and share skills that could later be spread more widely among students and colleagues.[17]

Along these lines, one of the conditions for seed money from USSALEP was that the workshop would provide an opportunity for artist exchanges between South Africa and the United States. It was with that stipulation that Peter Bradley was brought over as a guest visiting artist in 1985. According to Thupelo records, the other international visitors included American art critic Kenworth Moffett (1986), Canadian artist Graham Peacock (1987), British Painter John Hoyland and Canadian painter Robert Scott (1990), and British artist Andrew Sloan (1991).[18] Prominent local artists were also invited as honorary visitors, including Sydney Kumalo, Fikile Magadlela, and Ezrom Legae.[19] In the other direction, according to Thupelo records, the following artists were selected to travel to New York to attend the Triangle workshop: David Koloane and Ian Redelinghüys (1983), David

Koloane (1984), Garth Erasmus and Bill Ainslie (1985), Dumisani Mabaso (1986), Ian Redelinghüys and Lionel Davis (1987), Sholto Ainslie and Anthusa Sotiriades (1988), Durant Sihlali and Patrick Mautloa (1989), Chabani Cyril Manganyi (1990), Sam Nhlengethwa (1991), Madi Phala (1992).

Within the context of the Medu Art Ensemble in Botswana, Thami Mnyele, Mongane Serote, and their comrades had been eloquent polemicists in exile for the cultural policy of the African National Congress during the 1980s. They spoke clearly of the necessity for aligning artistic practice to the struggle against apartheid, and they conceived of the struggle as a phenomenon that would bring a new community into being. In their view art was something that serviced the needs of "the people" and in turn was informed by the community. Theirs was a creative model for community, but a reflective model for the relation of art to history and society. The Thupelo group followed a complementary trajectory for the making of community, but a somewhat contrary trajectory for the making of art. Its members' commitment to the struggle against the social effects of apartheid manifested itself in the making of a new community that was opposed to the racially separatist, culturally isolating, and developmentally demeaning status quo, rather than a literal illustration of the community-as-struggle in their art. For them the coming community was not just their wider audience, it was the working group of artists themselves. Community art, for them, became "a community of artists" working together in spite of racial and national divisions. In its small way, too, it was hoped that the resulting group would become a model to inspire change for a post-apartheid South African society. Owen Kelly, a participant in the community arts movement in Britain during the 1970s, described a position that resonates with that of the Thupelo group:

> Community...is not an entity, nor even an
> abstraction, but a set of shared social meanings
> which are constantly created and mutated through
> the actions and interactions of its members, and
> through their interaction with wider society...
> The community is not available for "development"
> by funders or "management" by externals. Rather
> it grows by member participation....One does
> not work "with" a community. One participates
> in bringing a community into being.[20]

The form Thupelo took, a two-week workshop where materials, lodging, and food were provided for the chosen artists, was similar to that of its contemporary sibling in New York, the Triangle international artist workshop. Triangle was closely related to Thupelo in that it had been inspired and initiated in part by British artist Anthony Caro and philanthropist Robert Loder, and in that each year an artist from Thupelo was invited to attend Triangle in New York. But the workshop method held a very different significance in South Africa. As I detail elsewhere, the idea for Triangle/New York was born in South Africa and in the end served to reinvigorate formalist, abstract expressionist art internationally as much or more than vice versa.[21] But whichever direction we might plot the vectors of influence, what at Triangle-U.S. was taken as an intensive refresher course for mid-career studio artists of the "New York School" sort, at Thupelo South Africa was an incredible luxury for the (mostly) black artists. This luxury provided more than a taste of the middle-class experience of white South Africa. It also allowed the possibility of thinking beyond the immediate needs of the present, beyond producing art for a market (or a political program) that made demands on content in black artists' work. A door was opened to thinking about what else art could be. It was opened by the community created around Thupelo and was composed in the form of experiments with modernist abstraction.

III. Beneath the Blanket Boycott

Given the "Ab-Ex" look of much of the work emanating from the annual Thupelo workshops, and given that during the mid-1980s the whole anti–Clement Greenberg and Cold War complicity backlash was in vogue in intellectual circles abroad, it comes as no surprise that accusations of American imperialism were laid against Thupelo by several (white) South African academics writing for the left-leaning press.[22] Therefore one of the curious things about Thupelo is that the anti-apartheid cultural boycott was never applied to the project. South African artists were not supposed to be traveling overseas, and international performers were routinely blacklisted by the progressive movement for playing in South Africa. But with Thupelo this does not appear to have been an issue. Why? When I asked about this, David Koloane explained:

> The Cultural Boycott was on already. From the
> beginning, the ANC Cultural Desk made a distinction
> between money meant for educational purposes,
> and other kinds of projects. We approached them
> for a black artist educational project [Thupelo], and
> were given a special concession…They knew me
> because I had curated the visual art section at the
> Culture and Resistance Festival…Bill [Ainslie]
> was also in constant touch with the ANC.[23]

From the pragmatic point of view of the ANC in exile, Thupelo looked like a sound project. But the deeper reason for their special concession is only hinted at in these remarks. David Koloane's "struggle credentials" were good, since he had helped organize the art exhibition shown in Gaborone.[24] Koloane had also known people like Thami Mnyele, Mongane Serote, Albie Sachs, Joe Manana (later the ANC Cultural Desk head), and others in the ANC upper ranks. They had all been regular visitors at the Ainslie household. Ainslie himself had shared his studio with these men, and he even helped some of them escape the country. Despite Ainslie's public comments about painting outside of ideology, his commitment to working in a nonracial manner and the company he kept lent Ainslie the profoundest respect among those who would later go on to leadership positions within the African National Congress. They gave the Thupelo Project a special concession because they already knew from personal experience what kinds of social riches the workshop method could produce, no matter what the art looked like. One might conclude erroneously, from the hardened positions taken by various actors on the South African art scene, that an artist like Thami Mnyele would have had little common cause with one like Bill Ainslie. Despite a sometimes angry-sounding dialogue in print these artists were actually part of the same social circle. What really mattered, the day-to-day politics of survival against the grain of apartheid, was hidden beneath polemic debates about the "commitment" of art to the struggle.

Following the clear gains of the UDF and the growing surge of cultural activism, ANC president Oliver Tambo announced in 1987 that the cultural boycott from then on would be applied "on a more selective basis."[25] Even before 1987 there had been special cases, like Thupelo, that had been given a pass by the struggle leadership in exile. During 1989–90, President de Klerk sped up the process of permanently dismantling apartheid from the inside. His decision to act, he claimed at the time, was only possible because the danger of an African Communism, perhaps the biggest fear of the Afrikaner Nationalists, had finally passed with the disintegration of the Soviet Union. As these events were unfolding, and as the ANC and other groups were unbanned and brought to the bargaining table, the ANC again adjusted their official cultural policy. The role of art became both wider and more diminished. Diminished since it was no longer needed as one of the few conduits available for money for the struggle, nor as a public platform for dissent, since opposition parties were now legal and could speak openly for themselves, no longer under the cover of "culture." Expanded because definitions of what "committed" art could officially be were relaxed. A document, titled "ANC Cultural Boycott Policy, adopted by the National Executive Committee of the ANC," was released by the ANC in Lusaka in May 1989. Its provision 1.3 states that "In order to grow and develop, this emergent culture of liberation needs to interact with and be exposed to the progressive intellectual and cultural currents in the rest of the world."[26] The shift in policy was noted in the South African press:

> The document represents a considerable rationalization of boycott policy, and extends the notion of a selective boycott adopted by the organization in 1986 and vigorously debated at various conferences since then—notably at the Culture in Another South Africa conference held in Amsterdam in late 1987, and a United Nations–sponsored conference in Athens late last year…The document notes that the culture of democratic South Africa, "though distinctly South African, is infused with an internationalist, humanist spirit that draws upon the best of the cultural heritage of all the population groups of our country and the rest of humanity."[27]

Then, following de Klerk's formal unbanning of the opposition in February 1990, the *Weekly Mail* published a portion of Albie Sachs' "Preparing Ourselves for Freedom," a position paper he had originally delivered at an in-house seminar of the ANC in 1989. Sachs, who had survived a car bomb attack by the South African government in Mozambique, and would later head the new South African constitutional court, suggested, somewhat tongue in cheek, that the ANC "ban" itself from saying "culture is a weapon of the struggle" for at least five years. He claimed, further, that such a narrow view of culture impoverished the struggle itself. He also proposed that rather than making images of petrol bombs and Casspirs (police trucks), poets and visual artists should strive instead for the kind of emotional depth achieved by musicians like Hugh Masekela and Abdullah Ibrahim.[28]

This was an important document. It set out new priorities for the politics of artistic representation after the fall of Communism and after the demise of apartheid. But what Sachs was suggesting was the kind of openness in the arts that those associated with groups like Thupelo had already been working on for at least half a decade—some of them since the 1960s. Thus it should come as no surprise that when, in 1990, David Koloane was asked by the ANC to curate exhibitions to accompany its Zabalaza Festival in London, the "committed" art he chose was made by Louis Maqhubela, Dumile Feni, and artists from the Thupelo group. These three generations of artists had all worked in Ainslie's workshop over the years and had tended toward the abstract in their compositions. While the politicians were busy trying to figure out what the new post-apartheid South African culture might look like, artists like Koloane were able to show what had been going on all along in the gray areas of art during those black and white years.

KWAITO: THE REVOLUTION WAS NOT TELEVISED; IT ANNOUNCED ITSELF IN SONG

Hlonipha Mokoena

When the popular soul singer Percy Sledge visited South Africa in 1970, the American Committee on Africa (ACOA)[1] issued a press statement, provocatively titled "Percy Sledge Sells Soul," condemning his decision and calling on other American artists and entertainers to heed the cultural boycott of the apartheid state. I remember Sledge's South Africa tour, though I was not yet born, because it marked the beginning of my uncle's rebellion. I know that my uncle defied my grandfather by going to a Percy Sledge concert. But when my family tells this story, the cultural boycott and the controversies around Sledge's visit are never mentioned.

As the ACOA's communiqué acknowledges, there remained, even in 1970, a great deal of naïveté about both the conditions of apartheid and what the world's response should be. The press release noted:

> In 1965 a number of American artists pledged
> to observe a total boycott of South Africa. Black
> artists included Harry Belafonte, Leon Bibb,

> Godfrey Cambridge, Diahanne Carroll [sic], Ossie
> Davis, Sammy Davis, Jr., Carmen de L. Holder
> [sic], Lena Horne, Eartha Kitt, Miriam Makeba,
> Johnny Mathis, Frederick O'Neal, Odetta, Sidney
> Poitier, Paul Robeson, Nina Simone, and Poppy
> Cannon White. Percy Sledge, and all those with
> him who defy this boycott, act in support of the
> white oppression of Blacks symbolized by South
> Africa; and therefore sabotage the struggle being
> waged today by the African liberation movements to
> liberate their country. Percy Sledge, in verbalizing
> naivite [sic], acts like the American businessman
> who denies that investment in South Africa is
> supporting a system of economic exploitation.[2]

However, Sledge was not the only musician to have ignored, or unintentionally violated, the cultural boycott. During the 1980s, numerous entertainers performed at the pleasure resort Sun City under the false impression or pretext that the homeland of Bophuthatswana—a Bantustan created in 1961—was an "old African kingdom."[3]

Although historical narratives and personal memories of the cultural boycott tend to focus on the successful implementation of boycotts against South Africa by international organizations and movements, a closer examination of the practice of cultural boycott shows that there was often confusion about who or what was being boycotted. As the sociologist Michael Drewett has shown, different organizations and individual artists often had competing ideas about what and whom they were meant to boycott, with the effect that local South African musicians were often barred from performing overseas even when they stood against apartheid. Drewett notes:

> Although the bigger picture was undoubtedly more
> important and far more sobering, musicians looking
> for creative outlets did feel frustrated when they
> were deprived of opportunities to at least perform
> overseas. Certainly, the fact that some anti-apartheid
> bands were prohibited from performing outside
> the country, and overseas protest musicians were
> strongly discouraged from performing in South
> Africa, essentially removed an important aspect
> of cultural struggle from the political contest.[4]

More importantly, the "cultural struggle" was not just being waged outside of South Africa. Internally, black South Africans continued to consume both local and international music despite the fact that they could not perform overseas, and the international musicians they listened to could not perform in South Africa. As the acclaimed documentary *Searching for Sugar Man* (dir. Malik Bendjelloul, 2012) illustrates, South African audiences, both white and black, often identified (or misidentified) with musicians regardless of whether they were censored in, banned from, or unwilling to travel to South Africa. Among other curious phenomena, Bendjelloul's film highlights the fact that wealthy and disenchanted white South Africans could idolize the rebelliousness of a musician even while they adopted a quiescent attitude toward the apartheid state and the actual social conditions in their surroundings.

In effect, the term "boycott" does not have a self-evident meaning, especially since "consumption," too, is often an opaque concept to define. For example, consider the South African runner Zola Budd (Zola Pieterse), who was given British citizenship and competed in the 1984 Olympic Games despite the sports boycott. Her story leads directly to another "Zola Budd"—the title of the hit song by Brenda Fassie, which immortalized the athlete even though she evaded the sports boycott by claiming British citizenship. Released in 1987 on the self-titled album *Brenda*, the song was not actually about the athlete but about the Toyota Hi-Ace minibus, which had been nicknamed "Zola Budd" because of its speed. This metonymic trade in symbols and symbolism illustrates how popular culture is a milieu without boundaries or pre-ordered systems of values, so that controversies such as Budd's athletic turncoatism can be obliterated and submerged by the popularity of a song or an artist. In the case of Brenda Fassie, her popularity and the innumerable monikers she has generated—"Madonna of the Townships" being one—meant that her song "Zola Budd" became a hit despite its association with an athlete whom the international anti-apartheid movement was attempting to discredit. The two Zola Budds thus became separate symbols, with the minibus taxi largely replacing the image of the barefoot athlete after whom it was named.

Fassie's career represents another complex aspect of the cultural boycott. If we assume that the main purpose of the boycott was to isolate the apartheid state while depriving it of the opportunity to use sporting and cultural events as propaganda, then two dimensions of the boycott presented problems for South African artists. The first dimension was that in South Africa, the radio and television stations were and are still owned by the South African Broadcasting Corporation (SABC), a de facto government institution. Any airplay constituted "sponsorship" by the government, and since radio and television stations were "ethnically" defined, it also constituted an endorsement of such segregation. Secondly, the absence of international exposure meant that South African artists had to rely on revenues generated in their own country. On the face of it, these two dimensions should have destroyed the power of state institutions to control "culture," but instead, as I will attempt to demonstrate, the cultural boycott boosted the South African brand of artistic production that is today epitomized in the phrase *local is lekker* ("local is cool").

In the 1980s, catchphrases like *local is lekker* did not exist, and musicians and artists were often identified by their allegiance to "protest" viz. protest literature, protest music, and protest theater. This dominance of "protest" cultural production would have continued had it not been for the sudden and unexpected emergence of "bubblegum" music.[5] In his recently published biography of Brenda Fassie, the cultural critic Bongani Madondo charts the singer's rise to fame and quest for stardom.[6] The story is part legend and part rehabilitation, but the thread that runs through most of it is that Fassie was a local South African star before she became known across the continent and the rest of the globe. This story of local fame first applies equally to her long-time producer and collaborator Sello "Chicco" Twala, who had been part of a rock-and-pop outfit in the 1970s before becoming a producer. Fassie's successful career (and eventual downfall) functions as a counternarrative to predominant histories of the cultural boycott, since it confirms the vitality of a local music industry that was able to produce and nurture stellar talent despite being deprived of the oxygen of international competition and collaboration.

The life and biography of Brenda Fassie are relevant to the history of the cultural boycott because unlike other South African artists, she did not go into exile. She was born Brenda Nokuzola Fassie in the Langa township of Cape Town in 1964. A precocious child, she formed a singing group called the Tiny Tots at age six. For a brief period in her teens, Fassie was the replacement singer for a girl band called Joy—the first black band to win in all the major categories of SABC's music awards, in 1979, with their hit "Paradise Road."[7] By winning Best Album, Best Produced Single, Best Producer, and Best Songwriter,

Gwen Ansell writes, Joy became the first black band to break the barriers of the SABC's awards criteria.[8] Airplay on SABC stations catapulted Joy into aural space that included both black and white audiences, and Fassie, joining the band in 1980, sang its hit song to huge crowds on the band's tours. Yet her real breakthrough came with the 1983 release of "Weekend Special," a catchy bubblegum song that became the fastest selling South African single of its time.[9] As Madondo points out, when Fassie burst onto the music scene, many listeners thought she was African-American.

Fassie's emergence onto the world stage coincided roughly with Paul Simon's *Graceland* album and tour, and its rejection by anti-apartheid activists. For all the protests *Graceland* generated, Simon's musical project also produced a swarm of musical "clones" and "offshoots," according to the musicologist Charles Hamm, who labeled these descendants of *Graceland* the "Folk Music Revival."[10] Riding this wave, in 1988 Fassie performed with Harry Belafonte at the Unicef Festival in Harare, and recorded an album with him, titled *Paradise in Gazankulu*, which was framed as a rejoinder to *Graceland*.[11] Yet, according to Madondo, she had not heard of sanctions or the cultural boycott and had to ask her PR person to explain the concepts to her. To Fassie's credit, such a degree of ignorance regarding the global anti-apartheid movement applied to most South Africans: since news (both print and electronic) was censored in South Africa, there was no airtime given to the activities of the anti-apartheid movement, especially the cultural and sporting boycotts.

Charles Hamm described the thin line separating *Graceland* and *Paradise in Gazankulu* in the following terms:

> The commercial success of *Graceland* has spawned
> a number of clones, such as Harry Belafonte's

Paradise in Gazankulu. In direct imitation of Simon,
Belafonte sings over the backing of black South
African pop stars: the Soul Brothers, Brenda Fassie,
Theta, the Makgona Tshole Band [sic], West Nkosi.
Unlike Simon, Belafonte did not go to South
Africa. His backing tracks were laid down in the
Powerhouse Studios in Johannesburg, under the
supervision of Hilton Rosenthal, Johnny Clegg's
manager, then sent to New York for overdubbing
and to Los Angeles for final mixing. Some of the
songs, written by Jake Holmes, are obliquely critical
of South Africa's racial policies; this has had no
adverse effect on the careers and lives of the backing
musicians, giving lie to Simon's claim that he avoided
political texts to protect his black collaborators.[12]

In terms of musical arrangement and studio production, there was
therefore no difference between the album produced despite the cultural
boycott and the one produced to strengthen it. Both Simon and Belafonte
relied on technology (and global courier services) to produce albums that
used the voices of South African artists without actually performing
in South Africa. Hamm further argues that Simon and Belafonte both
benefited from appropriating South African pop music to fit the image
of "folk" musicians: "[t]he beneficiaries were first of all the performers
themselves, whose careers as entertainers were launched or enhanced, and
the record industry, which saw soaring sales as the popularity of 'folk'
music spread from college campuses and folk clubs to a larger audience."[13]
As the continued popularity of musicians such as Miriam Makeba and
Ladysmith Black Mambazo attests, Hamm is not far off the mark. The
more controversial aspect of his insight is that the main beneficiaries were

~~the Paul Simons and Harry Belafontes of the music industry rather than~~ the South African musicians. This inequality in benefits could be said to continue since many of the less well-known musicians who collaborated with either Simon or Belafonte have died in poverty.

For Brenda Fassie, this brief association with Belafonte and the cultural boycott did not lead to her being a "folk" musician. A different kind of transformation has taken shape. At the height of her popularity in South Africa, her music became synonymous with "bubblegum"; posthumously it has been categorized as "Afropop" and even described as a precursor of the township house music genre called "kwaito." These multiple transitions and translations are themselves a product of the fact that when apartheid ended, and exiled musicians such as Miriam Makeba and Hugh Masekela returned to South Africa, South African musicians found themselves constituted into a motley welcoming party and the music industry had to produce a "sound" that celebrated the moment.

Prior to the transition to democracy, an unlikely song became the herald to the death of apartheid. Even before the return of exiles, the thawing of apartheid-era censorship was signaled by the uncensored airplay of Bright Blue's "Weeping" (1987). The song's lyrics referred symbolically to the whimpering sounds of a regime that was quickly running out of explanations and subterfuges. Importantly, the song used chords from the banned African national anthem, "Nkosi Sikelela i'Afrika"—a fact the censors ignored. The lyrics to the song are the perfect expression of what the local music industry achieved despite the cultural boycott:

WEEPING
Written by Dan Heymann (© Bright Blue)

I knew a man who lived in fear
It was huge, it was angry, it was drawing near

Assuming Boycott

Behind his house, a secret place
Was the shadow of the demon he could never face
He built a wall of steel and flame
And men with guns, to keep it tame
Then standing back, he made it plain
That the nightmare would never ever rise again
But the fear and the fire and the guns remain

It doesn't matter now
It's over anyhow
He tells the world that it's sleeping
But as the night came round
I heard its lonely sound
It wasn't roaring, it was weeping

And then one day the neighbors came
They were curious to know about the smoke and flame
They stood around outside the wall
But of course there was nothing to be heard at all
"My friends," he said, "We've reached our goal
The threat is under firm control
As long as peace and order reign
I'll be damned if I can see a reason to explain
Why the fear and the fire and the guns remain"

Although at the time I was too young to have understood the
political meaning of "Weeping" in full, the power of the musical score
and the "hidden" chords of "Nkosi Sikelela i'Afrika" infused my youthful
and impressionable mind with the delightful sensation of defiance. By
singing the song, it felt as if we were flouting the apartheid state right

in its own backyard—peering over the "wall of steel and flame." We felt a combination of fear and euphoria: fear that we could be caught and euphoria at the thought that the "enemy" we had been taught to fear was really a toothless tiger; that the majestic and seemingly omnipresent "system" was really a whimpering beast emitting its "lonely sound." And, as the song title suggests, this was also the beginning of a different kind of reckoning with sorrow; even at that age, I understood that my country would be spending many years in the future simply weeping—for lost opportunities, lost lives, and lost generations.

In the future many books will be written, and theories advanced, about what ended apartheid. Although it may seem controversial now, it is fair to say that apartheid did not end because of the cultural boycott—at least not as a single factor. The end of apartheid was a long and overdrawn process and no single agent or movement can claim that it dealt the death blow. What I have attempted to argue in this essay is that even at the time, the cultural boycott was an ambiguous tool of struggle, especially from a local South African perspective. In retrospect, what may have seemed like an organized and systematic boycotting of apartheid sporting and cultural events was anything but. Many artists and athletes found ways to circumvent the cultural boycott, either by emigrating, or, in the case of Paul Simon and Harry Belafonte, by appropriating South African music and globalizing it. Yet, rather than conclude that the cultural boycott was a failure, I have proposed a different interpretation. The globalization of South African music had the effect of boosting the local music industry by enhancing the appeal of already existing genres such as maskanda, isicathamiya, and mbhaqanga, and creating the conditions for emerging or soon-to-emerge genres such as bubblegum and kwaito. Thus, although kwaito is generally held to have emerged during the 1990s, after the end of apartheid, it is equally valid to define the genre as the late child of the cultural boycott.

Assuming Boycott

By giving a handful of artists international exposure, and preventing international acts from performing in the country, the cultural boycott forced local artists to innovate and experiment with new genres. Thus were born myriad surprising post-apartheid countercultures.

INCOGNEGRO: A MEMOIR OF EXILE AND APARTHEID [1]

Frank B. Wilderson III

The mood in Soweto was electric and unpredictable, alive with the promise of fire. The Defiance Campaign was in full gear, moving up to the Transvaal from the Cape. Residents in townships all across South Africa were angry and mobilized, so much so that rents and mortgages hadn't been paid in over a year and the government was paralyzed with no capacity to act even as a collection agent for the landlords. The mass mobilization of people had sent shock waves up the spine of civil society. On July 5, 1989, three weeks before I arrived, P. W. Botha had been compelled to meet Nelson Mandela, not in his prison cell on Robben Island but at Tuynhuys in Cape Town. And fifteen days after the braai Khanya took me to, Botha would be forced to convene the members of his Cabinet—also at Tuynhuys—and resign; his replacement would be F. W. de Klerk, the cunning pragmatist who had already taken the reigns of party leadership in March of that year.

It had been a brutal year for President Botha and the Nationalist Party: he'd suffered a stroke in January; in February there had been the hunger strikes by political detainees, a Defiance Campaign, and the trouncing of his party at the polls; in March, the rise of his nemesis, de Klerk; in May he received intelligence reports of a clandestine South African Communist Party congress held in Cuba at which the first new communist program since 1962 was produced by South African reds. Now this, in July: another unwanted meeting with Mandela and the rising smoke of another Defiance Campaign.

Emblazoned on the walls of Soweto's buildings were portents of its coming: Socialism Is Our Shield! Kill the Farmer! Kill the Boer! MK Lives! Viva SACP Viva!

Richard was a tall and muscular Zulu man nearly ten years my senior. Shirley, Khanya's cousin, was a nurse. How a nurse and a gangster had come together was beyond me. But in the five days I'd been in South Africa this dilemma was not by any means the most vexing. Simple things like knowing where I was in space and time at any given moment; or asking a group of people to speak English instead of an African language that I might know what's being said; or wondering at what point a police dragnet would materialize and catch me in it and what to do or say when it happens…These were the most pressing problems of those first few days. Who was dating whom, and why, would have to wait until I learned my ass from my elbow. There were five people in the car: Richard at the wheel, Shirley beside him, Khanya, Botsotso, and me in back. Botsotso was a young man in his late twenties. He was Richard's lieutenant. We were on our way to pick up Botsotso's girlfriend.

A haze of toxic carbons hung in the air like San Francisco fog. It was shot through with the setting sun's blue-amber light. This beautiful swath of tinted translucence laced the garbage heaps where children played, like a saintly halo, and wove around the low brick houses where their parents waited. Shirley told me the pollution came from plants that powered the homes and businesses of Johannesburg, while 40 percent of Soweto residents were without electricity. "The state coroner is forbidden to report levels of toxins found in the bodies of people who die here," she said.

We stopped at one of the countless small brick homes. Botsotso stood beside the car and whistled like a precious bird.

"You can't just go to a girl's house," Richard smiled at me in his rearview mirror. "'Now, who's this one and why is he coming for my daughter before I have my lobola?' That's what the father will say."

Everyone except me seemed to know why this was so funny.

"You can't even go out on a date without paying a bride price?" I said, effectively ruining the joke.

We waited five minutes or so. A light came on at the bathroom window. It went out, then came on again, and went out. Botsotso got back into the car and smiled. After a brief interval, a young woman stepped out of the front door and called some half-hearted promise, or lie, or both, to her parents inside. Mpo, a young woman who seemed as though she may have just graduated from high school, squeezed up front with Shirley and Richard. Now there were six of us in the car as we drove up to Richard's house. Shirley and Richard, Mpo and Botsotso, and Khanya and me: two gangsters, a high school student, a young nurse, a young law student, and me.

Two Afrikaner policemen were in the lane, standing next to their car as we approached Richard's house. It had been raining. Richard cursed as he saw them and drew up to the front so fast that he splashed their pants with mud. They were furious. Furious White cops, I thought, in sheer terror, furious and drunk. One of them hurled curses at us in Afrikaans. Richard and Botsotso hurled curses back in Zulu. The cops drew their guns. Botsotso was sitting in the backseat, passenger side—in the middle was Khanya, and I was behind Richard, the driver. Botsotso leaned across both Khanya and me and, following Richard's lead, stuck his gun out the window. Insults ricocheted back and forth. Khanya and

I were the only ones who seemed terrified. The police, the tsotsis, and Shirley thought it all quite normal.

Suddenly, and for reasons beyond my comprehension, it was over. The police got in their car and drove off. Botsotso and Richard climbed out of the car laughing their heads off. I was shaken but determined not to appear shaken. We went to the backyard, broke out the beer, and put steaks and chicken on the grill. The meat sizzled succulently as more and more people arrived. There were bus drivers, nurses, gangsters, and students. I marveled at this eclectic gathering and at how little my middle class, Kenwood, and Dartmouth College training had prepared me for it.

The streetlights in Soweto where Richard lived were three stories high. They rained down harsh garish beams on the residents like prison searchlights. As evening settled over Richard's backyard, most of the people left. Seven or eight diehards took the braai inside. We were all a little tipsy as we arranged ourselves in Richard's living room: Khanya, her cousin Shirley, Mpo, and one or two others. Richard, Botsotso, a couple of other men, and me. When the conversation turned to politics the women went into the kitchen. They carried on a soft but animated conversation in Pedi or Setswana as they sat at the kitchen table, while the men talked about the Defiance Campaign, which was sweeping north from Cape Town, and argued about whether F. W. de Klerk could really dethrone P. W. Botha. I felt a slight unease. It was as though anything could happen at any moment (like when Botsotso had thrust his gun out the window at the two policemen). There was an inner tension, mine. There was an outer tension, theirs. The source of their tension revealed itself in short order.

Khanya had remained seated in the living room. Not only was she still in the living room, but she was drinking Richard's good liquor with even greater alacrity than Botsotso, his own henchman. And, as regards the discussion, she was debating with the best of them, providing as much political analysis and as many cold hard facts about the Defiance Campaign as anyone in the room. Every so often Richard's eyes flashed at Botsotso. Botsotso mirrored his boss's exasperation. Khanya was oblivious to it all. She continued to hold forth. She explained why it was necessary for mortgage loan boycotts to run coterminous with rent boycotts. This, she pointed out, would force the cautious and conservative Black bourgeoisie to be carried along by the militant energy of the Black working class and not vice versa. And it would bring landlords and the government to the table more quickly. She said that P. W. Botha could afford to sacrifice a few landlords but a mortgage boycott would affect the banking industry more directly and would bring the economy nearer to a stock market meltdown—and bring *us* that much closer to victory. It was a brilliant analysis and it would have carried a heretofore-anecdotal debate forward, if not for the fact that Richard had grown cold and silent.

"Botsotso," he said, as he kept his eyes on me.

"Yebo, induna," Botsotso said, respectfully.

"Did I tell you I lived in Harlem for three years?"

"Many times, induna." I braced myself.

Richard had studied in New York to be a dentist. When he got back to South Africa, the apartheid government wouldn't let him practice. Well, he had thought, if I can't be a dentist, I'll fix them, I'll show them, I'll become a smuggler instead.

"Now, Botsotso."

"Yebo, induna."

"Remember what I said about the Black man in America—about his problem?"

"Some of us should hear it again, induna."

Richard thrust his drunken face closer to mine and said, "He can't control his woman."

I laughed at this. It was a nervous, fitful laugh but he thought I was laughing at him. No one else laughed, not even Khanya. But something in the laughter may have emboldened her, for she launched into a long attack on African men and their lack of appreciation for the contributions of African women to the liberation struggle. The more she spoke, the more tentative I became. I felt that she and I were in a paper canoe being pulled toward the falls.

Richard was standing now, looking down at both of us. *If he hits her I'm going to have to fight him which means I'm going to die. Even if I could take him, Botsotso would jump in and that skinny guy with dreads sitting in the corner, too—it'll be three against one. What am I doing in this country?*

Richard and Khanya were yelling at each other. She shook her finger in his face. I thought the walls would burst apart at any moment. I finally made an interjection that was heard: "What she's saying is true, Richard, and you'd know it if you'd read *The Handbook for the Black Revolution*." That stumped him. I am only now beginning to understand what really stumped him. It was not the authority of a foreigner who "could not control his woman." Nor was it the reasoned and well-informed arguments of an African woman, her status as a law student notwithstanding. It was the authority of a book. For most of his life he had sweated and toiled at his kitchen table in the township while other boys were out playing soccer. He'd been studious, steadfast in his conviction that books held a mystical, emancipatory power that could break the shackles of apartheid. But it wasn't true. He'd found far more freedom in six years of gunplay than he had in sixteen years of study.

Nonetheless, the truth of guns had not shaken his faith in books. For he was still a traditional intellectual at heart. So the mention of a "handbook" that he had not read, and that challenged his basic assumptions, gave him pause.

"What handbook?" he said.

"*The Wretched of the Earth*, by Frantz Fanon," I said.

He regained his balance and was about to run roughshod over me when the silent dreadlocked man in the corner said, "Let him speak."

The room quieted. Botsotso looked at Richard. Richard looked at the slight but able-bodied man in the corner, who was no more than twenty-five years old, a good twenty years younger than Richard. A cultural axiom (a youth does not order an elder about) had been trumped...but why, I wondered. Who is this young man and who is he to Richard? Now, we could hear the soft jazz music from the phonograph that was heretofore drowned out by the roar of argument.

"I'd like to hear his views on Frantz Fanon," the young man said.

"Sure, Jabu," Richard said, "why not. Go ahead, m'china," he said to me, "speak."

Having taught Fanon's *Black Skin, White Masks*, as well as *The Wretched of the Earth*, I was in my element and all too happy to hold forth in the same way that Khanya had held forth. When I paused, Jabu said, "What, tactically, would Fanon advise in this dispensation; say, or the Defiance Campaign?"

"I don't know if he'd advise anything, he was a theorist, not a tactician. But I know what he'd want."

"And that is?"

"For Nelson Mandela to be released immediately from prison." Everyone cheered and raised their fists, including the women in the kitchen, who had moved to the threshold to get a glimpse. It was as though the fight in the living room hadn't happened. They were all happy, in agreement, ready to forget the "woman question" and the question of "weak" Black American men and to celebrate the fantasy of Mandela's release.

"And then he should die," I said, "of natural causes, of course. But quickly, before he can do the revolution any damage."

Suddenly the sea changed. The room howled curses of anger
and indignation at me. Even the women in the kitchen were enraged.
Richard and Botsotso leapt to their feet. Khanya was wide-eyed and
sober—torn between her affection for me and anger. *Well, there goes your
chance with her.*

But Jabu was neither angry nor enthused. "Let him finish," he
said, soberly, to Richard and Botsotso, who were threatening to kill me
lest I leave the house that minute. Richard protested. But Jabu raised his
hand. "Let him finish," he said.

I told them that apartheid was no longer the problem; liberalism
was the problem, laissez-faire White supremacy was the problem.
Though it was clear that Mandela wanted an end to apartheid, it should
also be clear that he would not help people like Chris Hani or Winnie
Mandela usher in a socialist state. "How do you know?" retorted
Botsotso indignantly, "Have you been visiting him in prison?" I said
that all anyone had to do was read the symptoms of his letters to the
world; those bits of pieces of his thought that have reached us from
Robben Island. "The man's a Christian and a lawyer; that's the worst
combination," I said. "From what I've heard from him, he'd take a
jaundiced view toward rent strikes and mortgage loan boycotts. Sure, he's
against apartheid, but how radical is that? It's like saying you're against
starvation or torture. Hardly the grist of revolutionary thought."

"So, you're Mandela's pen pal," Richard laughed, and so did
everyone else. "Tell us what his mail says, m'china."

"It's not what's in the letter that counts," I said, "it's who it's to:
none of his letters are written to anyone in this room. They're written
to liberals for a liberal consensus. His letters say we should have the
right to eat in Hillbrow if we want to eat in Hillbrow. We should live in
the suburbs if we can afford to live in the suburbs. But whatever we do
we should go to work, pay our taxes, and get the same gold watch the

Whites get at the end. He wants a White state with a Black face. Is that liberation?"

"You're lying!" said Botsotso.

"So what's the truth if I'm lying?"

"You can't come to our country and slander our leaders!" he blurted out.

"You're moving the goal posts."

Richard now sat forward on the edge of his chair and put his hand on Botsotso's arm as if to say, let me handle this. He shook his finger at me and the ice knocked about in the glass he held in his other hand and his drink almost spilled on the floor.

"Hey, m'china! You're talking about a man who's been locked up for twenty-five years. Who are you, anyway?"

"I'm no one." The liquor had gone to my head as it had to all of theirs; in my peripheral vision I noticed the women at the kitchen door listening to every word. Khanya touched my arm, as if telling me to come back to shore; these waters are too deep and too dangerous, Frank.

"I'm an uncredentialed kaffir," I asserted, unheeding Khanya's hand on my arm, "just like you, Richard."

Richard rose to his feet, his fists balled. I thought he was going to drive his fist through my skull. But the young man with dreads said, "You're suggesting we struggle to free Madiba from prison and then kill him once he's released—I'd like to understand the analysis behind such a provocative statement."

Richard was stymied by the question, and curious to boot, so much so that he sat back down. Still, he managed to thrust a finger in my direction and say, "We should kill him!"

"You're being provocative," I said to Jabu, ignoring Richard's latest ballot initiative, "needlessly provocative."

"Am I?" Jabu smiled, as though he alone knew where this would lead.

"I didn't say we should kill Mandela. I said it would be nice if he died of natural causes. He would be of great service to the revolution—dead. Just as he's of great service to us now—in prison."

"So, he'd be an asset to the Boers if he were out of prison and lived too long?" said Jabu.

"Yes, but more to the Brits than to the Boers; and even more to U.S.-style 'liberal democracy' than to the local Brits. Mandela will ripen the terrain for the 'peaceful' invasion of U.S. multinational corporations. The Boers aren't the problem."

Botsotso was incredulous: "The Boers aren't the problem, he says." He motioned to Richard as he spoke, as if to say: I vote "yes" on the referendum to take him out back and beat the shit out of him. "So those weren't Boers waiting for us when we arrived this afternoon? Those aren't Boers driving through Soweto *sjamboking* children and shooting at us?"

"The world is changing, Botsotso. The Afrikaner's hard line is isolating him. The *sjambokings*, the shootings—you'll long for those days if Mandela is allowed to usher in a liberal consensus."

"One of my professors says the English are as angry at the Afrikaner as the Blacks," noted Khanya.

"Yes," I said, and I felt how the sway of the room had shifted in my favor. It could not be registered at the level of agreement, not even the curious man in the corner had shown any signs of alliance with either me or the blasphemous oracle from which I read; but they all had shifted from aggression to curiosity, which meant that I had been granted the power to pose the question. *And the power to pose the question is the greatest power of all.* "But your English professor is not vexed with the Boer for the same reasons you or I are vexed with the Boer. Your professor is troubled by his own exclusion from a cosmopolitan West, not with your degradation at the hands of the state. Apartheid has isolated the Brits in this country culturally, intellectually, and economically, but most of all, at the level of esprit de corps from the rest of the Western world. In other words, he doesn't want to be the only White of Africa; he wants to be a member of a global Whiteness, the enlightened and cosmopolitan Whiteness of Europe and America."

"According to your theory," said Jabu, reflectively, but with a pinch of skepticism, either because he was skeptical or because he did not want to tip his hand at too great an angle toward mine, "Nelson Mandela is the White English liberal's only hope, not only for the rejuvenation of finance capital but for the stabilization of a more subtle, nuanced, and, what you seem to be describing as international, form of White supremacy."

"That's it, in a nutshell."

"Is there anyone in our movement who you approve of," said Jabu, "since you disapprove of Madiba?"

"Chris Rani. Winnie Mandela."

"Anyone else?"

"You." This made him smile. "Khanya. Shirley. Mpo. The other women in the kitchen. Botsotso. Even Richard."

"A little late to be licking arse, m'china," Richard sneered and poured himself another drink.

"I'm not licking ass. I didn't say I liked you. I said I approved of you, politically. I'm making an analysis. Despite your reverence for Nelson Mandela, he would hardly approve of you. Chris Rani and Winnie Mandela may be the only people with Nelson Mandela's stature, but who aren't manacled by his vision. Their leadership is essential to a political project that Fanon would be devoted to; one that could validate and mobilize the energy and split-second analysis that you, Richard, and you, Botsotso, showed when you drew your guns and made those cops stand down; one that can validate and mobilize the energy and split-second

analysis that sprung from Khanya when she decided to stay right here
in this living room and enlighten us as to the importance of a mortgage
loan boycott as well as a rent strike instead of going quietly to the kitchen.
Mandela would have paid lip service to Khanya's actions, told you two to
put your guns away, and he damn sure wouldn't support a mortgage loan
boycott or the meltdown of the stock market."

Richard appealed to Jabu, "Do you believe this nonsense?"

"It's a theory," said Jabu.

"Voetsek! I want him and his talking-woman out of my house!"

"Your words could precipitate internecine conflict within the
ANC," said Jabu. "There's always that danger."

"The conflict already exists—my words would just make me a
scapegoat."

"But, still, we don't want in-fighting in the ANC," said Khanya.

"I don't want in-fighting, either," I said. "But it seems to me that
a struggle for hegemony is inevitable. It's either our ANC or it's their
ANC. We can't very well share it."

"Nor should we kill Madiba," said Botsotso.

"You're twisting my words again!" I said. "What I said was that
if he's released from prison he'll use his biblical stature to sanctify an
accommodationist stance through which cosmetic changes would be
heralded as essential changes and the revolution would be up shit's creek!
We need his legacy but we don't need him."

In the kombi from Soweto back to Braamfontein, Khanya was
still unnerved by the way I'd spoken about Nelson Mandela. It was not
my analysis that disturbed her, for my analysis had simply built upon
what she'd said about rent strikes and mortgage loan boycotts as means
of mobilization. Rather, she shared, with Richard and the others (except
Jabu, who never showed his hand), a feeling that whereas Mandela's ideas
could be debated, Mandela the man was sacred.

"You talk like he's your father," I scoffed.

Her anger at my cavalier response prompted her to say: "He is my father!" But the look in her eyes that immediately followed was one of regret and embarrassment at her outburst.

We were silent as we walked from the kombi rank on Bree Street up the hill to her dormitory at the University of the Witwatersrand. The air was cool but not too cold for a midwinter's night in July and the moon was high and glistening. It was a perfect night for love. But love, I feared, was not in the air. To my surprise we kissed goodnight and promised to meet the next day.

BDS AND THE CULTURAL BOYCOTT OF ISRAEL

Launched in 2005 by a coalition of Palestinian civil-society organizations, the Boycott, Divestment, and Sanctions (BDS) movement is a nonviolent campaign to spark international action against the Israeli government's systematic violations of Palestinian human rights. Adopting tactics pioneered by anti-apartheid activists, BDS aims to apply cultural, economic, and political pressure on Israel to render it a pariah state if it does not radically change its policies toward Palestinians. Significantly, the movement's three central tenets—an end to the Israeli military occupation of Arab lands, full equality for Palestinian citizens of Israel, and the right of Palestinian refugees to return to their homeland—constitute a comprehensive political platform that unites a multiply fragmented population.

Both the demands and the tactics of BDS are highly controversial. First, at the tactical level, the cultural and academic boycott of Israel—initiated in 2004, before the formation of the full BDS call—finds particular opposition, raising two major objections: it is said to isolate and harm those elements of the Israeli population most critical of their government's policies, and to diminish the unique capacities of the arts and education to foster understanding and spark difficult conversations. Critiques such as these find in-depth *responses as well as rebuttals in this section, for which the cultural boycott is a priority given this anthology's themes of artist-led resistance and cultural production. Secondly, at the level of demands, BDS' three tenets find uneven support. While the goals of ending the occupation and granting Palestinian citizens of Israel equal rights are actively pursued by a wide swath of liberals and progressives around the world, the right of return (which would apply to as many as 7 million refugees) is far more contested, because it would fundamentally alter Israel's self-definition as a Jewish state. The question of Palestinian return is thus another focus for many of the essays included in this section, all of which take for granted the need to struggle against the oppression of Palestinians by radically transforming Israel—and not just ending its fifty-year-old occupation. The contributors featured here, who are Jewish Israelis and Palestinians living in either Israel-Palestine or the United States, address these and other questions central to the debate surrounding BDS, while further asking how cultural producers can help foster "co-resistance" among Palestinians, Israelis, and committed artists and activists around the world.*

Returning not just to Israel's foundation but to the origin of political concepts such as sovereignty, citizenship, and self-determination, media theorist and curator Ariella Azoulay's essay parses BDS' long historical backdrop in an attempt to articulate the conditions that could generate new civil alliances between Jewish Israelis and Palestinians. For Azoulay, BDS rightly targets not only the occupation but the entirety of the "regime-made disaster" that has resulted in the ongoing dispossession of the Palestinian people since 1948. Where BDS directly addresses citizens in other parts of the world, however, Azoulay asks how Israelis can engage with the movement from their position as "citizen-perpetrators" whose national belonging is structured by the expulsion and exclusion of Palestinians. She proposes that Jewish Israelis adopt BDS as "a call to redefine the nature of their citizenship altogether," clearing the way "to start imagining new forms of partnership devoid of any claim for Jewish supremacy." Thus, in addition to the rights asserted by BDS, Azoulay adds another: "the right not to be a perpetrator."

Human rights lawyer and Jadaliyya *co-editor Noura Erakat, meanwhile, offers an incisive perspective on the more recent political conditions that have given rise to BDS. Analyzing the impact of the Oslo Accords, Erakat argues that the so-called "peace process" facilitated more rapid Israeli settlement in the occupied West Bank, fragmented and segregated the Palestinian population, and weakened a Palestinian leadership once devoted to national liberation. "Rather than end the occupation," she writes, "[Oslo] signaled a new phase of Israeli domination—one in which Israel maintained its occupation regime while outsourcing its day-to-day security needs to the Palestinians and footing the bill to the United States." In this context, Erakat views BDS as significant in uniting Palestinian civil society across its Israeli-imposed divisions and despite its corrupt representatives in the Palestinian Authority. And under these conditions, she asserts, culture cannot merely facilitate dialogue, but "must begin by disrupting collaboration and establishing the grounds for collaborative resistance."*

In an interview that explores both existing and hypothetical models of co-resistance in Israel-Palestine, the architect and political theorist Eyal Weizman speaks about the ways the academic and cultural boycott can lead to new, decolonized forums for cultural production and education. Analyzing BDS in light of theories of the general strike that underscore its generative, community-building potential, Weizman asks, "How do we move from a stage of undermining Israel's legitimacy by applying the force of withdrawal to a next step of building alternative, egalitarian spaces?" Even as he sees such radical transformation as the horizon for co-resistance, however, he grapples with the benefits and pitfalls of engaging with existing Israeli state institutions in order to advance Palestinian rights, navigating what he calls "the gray zone of tensions between the tactics of boycott and the general strategy of resistance."

Reviewing critiques of BDS leveled by writers who oppose the Israeli occupation, the political theorist Nasser Abourahme parses their objections to the most controversial of the movement's three tenets: the right of Palestinian refugees to return to their homeland. In Abourahme's analysis, not only do these otherwise left-leaning commentators equate Palestinian return with a denial of Jewish self-determination, but "return is always read as a euphemism for (vaguely defined) destruction." Confronting this fear of retaliatory violence, and the conflation of self-determination with demographic dominance it implies, Abourahme also challenges a prevalent assumption that return means turning back the clock. He presents the Palestinian desire for return not as a naïve longing for a time before the Nakba, but a refusal to see the continuation of Israel's foundational violence as inevitable. The BDS call, in Abourahme's view, is "an invitation to a future no longer bound to the trajectories of the colonial encounter, or the antagonistic identities forged in that encounter's primal event."

Examining BDS through the lens of political economy, the curator Joshua Simon situates the movement within what he calls—following the philosopher Michel Feher—a period of "neoliberal sovereignty," in which sovereignty is not held by citizens of a state but by its external investors and debt holders. In this context, Simon laments that BDS addresses neither the Israeli public as a whole nor its working class in particular, calling it "a form of neoliberal protest" and "an acute symptom of post-Oslo Palestinian dependency on the international community." At the same time, he recognizes the strategic necessity of targeting the international class of investors to which the Israeli government is financially accountable. Simon's analysis of BDS as a symptom of and response to global neoliberal capitalism is thus rife with ambivalence; for him, BDS symbolizes the dissolution of both common Israeli-Palestinian projects and a Palestinian politics of national liberation, but it may nonetheless challenge the political-economic realities that circumscribe its present strategy.

In a manifesto-like text, the artist Yazan Khalili proposes a radical amplification of BDS demands, aimed at structurally transforming Israel so that it is no longer defined as a Jewish state. Arguing that Zionism has trapped Israel's Jewish citizens in a racial logic that merely extends European *anti-Semitism, Khalili suggests that BDS can bring about the emancipation of Jewish Israelis as much as Palestinians. Together, he argues, Israelis and Palestinians must boycott Israel as a repudiation of Zionism that sees a revolutionary horizon not in a two-state solution or a one-state solution, but in the dissolution of nationalism and even the state itself. With its proposition of what one might call a "no-state solution," Khalili's text moves beyond the paradigm of sovereignty critiqued in various ways by each of the authors included in this section, recoding the human rights for which BDS advocates with utopian imagination.*

"WE," PALESTINIANS AND JEWISH ISRAELIS: THE RIGHT NOT TO BE A PERPETRATOR[1]

Ariella Azoulay

1. Who Is Called on to Boycott Israel?

The Boycott, Divestment, and Sanctions (BDS) movement is a way to achieve three things: (1) to expose the mechanisms of dispossession, segregation, and legalized discrimination against Palestinians that are part of the Israeli democratic regime; (2) to publicly and internationally express solidarity with the Palestinians as a people, confronting the Israeli regime's continuous efforts to fragment them into groups that are governed differentially within and beyond the green line; and (3) to mount pressure capable of impacting daily life for the privileged group of the governed population, i.e., Jewish Israelis, in order to radically alter the conduct of the Israeli regime or transform it altogether. A call for boycott is based on the assumption that sovereign states are actors in an international arena, and hence individuals, groups, institutions, and states can suspend their interactions with particular regimes until the justice of certain demands are recognized and adequately addressed. The

Palestinian-led BDS movement thus aims to mobilize the international community to respond to a triple call from within that advocates: full equality for Palestinian citizens of Israel, an end to the military occupation of the Palestinian territories, and the right of Palestinians who were expelled in 1948 to return to their homes, on which more later.

The 2005 call for BDS is a way to reverse what the state of Israel has achieved since 1948—on the one hand containing "the conflict" as an internal affair between a sovereign state and its subjected population, and on the other hand determining who among the Palestinians can be "partners" for peace negotiations. Denied their rights to shape the regime or participate in its ruling apparatuses, Palestinians were thus deprived of their status as political actors both internally and internationally.

The boycott targets the Israeli regime, not Israeli citizens, unless they act as representatives of the regime. What, then, is the position of Jewish Israeli citizens with regard to this call? They may not be able to suspend their relations with the state completely, as BDS leaders themselves acknowledge. However, they can narrow them down. Occasionally, when they are able to mobilize symbolic power, they can publicly boycott particular events, prizes, and ceremonies, and avoid giving services that they are required to give. In this sense, their responses to the crimes and abuses practiced by their own regime do not come from an external position and hence do not consist of solidarity of the sort offered by citizens of other countries. Jewish Israelis are governed alongside Palestinians, and they are subjects of the same political regime; their citizenship is not external or incidental to the abuses of Palestinians under this regime, but its constitutive element. Unable to endorse the boycott from the outside, Jewish Israelis can still take part in it, and their participation, as citizens denouncing their own political regime, makes the BDS movement's call a call to redefine the nature of their citizenship altogether.

2. Why Call for a Boycott?

The Israeli occupation regime has governed the West Bank and Gaza through military rule that employs disastrous measures such as concentration sites and camps, blockades, destruction, dispossession, and lethal violence. "The occupation" lies at the center of the effort to mobilize people to support the boycott. When measures employed in the occupied Palestinian territories become more visible through their imprint on the bodies of the regime's direct victims, and when these harms are associated with the Israeli regime that bears direct responsibility for their infliction, the reasons for BDS become clear and the movement gains supporters around the world. This is not a negligible achievement. Criminalizing Israel, as is well known to those who seek to expose the state's crimes, is an extremely difficult task. The growth of the boycott movement is an indication that the filters implemented globally by the Israeli propaganda machine are no longer as effective as they used to be. Many are beginning to realize that the Israeli regime is directly responsible for the disastrous conditions under which Palestinians live.

And yet, the occupation is not the sole reason for supporting the boycott. Already in the initial 2005 call for BDS, its authors made clear that at stake is also "Palestinian people's inalienable right to self-determination" and "[r]especting, protecting and promoting the rights of Palestinian refugees to return to their homes and properties." It is important to note that these two rights, of self-determination and of return, are formulated differently. The first is stated as an "inalienable right" while the second is formulated more hesitantly, as a right in need of "respect, protection and promotion." The latter statement seems to petition for the very acknowledgment of this right, rather than to demand that the entitled persons be able to freely exercise this right. The hesitant tone anticipates, based on past experience, Israel's

possible response to such a petition and the type of support that can
be expected in the international arena, especially from other states.
It is not a coincidence that these two rights are expressed differently.
These are two distinct types of rights: the first reassesses the imperial
policies required for the creation and maintenance of sovereign states,
such as the acts of partition and deportation necessary for a people to
achieve self-determination (at the expense of another people); while the
second threatens to reverse the authority of sovereign states to decide
who will be included in their body politic and what status they will be
given. The difference between these two rights testifies to the way the
civil imagination is bounded by a post–World War II consensus on the
legitimacy of sovereign states constituted by differential rule.

In the years following WWII, armed Jewish forces in Palestine
devised and embraced imperial measures that formed a part of policies
aimed at implementing a "new world order" in and beyond Europe.
Those policies, such as partition, massacres, deportation, destruction,
and looting, helped to construct a body politic in which the most
populous group—Palestinians—became an exception to the rule, that
of Jewish self-determination. Though the numbers are widely known, it
is still important to mention them. With the foundation of the state of
Israel in 1948, 750,000 Palestinians were expelled and the remaining
150,000 became a minority. Meanwhile, almost 700,000 Jewish refugees
and immigrants, most of whom were oblivious to both the scope of
destruction that preceded their arrival and the fabric of the mixed society
that had lived there before 1948, nothing of which remained after they
arrived, were incorporated into the new nation-state. These immigrants
were immediately recruited to partake in the war against the "enemy,"
whose identity was intentionally blurred. The "enemy" was a result of the
conflation of the British colonial power with "Arab armies" and the local
Palestinian population. Thanks to this deception, the neocolonialism

pursued by the nascent state of Israel could pass as anti-imperial struggle and provoke international support.

The destruction of Palestine as a mixed society involved the expulsion of the majority of Palestinians, the dispossession of their property, and the refusal to allow their return. Those expelled were confined to sites and concentration zones ("refugee camps," ghettoes within cities such as Jaffa, Ramleh, and Lydda, and geographical regions such as "the triangle" and zones of the West Bank and Gaza Strip), many of which still exist today. There, for years to come, those expelled were exposed to the accumulating consequences of a regime-made disaster. The constant refusal to allow their return, which has been reaffirmed by every Israeli government since the state's foundation, makes Israeli Jews both preservers of the consequences of crimes committed when the country was founded and perpetrators of new crimes. Under the emergency regulations that have not been revoked since 1948, and whose purpose has been to maintain the principle of differential rule, to be a good citizen means being involved, in more or less direct ways, more or less enthusiastically, in exercising the violence necessary to maintain this principle. Therefore, from the point of view of an Israeli citizen, the call for boycott can also be the beginning of the recognition of a right that Israeli Jews have been consistently deprived of: the right not to be perpetrators.

The crimes that justify the boycott of Israel, crimes perpetrated against the Palestinians, are not just crimes against Palestinians but, to use Hannah Arendt's expression, crimes against humanity.[2] Stopping crimes against humanity and addressing the plight of their victims, providing reparations, and inventing forms of compensation should not remain the interest of Palestinians alone. These should be, first and foremost, the obligations and interests of Israeli Jews and the Jewish community worldwide, of all those who were implicated in committing and perpetuating these crimes, all those who—by collaborating with the political regimes that have ordered the crimes, refused to acknowledge them, and spread misinformation about them—have been deprived of their inalienable right not to be perpetrators.

Since the institution of popular sovereignty in the eighteenth century, and more intensely in the wake of WWII, with the consolidation of an international system of sovereignties based on mutual protection (often against their own governed populations), the "inalienable right of self-determination" has been the most sacred right protected by sovereign states. The recent recognition of a Palestinian state by several European parliaments, including that of the European Union, even before such a state has been established and without any significant changes in the lives of its inhabitants or reparations for past crimes, is symptomatic of this pact among sovereign nation-states. The return of those expelled, on the other hand, is somewhat like a Pandora's box for sovereign states, many of which would refrain from endorsing such a demand for fear of exposing themselves to a *tu quoque* objection. The qualified formulation of the right of return in the BDS movement's foundational statement betrays a tacit acknowledgement of this pact among sovereign nation-states and shows how this pact limits what the movement knows it can expect from the Israeli regime—if, that is, Israel is ever ready to comply with some of the BDS movement's demands. This is, again, symptomatic of the power that the Israeli regime has acquired since it was founded on the ruins of Palestine and the mixed society that lived there.

The right of self-determination foregrounded by the BDS movement is a particular form of rule that was invented in the late eighteenth century by imperial powers through the American and French revolutions and was proposed to colonized peoples against whom crimes were committed. In the name of this right, regime-made disasters spread across the world. Crimes were committed in Palestine in the name of Jews' right to self-determination, a right that was recognized by the UN General Assembly in 1948.[3] These crimes require absolution: Palestinians' place in an undifferentiated body politic should be acknowledged, and Israelis should be free to exercise their right not to become or remain perpetrators. The return of those expelled and the liberation of Israeli Jews from their role as perpetrators are linked and can be achieved only through processes of undoing this regime-made disaster rather than through more partitions, transfer, and cleansing.

3. What Makes a Civil "We" Possible?

The citizen-perpetrator is not only a particular kind of perpetrator but also a particular kind of citizen. Distinct from those high up in the state hierarchy, who plan and order the crimes, and unlike the "thoughtless" Nazi perpetrator described by Arendt,[4] citizen-perpetrators are deprived of the choice not to be perpetrators. For the most part, they act within the capillaries of regime-made disaster and, hence, may at best alleviate the plight of Palestinians, be "more humane" or generous toward the Palestinians in different spheres of life. Even refusal to serve in the army, which few exercise, does not spare them the role of citizen-perpetrator they automatically reassume as soon as they are released from jail. Nothing short of a complete transformation of the principle that organizes the body politic can spare them from assuming this role. Studying the conditions of citizen-perpetrators within a regime based on differential rule, and understanding these conditions as part of the disaster, is a first step toward recognizing the disaster as inseparable from the political regime that generates it.

Implicit complicity with the reproduction of the regime awaits every newborn Israeli Jew. Her situation is not very different from that of the new Jewish immigrants of the late 1940s, thrown into a situation construed as an "existential war" in which they had to do their share in order to become good citizens. True, enough information about the disaster has always been available, but always in bits and pieces—and always mingled with lies. People could have known that this or that war they were recruited to fight was not really a war of "no choice" and that they did not fight for their very existence. More generally, people could have known that crimes had been committed, that Palestinians had been wronged, that they were made into enemies and not born so, and that the Israelis were constructed as natives in order to make the political regime appear as a fait accompli. However, assembling the numerous pieces of the puzzle into a coherent picture, while this fragmented information is almost always distorted, concealed, and scattered, framed as part of a story of "nation building" or as another response to "existential threat," and buried under lies and misleading axioms, is as difficult as it is to persuade people to support the boycott. It takes a lot of time and some civic courage to invest political structures and situations with meanings that would counter those produced by the state. It takes more than a few individuals to propagate *as crimes against humanity* deeds that were originally made to appear as natural and necessary acts of self-defense.

The ongoing catastrophe visited upon Palestinians is inseparable not only from the structure of the Israeli regime and its system of citizenship but also from the fact that the very nature of this regime remains concealed from most Jewish Israelis, who take the differential rule at its foundation as either natural (in "Israel proper") or temporary (in the occupied territories) and cannot understand that—or why—their regime should be dismantled. This collective blindness is an essential aspect of the catastrophe, produced and distributed along the dividing lines of the differential body politic in Israel-Palestine, and is what makes it a regime-made disaster. This disaster is constitutive of the regime, not incidental to its functioning, and contributes to its self-preservation. Most Jewish Israelis do not perceive themselves as perpetrators and do not recognize their regime as one whose end is long overdue; at the same time, conflating the state, the regime, and the people, they perceive calls to dismantle their regime as calls to destroy their country and annihilate its Jewish population. Today, Jewish citizens comprise no more than 52 percent of the governed population in Israel-Palestine. The unreserved support for and unconditional legitimization of differential rule by this group is necessary for the perpetuation of the Israeli regime.

In a decades-long process, the Israeli regime has succeeded in making it almost impossible either to imagine civil life in Israel-Palestine or to recognize the common history of Jews and Palestinians as a point of departure for any process of Palestinian reparation. The engaging call of the BDS movement—"Let us harness solidarity into forms of action that can end international support for Israel's crimes"—should be understood as addressed to the international community. Israelis cannot allow themselves the luxury of solidarity, as if the struggle to overthrow the Israeli regime and the history of almost seven decades of regime-made disaster is a Palestinian cause they support from the outside. Israeli Jews should engage in the BDS movement's call, but they should also do much more. It is their duty to start imagining new forms of partnership devoid of any claim for Jewish supremacy, working to recover pre-1948 modes of civil coexistence, which had not yet been nationalized, and which many of their ancestors opted for at the time.

They should do this not because the BDS movement requires or even welcomes such shared effort and common work of political imagination. Regretfully, it does not. The movement was initiated by Palestinians, in the name of Palestinians, and for the Palestinian cause, as if dismantling a regime-made disaster should be the onus of its direct victims alone. To the contrary, it is only through shared work by Israelis and Palestinians toward a total transformation of the regime under which they have been ruled together as perpetrators and victims that a fertile common ground can reemerge. That said, Palestinians cannot be blamed for not seeking Israelis as partners and collaborators. For decades, they have been deceived by Israeli Zionists who presented themselves as leftists but didn't acknowledge the Nakba, and continued to support the Israeli regime's militaristic logic and principle of differential rule, while rejecting expelled Palestinians' right of return.

Acknowledging the Nakba is a prerequisite to join the BDS movement, but it cannot be enough for Israeli Jews. The destruction of pre-1948 Palestine should concern them not only as a problem of or a catastrophe for the Palestinians, but also as a *crime against humanity* for which they bear responsibility. Hence, in recognizing Palestinian rights, they should also supplement them with a right of their own—the right not to be perpetrators, the right to refuse to inhabit the position allocated to them by the Israeli regime. In the context of this regime, under which Jewish responsibility for the destruction of Palestine and the perpetuation of the catastrophe is still widely denied by many Jews, the universal value of the right not to be a perpetrator can be acknowledged today mainly by Palestinians and within the BDS movement. This universal right should be at the foundation of a different civil contract, which would emerge through a process of catastrophe reversal, including recognizing and promoting the right to return and reparations. Such common work on reversing the outcome of the catastrophe should include the inalienable right of all citizens to refuse to become perpetrators. This right could serve as the foundation of a new Palestinian-Jewish partnership. On this basis, a civil "we" might finally be uttered again.

THE CASE FOR BDS AND THE PATH TO CO-RESISTANCE

Noura Erakat

The following text is a version of the speech Noura Erakat gave at the Vera List Center's April 2015 colloquium, "Assuming Boycott: Resistance, Agency, and Cultural Production." It has been lightly modified and expanded by Erakat, together with the editors of this book.

Why BDS?

The strength of the Boycott, Divestment, and Sanctions movement (BDS) is built on twin pillars, each of which arises from the essential fact that it is a Palestinian-led movement. The first of these pillars is that it represents the largest swath of Palestinian civil society to emerge from the political vacuum created by the collapse of the Palestinian Liberation Organization (PLO) into the administrative mandate of the Palestinian Authority (PA). This shift was a result of the Oslo Accords, which mandated limited Israeli withdrawals from Gaza and the West Bank, while fragmenting the latter into three administrative Areas. The Accords ushered an autonomy framework for Palestinians without any guarantees of independence or sovereignty, without resolving issues related to Jerusalem, the right of Palestinian refugees to return to their homes, or the proliferation of settlements in the West Bank. The PA, meant to be an interim body, supplanted the PLO and debilitated a national liberation program and replaced it with a containment process euphemistically portrayed as a peace process for state building. The second of these pillars is the total suppression of Palestinian resistance, to which I will return after examining the ever-worsening condition for Palestinians living in the wake of Oslo.

In the two decades since the Oslo agreements, Israel has torpedoed the possibility of a sovereign Palestinian state. It has increased the population of Israeli settlers in the West Bank (including East Jerusalem) from 200,000 in 1993 to nearly 600,000 by March 2015.[1] It has built a Wall, declared illegal by the International Court of Justice, whose length spans mostly through the West Bank and effectively expropriates 13 percent of the territory.[2] More generally, Israel has accelerated its settlement-expansion program in Area C, or 62 percent of the West Bank.[3] It has declared 18 percent of that territory a military firing zone, precluding the residency of Palestinians living there and necessitating their forced displacement.[4] Israel's Military Order 1650 on the Prevention of Infiltration prohibits Gaza's residents from living, working, or studying in the West Bank.[5] Together with Israel's naval blockade and land siege, it has exacerbated the social, economic, and political distance between Palestinians in the West Bank and their counterparts in Gaza— otherwise intended to constitute a single civic and national polity. Israel's ongoing siege of the Gaza Strip, together with systematic military onslaughts, have risked making conditions in the coastal enclave unfit for human survival.[6] Finally, the state's Judaization campaign in East Jerusalem continues to diminish the presence of Palestinian Jerusalemites in what amounts to an ethnic cleansing campaign.[7] Israel uses a matrix of laws and policies including home demolitions, residency revocations, and exorbitant retroactive taxes to manufacture a Jewish demographic majority. In 2008 alone, Israel withdrew Jerusalemite residency for nearly 4,600 Palestinians—hardly preparing East Jerusalem to become the future capital of a Palestinian state.[8]

Far from resisting these conditions, the official Palestinian leadership has facilitated them.

The high cost of occupation, both financially and politically, drove Israel to enter the aforementioned peace negotiations in the early 1990s.[9] Rather than end the occupation, this initiative signaled a new phase of Israeli domination—one in which Israel maintained its occupation regime while outsourcing its day-to-day security needs to the Palestinians and footing the bill to the United States, thereby reducing its own costs.[10] The outcome is that the Palestinian leadership has become a proxy arm of Israel's occupation, whereby it protects Israel's illegal settlement enterprise from Palestinian resistance, rather than protecting Palestinians by resisting the occupation. Consider that in the course of its twenty-two-day military onslaught of the Gaza Strip during the winter of 2008–2009, Israel was able to deploy its troops from the West Bank to the besieged enclave because of their reliance on Palestinian security forces. As the U.S. lieutenant general Keith Dayton, who trained those forces, put it:

> The IDF also felt—after the first week or so—that
> the Palestinians were there and they could trust them.
> As a matter of fact, a good portion of the Israeli
> army went off to Gaza from the West Bank—think
> about that for a minute—and the commander was
> absent for eight straight days. That shows the kind
> of trust they were putting in these people now.[11]

This is just one glaring example illustrating how Israel, together with U.S. support, has co-opted and neutralized the Palestinian leadership within the framework of the peace process.

To anyone paying attention to the realities obscured by American media outlets and Israeli hasbara, the two-state solution has long been dead. In fact, now it would take effort to ignore this predicament, in light of Israeli leaders' repeated pronouncements that there will never be a Palestinian state. They have made clear their intentions to retain full control over the West Bank and to deny any measure of meaningful Palestinian sovereignty.[12] Israel is intent on pursuing its settler-colonial policies in Mandate Palestine, and toward all Palestinians irrespective of their geographic residence or legal jurisdiction, through an interlocking process of dispossession, removal, and concentration. It achieves these goals using martial law in the West Bank, a mix of martial and administrative law in East Jerusalem, civil law within Israel, and all-out warfare in the Gaza Strip.[13] The co-optation of an effective Palestinian leadership left a political vacuum; the civil society initiative calling for BDS has been one effort to fill that void.

The second pillar bolstering BDS, then, is the near-absolute foreclosure of effective resistance. Israel has effectively delegitimized all forms of Palestinian political struggle. Even the tepid invocation of international law by the PA is framed as an affront to peace building; direct actions are ignored and/or severely repressed; and every turn to armed resistance has been labeled terrorism, even when targeting Israeli soldiers, and even when launched in direct response to Israeli attacks.[14] Moreover, the United States has disabled and dismembered other forms of international legal mechanisms ranging from the fact-finding missions of the UN Human Rights Council to attempts by national courts to apply universal jurisdiction, to the reach of the International Court of Justice, and arguably the reach of the International Criminal Court as well.[15] If it were up to the United States, even the UN General Assembly would be an unavailable forum to the Palestinians. Working together, Israel and the United States have successfully leveraged power politics to meaningfully incapacitate legal, diplomatic, and military resistance to Israel's settler-colonial regime. They have neutralized and co-opted the Palestinian leadership, disabled international mechanisms for justice, and delegitimized Palestinian resistance. Meanwhile, Israel's settlement project continues to expand, steadily and ceaselessly.

Under these conditions, it is ever more incumbent on an international community to find new ways to stand in effective solidarity with Palestinians, especially by heeding direct Palestinian calls. For cultural workers and artists, such solidarity has taken the form of endorsing the call put out by the Palestinian Campaign for the Academic and Cultural Boycott of Israel (PACBI), an essential facet of BDS.

Settler-Colonialism and BDS

The tripartite call of BDS, which is based on human rights norms and international legal principles, seeks to bring about the right of return for all Palestinian refugees, the end of Israeli occupation, and equality for the Palestinian citizens of Israel who comprise roughly 20 percent of its population. And yet these rights-based demands have been maligned as bigoted toward Jews. Not because they target Jewish people—to the contrary, BDS is an anti-racist, intersectional movement, embraced by Jewish advocacy groups, labor unions, racial justice organizations, faith-based institutions, and a constellation of formations constituting the U.S. Left. Rather, Israel declares that BDS, a nonviolent, global, rights-based movement, is the second most significant threat to Israel after a nuclear-capable Iran because of the threat it poses to its demographic balance in particular, and its settler-colonial project in general.[16]

Zionist logic, as articulated by its founding father and two-time prime minister, David Ben-Gurion, requires an 80 percent Jewish majority where a native Palestinian population already existed.[17] To achieve this, Palestinians had to be removed. Israeli forces displaced and forcibly exiled 700,000 native Palestinians through May 1948, who today constitute a 6.6-million-strong refugee population. This removal, however, is not simply a one-time historic practice—it is ongoing.[18] Today, Israel continues to dispossess and segregate Palestinians regardless of their geographic location or status as citizens, residents, or civilians under occupation. Within its 1948 borders, the state of Israel bifurcates Jewish nationality and Israeli citizenship in order to facilitate the immigration of Jews and diminish the rights of its 1.2 million Muslim, Christian, and atheist Palestinian citizens, sometimes dispossessing them of their lands and removing them altogether—as evidenced by the Prawer Plan targeting 40,000 Palestinian Bedouins in the Negev and the Ban on Family Reunification that disproportionately impacts Palestinian-Israelis. In the West Bank, including East Jerusalem, Israel has carried out similar dispossession by martial and administrative law, often using "security" as a nebulous, catchall justification.[19] Between 1967 and 2004, Israel revoked the residency of 140,000 Palestinians in the West Bank without due process, thereby prohibiting them from a right to entry.[20]

In this context, BDS poses a threat to Israel because the state is based, and has been based since its foundation, on a racist logic of demographics and a right to race-based discrimination that privileges Jews at all levels. Israel is, after all, legally defined as a Jewish state, and as such, it discriminates as a matter of fact—the only question is how much and by which means? While the BDS movement is not a settler-decolonization movement, its terms work to destabilize the normalcy of Israeli settler-colonialism. It thus possesses the germ for much greater possibilities necessary for meaningful emancipation for both Jews and Palestinians. As a tactic, the three-pronged demands of the Call explicitly put into question the race-based distribution of fundamental rights such as those to family, water, land, livelihood, culture, and nationhood. It effectively highlights the abnormality of Israel's racially stratified regime of rights and privileges. By representing Palestinian interests as a holistic national body, the Call shatters the violent demarcations that fragment Palestinians. It insists that Israel maintains a uniform policy toward all Palestinians regardless of legal jurisdiction and geographic residence. The movement also upends a narrative of peacemaking between two counterparts. Instead, it highlights the power disparity inherent in a settler-colonial relationship between colonial power and colonial subjects.

Art as a Bridge?

When it comes to Palestine and Israel, everywhere one turns there are calls for dialogue. It's a concept with universal appeal—what kind of person could be against talking a conflict out? But not all dialogue is the same. It can be meaningful if undertaken with a critical perspective on power relations. However, it can also be counterproductive in ways that have grave consequences when applied without attention to the imbalance of power that shapes the Palestinian-Israel conflict. Dialogue is a powerful tool, for example, in a transitional justice framework, where it builds a bridge from the end of a conflict to a new and sustainable status quo. On the other hand, dialogue during ongoing conflict is paralyzing and serves to reify the current status quo. Rather than rectify gross imbalances of power, it elides them and supplants a political analysis with a cultural one. "Interfaith dialogue" presumes that religious extremists "on both sides" fuel waves of irrational violence, directing attention away from an apartheid system rooted in settler colonialism. "Intercultural dialogue" implies that the conflict comes down to a battle between competing nationalisms, as if Palestinians and Israelis belonged to neighbor states with remotely comparable power, which would stop fighting if their peoples just understood one another better. In fact, Palestinians understand the Israeli side all too well. Like other marginalized groups whose perceptions remain unobstructed by the blinding shades of institutionalized privilege, they are deeply attuned to Israeli concerns and perceptions of reality.

The problem is that Israelis never have to learn about Palestinian history, culture, or daily life, and do not fully appreciate their roles as members of a settler-colonial regime. Instead, their pedagogical curricula reinforce a revisionist history of the land and its peoples, U.S.-afforded diplomatic immunity shields them from any meaningful consequences available in multilateral fora, and urban planning from within Israel and extending into the West Bank segregates and concentrates Palestinian populations—be they citizens or persona non grata as civilians under occupation—so that they almost never have to see a Palestinian.

If that were not enough, the Knesset has passed legislation proscribing even the exercise of education and awareness. Take the 2011 Nakba Law, which targets groups dedicated to revealing how Israel's establishment as a Jewish state with an 80 percent majority necessitated the *ongoing* forced removal, dispossession, and concentration of native Palestinians. The act threatens to revoke state funding for NGOs teaching this history, such as Zochrot, an organization that advocates for decolonization and the Palestinian right of return. In 2011, the Knesset also passed the "Anti-Boycott Law," authorizing the Finance Minister to revoke funding or remove tax breaks from Israeli NGOs that support the boycott of any Israeli products, even if limited to those made in illegal settlements.[21] These laws effectively prohibit the sort of conversation that would challenge institutionalized supremacy and apartheid.

That's why any "dialogue" must begin by disrupting *collaboration* and establishing the grounds for collaborative *resistance*. Artistic, cultural, and faith-based collaboration should overturn settler-colonial myths and violent processes, which impact both Palestinians and Jewish Israelis. In contrast to the deployment of dialogue as an opportunistic tactic aimed at reinforcing and reproducing the status quo, dialogue must begin with an understanding and appreciation of Palestinian rights and demands, if it is to lead to co-resistance. It must begin with awareness that Israelis are not neighbors, or even occupiers, but colonial masters and beneficiaries of ongoing Palestinian deprivation.

Within this context, it is perplexing to encourage cultural dialogue and engagement as the prescription. These pat "solutions" do not properly address this condition. Worse, perhaps, they place the onus on Palestinians to educate their colonial overseers. Instead, Israelis should bear that responsibility, supported by a robust global movement based on international law and human rights norms, to join with Palestinians in a difficult but vital process of settler-decolonization. Cultural boycott is not the prescription to settler-colonialism, but it is an effective intervention from which co-resistance can spring.

EXTENDING CO-RESISTANCE

Eyal Weizman and Kareem Estefan

Kareem Estefan: Like other boycotts and political campaigns predicated on collective withdrawal from events and institutions, the Boycott, Divestment, and Sanctions (BDS) movement is generally considered to wield a negative form of agency. The cultural and academic boycott, in particular, is said to obstruct—or, its opponents would argue, censor—cultural production. While it is no doubt true that BDS has impeded certain events from proceeding, such a perspective overlooks the more significant fact that a cultural boycott engenders conversations about the political stakes of art, in and beyond the context of Palestine/Israel, which otherwise would not take place. For example, a boycott campaign launched against an exhibition supported by the Israeli Ministry of Culture, far from shutting down all conversation, will redirect the energies of mounting an art show toward the work of raising awareness about Israel's settler-colonial violence, and where Israeli cultural production stands in relation to the state's political policies. Such efforts can transform discourse about the symbolic politics of representation—what art depicts, *and how—into debates about the concrete political effects of representation—what art* does, *and in what context—in normalizing or resisting segregation and colonization. From this perspective, the cultural boycott of Israel is a demonstration of extraordinary positive agency: the power to shape conversations about culture that bring the long-repressed rights, demands, and analyses of Palestinians to the forefront.*

Speaking at a panel on the meaning of BDS in the Vera List Center's "Assuming Boycott" series last year, the architect and political theorist Eyal Weizman invoked the concept of "co-resistance," referring to acts of civil disobedience undertaken in West Bank villages like Nabi Saleh and Bi'lin, where Israeli and international solidarity activists have joined Palestinians in weekly nonviolent protests of the occupation. Co-resistance is one way to frame adherence to the BDS guidelines that underscores the active engagement that solidarity entails, even when it means declining an invitation to speak at a university or deciding not to make art commissioned for a major exhibition. In the context of a boycott campaign, co-resistance unsettles the binary of action and non-action, instead channeling creative social energies from one field of action to another. With this in mind, I asked Weizman how more cultural platforms could become sites of co-resistance, pursuing an analogy he introduced at his "Assuming Boycott" talk: BDS as a form of withdrawal and production akin to the general strike.

Eyal Weizman: I support the BDS movement. It is a form of civil action directed at Israeli colonial practices and simultaneously at those Western governments, above all that of the United States, which support nearly all of Israel's actions and continually reward the state with unparalleled financial, diplomatic, and cultural support. It has become popular in part because, at its most basic level, it turns *non-action* into a form of activism. This helps people living in the United States or Europe to avoid institutional relations with Israel; however, the demand that it poses on people closer to and more involved in the issue is different. Withdrawal needs to be complemented with other avenues for action. Wherever BDS cuts off or impedes a relation with a state institution, the movement should find—perhaps even create—new forums for solidarity and cultural production.

One of my favorite parts of the PACBI guidelines makes the distinction between cohabitation and co-resistance, explaining that in a situation of structural violence, mere cohabitation maintains the status quo. Along these lines, I think that the academic and cultural boycott needs to be seen as an intervention in the production of knowledge, rather than simply a series of obstructions. Since taking up the call of BDS, I have started lecturing locally only in association with select, committed human rights organizations, such as Zochrot, Yesh Din, Al Haq, or the Regional Council of Unrecognized Villages of Negev, and through the Decolonizing Architecture Art Residency (DAAR) studio in Beit Sahour, in which I'm a partner. These groups promote new means to understand and creatively grapple with the ongoing social, political, and spatial effects of Israeli colonization, and given the way the Israeli government persecutes them, they need support.

Once we understand it as a movement channeling intellectual and political energy away from Israeli institutions, BDS becomes part of a wider spectrum of political actions that *block* non-democratic and unequal platforms and *open* democratic platforms for co-resistance. It is a matter of forging communities of practice, wherein action produces political constituencies and radical subjectivities among those who withdraw from the state. Of course, withdrawal is in itself action—a good example is the general strike. Consider theories of the general strike from the early twentieth century, like those of Rosa Luxemburg, in which the strike is not only a form of non-action or a means to avoid work; its purpose is also to build solidarity, steal back time, and make space for other forms of living. A strike is labor directed to new ends: it opens up sites for organization and contributes to resistance, resilience, and the communal production of knowledge. It is also an important stage in the process of revolution and political transformation. The strike already has a great tradition in the Palestinian struggle. In the first intifada, for example, strikes led to the closures of schools, and informal academies popped up in the very places—garages, workshops, shops—that were shut off from the outside world, including the Israeli economy.

The challenge for the BDS movement is to find and create platforms that are egalitarian and democratic—to provide alternatives to the forms of culture and politics that exist. So, if we consider theories of the general strike as a withdrawal and an interruption, we should also ask, where is the site of creation in BDS? How do we move from a stage of undermining Israel's legitimacy by applying the force of withdrawal to a next step of building alternative, egalitarian spaces?

To put it differently, not only do we need to boycott Israeli universities because they serve the apparatus of Israeli domination; and not only do we need to boycott Israeli galleries and museums because they put a lick of paint over colonialism; but equally, we need to open universities and art spaces that adhere to the principles of BDS and can become sites of co-resistance, and not, as is often contended, sites of separation. Building activist institutions such as these would also help counter the false claim that the cultural and academic boycott restricts freedom of expression and academic freedom.

K.E.: I agree: it is important to emphasize the conversations, relations, ideas, and institutions that develop through boycott, especially in light of critiques of BDS as an impediment to academic and cultural activity. But what would a general strike look like in Palestine/Israel, where populations are not only fragmented but, as Ariella Azoulay and Adi Ophir have shown, differentially governed? What are the conditions in which co-resistance can emerge, when you have so many segregated groups afforded different rights and facing unequal economic and political conditions? The implications and impact of withdrawal for Palestinians in the West Bank, for Jewish Israeli citizens, and for Palestinian citizens of Israel, for example, are radically dissimilar. Meanwhile, Palestinians in Gaza have already been effectively removed from

*the Israeli economy, not to mention Israeli citizens' field of visibility, through
a decade-long blockade. In a context in which Israel has concentrated most
Palestinians in discrete territories apart from its own economic centers, how can
the general strike build alternative communities of the sort you describe? How
can it negate the differential impact of Israeli rule, which subjects Palestinians,
to varying extents according to their structural positions, to economic, political,
and military forms of violence?*

E.W.: First, one would have to ask: What are you withdrawing
from, what are you striking against? The brutality of the Israeli military
apparatus and the settlers is abundantly clear to anyone paying attention.
But we need to look at the more intricate ways in which cultural
and academic production in Israel is connected to these systems of
domination. This is not just about the exclusion of Palestinian students
from Israeli universities and other educational institutions. Nor is it
only about the research and development functions of universities
that are built upon and benefit from political violence enacted against
Palestinians, for example through military technologies such as drones,
cyber-weapons, and armed bulldozers. Nor is it only about the soft
acquiescence of most Israeli academics, excepting several important
voices, like Anat Matar or Neve Gordon (who support BDS), to the
injustices they witness within and around their own institutions.
Universities also develop more intricate lines of legitimation, both legal
and ethical, whose overall effect is to authorize the actions of the Israeli
regime. Legitimation is not simply an aftereffect of repressive actions,
or a process external to them; legitimation is the condition of possibility
for ongoing perpetration. If denial is directed to the past, legitimation
is aimed at the future. It is thus more dangerous and more urgent to
address. The incredible apparatus that Israel has constructed exercises
both the hard power of physical transformation and the softer power that
has managed to legitimize injustice to the extent that calling it criminal

has itself been criminalized. To face this challenge, BDS must become a site of knowledge production in another way: it must continuously map all the intricate ways in which knowledge flows, and academic, legal, and political networks intersect, to legitimize the state of affairs.

Luxemburg's model of the general strike should have—and could have, according to her—united the workers of Germany and France in their refusal to fight and kill each other. It could have succeeded, that is, only by transgressing national borders. To continue the analogy, BDS unites activists in Palestine within the '67 or '48 borders and impacts the entire domain of colonial domination, from taxing and infrastructure to court decisions and military actions, in addition to reaching abroad. Through rupture it can connect the separate actors within a field it creates.

K.E.: Let's step back for a moment and consider where BDS stands today in relation to what could be called its "intended audience": citizens of the Western countries that have historically provided the most significant political and financial backing for the Israeli occupation regime. In the United States, BDS activists have recently celebrated victories like the endorsement of the academic boycott of Israel by the American Studies Association, major divestments from the occupation by the Presbyterian Church and the United Methodist Church, and widespread endorsements of the cultural boycott by prominent artists and musicians. A Pew Research poll conducted in May 2016 showed that, for the first time, Democrats who identify as "liberal" (the only other options it provided were "moderate" and "conservative") sympathize more with Palestinians than with Israel, a shift that enabled frank debate about the occupation and BDS to publicly unfold on the Democratic Party platform committee, thanks in large part to appointees of Senator Bernie Sanders, namely Cornel West and James Zogby.

At the same time, combatting this surge of support for Palestinian rights are politicians of both major U.S. parties, who have enacted state-level legislation blacklisting organizations that boycott Israel. Anti-BDS bills have become the law in New York and roughly a dozen other states, according to Palestine Legal. What are your thoughts about the status of BDS in the United States and Europe today? How are debates about the Israeli occupation and Palestinian rights evolving, in light of both on-the-ground conditions in Palestine/Israel, and other developments like the Syrian refugee crisis, the rise in xenophobic right-wing populism, and the simultaneous ascendance of left-wing protest movements targeting white supremacy, economic inequality, and climate change?

E.W.: The fact that the United States and many European nations have lined up to support Israel's campaign against BDS signals to me that these countries have given up on ending the occupation and resolving the conflict—if they ever had such aims at all. The BDS campaign should be an uncontroversial appeal to universal human rights, but it is being criminalized because it represents the last challenge to Israeli hegemony. This creates a big division between Western governments and their citizens, as support for Israeli actions has seen a steady decline, and, as you note, more and more people—especially young people—are eager to support Palestinian equality and self-determination. By supporting BDS as a resident of New York today, you protest both Israel and U.S. policies in the Middle East—and, absurdly, *you* will be boycotted, in the sense of being sanctioned, by the state. The stakes are much higher because of the alignment of the entire political class against BDS. In this context, BDS can become a revolutionary force against Western leaders.

At the same time, reactionary, xenophobic politics is clearly on the rise in the United States and Europe, exemplified in the figures of Donald Trump, Nigel Farage, and Marine Le Pen. Indeed, as Israel continues to govern Palestinians as non-citizens, or as second-class citizens, it looks to Europe, and it is now satisfied to see that many right-wing parties are thinking about refugees the same way it has for decades. Indeed, both the United States and many European nations are now reluctant to accept Muslim refugees from the Middle Eastern wars they have launched or helped to create, and they continue to support Israel's refusal to even discuss the readmission of Palestinians it has expelled. Today Israel looks like a pioneer in the management of unwanted refugees, the poor, and the dispossessed, in a politics of separation and containment. The control of Palestinians has become almost absolute: even if we see, here and there, acts of resistance, think of how few there are, given that millions of Palestinians are suffering under occupation! This system of managing people has been honed and perfected. Israeli society pays a very low price for holding down millions of Palestinians. So rather than European politicians saying to Israeli politicians, *stop what you're doing*, Israelis are saying to Europeans, *Look what we can do*. And facing an unprecedented refugee crisis, the European political class is eager to listen.

The rising fascism in Europe and the United States mirrors rampant fascism in Israel, and we need to protest both before more and more Israeli technologies and policies of domination spread. Israel treats Palestine as a laboratory for military and political control; we must instead look to Palestine as a place where modes of civil-society resistance are being developed.

K.E.: At your Vera List Center talk, you said of BDS, "The more proximate you get to the situation, the more complex the picture becomes." Can you expand on what you see as the differences between adhering to the boycott internationally and participating in it from within Israel or the occupied territories?

E.W.: The problem of working from inside is more complicated, of course. Adalah, the advocacy organization for Palestinian citizens of Israel, has a deep understanding of the idea of resistance from within and across the spectrum. In fact, the '48ers are posed with the greatest dilemmas. Part of the struggle is to turn Israel into a democratic state of all its citizens, and prominent figures like Hanin Zu'abi—leader of the progressive Balad party, now part of the alliance of Palestinian-led parties known as the Joint List—have been elected to the Knesset to assert the equality of Palestinians who are otherwise considered second-class citizens.

Yet this kind of action is not without its problems. In Forensic Architecture, we work with Palestinian petitioners across all areas of Israeli control, and we know that the courts in Israel enact the laws that propel and legitimate dispossession. Israeli spokespersons, meanwhile, claim that the state does everything in its power to investigate soldiers and charge them for criminal offenses where appropriate, rendering international process redundant. International humanitarian law is bound by the principle of "complementarity." The International Criminal Court (ICC), for example, is mandated to be a "court of last resort" that will step in only if states show themselves unable or unwilling to launch processes to address violations of international law. Prosecuting a few cases here and there is a useful way for states like Israel to demonstrate that its legal system is competent and willing to examine itself. But its overwhelming purpose is to protect perpetrators and legitimate Israel's ongoing violence and land grabs.

In 2014, despite several isolated legal successes, we at Forensic Architecture determined that withdrawal is preferable to cooperating with the Israeli legal system, that confronting Israel's regime of domination is more effective outside of the state's legal institutions, and that despite being compromised in other ways, international forums provide a better chance at an even-handed process. We have decided we will no longer undertake forensic analysis on behalf of cases presented in Israeli legal forums, nor pass on material to Israeli legal institutions (though for the moment we continue work on cases we have already initiated). But we remain committed to investigating and publicizing Israel's human rights violations, at the same time as we will expose and denounce the violence perpetrated by Israeli legal institutions themselves.

K.E.: The Joint List represents something of a tactical shift away from boycott; many Palestinian citizens of Israel who had always boycotted elections decided to participate for the first time in 2015, as a result of this new alliance. The Joint List now represents the third largest bloc in the Knesset, holding 13 of 120 seats. How do you interpret this development, which on the surface may appear to contradict the ethos of BDS, encouraging further engagement with an oppressive system, rather than total disengagement?

E.W.: As a supporter of the BDS movement, and an artist and professor adhering to the call of PACBI, I would like to see the expansion of the boycott's terms, and productive variations of its tactics. For academics in the United States, who are personally removed from the situation and have little ability to intervene directly, disengagement from Israeli institutions is absolutely necessary. When you are working in Palestine-Israel, especially in '48, the issue is no longer abstract, and decisions in relation to BDS frequently have to be undertaken anew. The closer you are, the more powerful, the more meaningful, such decisions become. Within this context, I find the Joint List very inspiring and consider its existence an act of resistance. As with every Israeli election, many Palestinians with Israeli papers debated whether to boycott the elections. I support the Joint List and think of it as an important part of an anticolonial movement.

Recently, I've been involved in legal support for Bedouin Palestinians. The Bedouin are the only community that has returned to the places from which they were evicted in 1948. For enacting the right of return, for putting this right into practice, they have been beaten down and evicted countless times. They have brought cases to Israeli courts. Of course, Israeli courts adjudicate by adhering to Israeli laws that often guarantee the right of the Israeli state to evict Palestinians from their homes; fundamentally, they are mechanisms for dispossession. But I am drawn to a paradox in this example, as I am with the Joint List in the Knesset: these forums can be transformed by using them to articulate radical claims.

Supporting Palestinian rights within Israel requires a much more nuanced critical practice of measuring degrees of complicity and degrees of resistance. What interests me in this practice is the gray zone of tensions between the tactics of boycott and the general strategy of resistance, or more precisely, co-resistance toward the aim of decolonization. When those two principles contradict, one must map the situation and make a decision. And one of the important things about BDS is that it forces you to do your research, to decide what position to take in such situations.

Anti-colonial struggle can turn the tribunal into a tribune—into a theater where the law itself is put on trial. Here I follow the great French lawyer Jacques Vergès, and the possibilities that he articulated with his theory of *rupture*. Vergès insisted on performing his legal duties during the French occupation of Algeria, within the most compromised institutional mechanisms of French colonization in Algiers, in order to turn the court into a platform where people could articulate claims that would not otherwise be heard. Gandhi and Mandela worked in a similar way. Think of Mandela's famous speech in the Pretoria Supreme Court, the highest judicial apparatus of apartheid, in which he condemns the increasingly repressive legislation of the apartheid state, which forced the ANC to take up arms, and declares that he is willing to die for the principle of a non-racial democracy.

K.E.: How do such decisions connect to your work with Decolonizing Architecture? How does Decolonizing Architecture—a collaborative project with the architects Sandi Hilal and Alessandro Petti that has evolved into an art residency in Beit Sahour, near Bethlehem—either take up or challenge the framework of the cultural boycott?

E.W.: In Decolonizing Architecture, we have been thinking about action vs. non-action in terms of the dilemma of Palestinian refugees. In fact, Sandi, Alessandro, and I set the practice up in part to think about the condition of refugeeness—specifically, the principle of not becoming too comfortable in a place that is not home, not making a new home, because this would normalize Israeli dispossession and surrender the right of the refugee to return home. This is a similar dilemma of engagement and collaboration.

The right of return is the most important act of decolonization; it is, in fact, *another name for decolonization*. In other words, Israel could *not* remain Israel if the right of return were granted. It would have to become another place completely—and that's the hope. Indeed, I think Palestinian return is our only hope, and the principle by which all tactics should be measured.

K.E.: By naming the right of return as a decolonial act, it strikes me that you're saying it must be as transformative—as much of a rupture—as 1948 was, but in a sense that we don't yet know how to define. It involves return as an overturning—not a return to the past, but to a new collectivity.

E.W.: A return is not an inversion of time. It is a creation of a new situation and a new mode of living together as equals. A return is also always a return to the urban, though ethnic cleansing has also taken place in rural areas. The urban is not just a dense concentration of buildings and people, but a complex heterogeneity and intensity of relations. And returning to it requires the subversion of the architectural fabric, so there is again an engagement with the very thing that displaced you, the very thing that oppressed you, the very thing that dispossessed you—the cities, villages, and settlements of the colonizer. It will require learning to live with your enemy. To live in the house of your enemy is a critical practice.

BOYCOTT, DECOLONIZATION, RETURN: BDS AND THE LIMITS OF POLITICAL SOLIDARITY[1]

Nasser Abourahme

Sovereign States, Sovereign Anxieties

It is fair to say that the Palestinian-led Boycott, Divestment, and Sanctions (BDS) campaign has today achieved a certain (belated) level of legibility, or audibility. Its opponents still vociferously and viciously fight it but in the U.S. and European academy it has, with some effort, gained the right to be heard. This is not to say that supporting BDS is a safe political or professional stance. On the contrary, the risks associated with BDS seem only to grow with its wider uptake. Today in the United States, despite the absurdity of drafting law to essentially punish inaction, a host of anti-BDS resolutions and bills have been passed at various legislative levels, and the threat of sanction by university administrators remains real. Nonetheless, BDS is, in many Left and even liberal circles, an acceptable topic of debate and conversation. As with any address to a broad and politically diverse audience, however, such audibility quickly leads to questions of reception. More specifically, in this case the growth of the Palestinian-led BDS campaign challenges us to think about, and qualify, the varied forms of political solidarity it engenders.

Here, I examine recent critiques of BDS put forward not by Israel's vociferous defenders, but rather by American and Israeli intellectuals broadly identified with the Left, who oppose Israel's ongoing occupation of Palestinian land, but nevertheless take issue with key aspects of BDS, above all its promotion of the right of Palestinian refugees to return to their homes. These critiques—written by figures including the political scientist Norman Finkelstein, the sociologist and New Left activist Todd Gitlin, and the philosopher Adi Ophir—warrant engagement, I argue, because they mark a certain limit of solidarity with regard to the BDS call among noted voices of the anti-occupation Left in Israel and the United States—a limit that seems to harden around the question of Palestinian return.

Take Norman Finkelstein's dismissal of BDS on the grounds that return means "the end of Israel," because, he claims, "if we end the occupation and bring back six million Palestinians and we have equal rights for Arabs and Jews, there's no Israel."[2] Or, read a recent commentary by Todd Gitlin, which opens by assuring us that he is "devoutly" committed to ending the occupation, but opposes the boycott, because, "In the endgame envisioned by BDS, one set of pieces is left on the board, and the other removed."[3] Or, consider the opinion of M.J. Rosenberg, who writes, "There is no place for any form of Jewish sovereignty in BDS Land, a land in which the Jewish majority is replaced by a refugee-created Palestinian majority, a majority that would not, one can safely predict, permit Israel (or whatever it would be called) to remain a guaranteed refuge for Jews."[4] Aside from the obvious question—what kind of "refuge" requires the continuous dispossession and displacement of others to function as such?—one is struck by how return is always read as a euphemism for (vaguely defined) destruction. For these critics, return is the point at which a certain ineffable threat appears; none of them can tell us why or how the return of refugees would necessarily result in "bloodshed," but each expresses a fear that transmutes the horizon of equal cohabitation into the inevitability of irrational violence.

In all of these critiques, the call for return presents a kind of "smoking gun"—the incontrovertible evidence through which the BDS campaign unveils its true (sinister) self. Finkelstein accuses the campaigners of being "clever," adding, "they understand the arithmetic perfectly well." Gitlin reads dissimulation in the call's stipulations, arguing, "The language masks (however thinly) the desire of one of the parties to the horrendous Israel-Palestinian conflict that the other one disappear." Israeli anthropologist Dan Rabinowitz takes the cloak and dagger imagery even further: "The demands from Israel, designed to be interpreted by innocent bystanders as a call for a two-state solution, obfuscate a more sinister vision that has no place for Israel."[5]

Cleverness, masks, obfuscation, sinister visions. What political common sense produces this sensationalist prose and the confidence of its deductions? What exactly is being defended against existential threat here? While the BDS campaign has not offered a vision of a political future, focusing instead on the minimum needed to eventually lift the boycott, it is no secret that the Palestinian liberation movement has always rejected the racial character of the Israeli state; most involved in this struggle have long maintained that Israel has neither a natural nor a historical right to maintain forms of political membership and statehood that are racially discriminatory. In a sharp riposte to Rabinowitz, Nadia Abu el-Haj makes this clear: "Yes, this is a challenge to the state's future—that is, those of us advocating for boycott and divestment think that the Israeli state has no right to continue to exist as a racial state that builds the distinction between Jew and non-Jew into its citizenship laws, its legal regimes, its educational system, its economy, and its military and policing tactics."[6] The imperative, then, is not as Rabinowitz presents it, that BDS campaigners "must come clean about seeking a post-Israel endgame," but quite the contrary: the detractors of this campaign should make clear what exactly they defend under the proper name Israel.

What kind of political form faces "existential threat" from the end of military occupation, the legal guarantee of substantive equality, and the restitution of rights to the dispossessed? What does Palestinian return pose a threat *to* exactly? That the return of people to their appropriated homes and land and the restitution of their rights, if only within a liberal-bourgeois conception of private property, need not necessarily involve injury to those who have since then accrued "rights" to that property is easy enough to demonstrate (and has been).[7] But this does not seem to be the issue. There is no *necessary* contradiction between the return of the refugees and maintaining some kind of Jewish self-determination in Palestine. The question then becomes, is Jewish self-determination in Palestine contingent upon a majoritarian advantage? This seems to be the assumption in the open demographic anxiety at play in Finkelstein's "arithmetic" and Rosenberg's "refugee-created majority." If it is, then the line between the self-determination that these writers want to hang on to, and the supremacy they want to disavow, begins to thin.

A concern with self-determination also animates Adi Ophir's introduction to a collection of essays he commissioned and edited for the journal *South Atlantic Quarterly*, titled "Israeli Jews Address the Palestinian Boycott Call."[8] Ophir insists that Jewish Israelis "should force themselves to become addressees of the BDS's call"[9] but grapples with the difficulty, or near impossibility, they face in heeding this call. Again, Palestinian return is the insurmountable obstacle. For most Israeli Jews, he writes, "this demand, especially the call to allow

Palestinian refugees the right of return, means a call for 'the elimination of Israel.'"[10] With their insistence on respecting the right of return as a condition for lifting the boycott, BDS organizers "have made it clear that they target Israel not only as a regime of occupation and colonization but also as a Jewish state (implicitly denying Israeli Jews the right of self-determination for the sake of respecting the same right of Palestinians)."[11] It is not clear here if Ophir is paraphrasing a wider anxiety or passing his own judgment. Nonetheless, the presupposition is left intact: no Jewish state means no Jewish self-determination. That becoming an addressee of the BDS call might necessarily entail a reckoning with forms of collective self-determination beyond racial, territorial sovereignty is never really considered. Instead, Palestinian self-determination is itself inscribed into the same formula—that of a sovereign right to a racially defined state. But neither the BDS call nor most of the political history of the Palestinian liberation movement posited such a conjunction.[12] As the political theorist Raef Zreik points out, the lack of an independent state for Palestinians has had little bearing on their national identity: "For Palestinians, sovereignty lies at the margin of identity, while for Zionist Jews it sits squarely at the center."[13] To make the comparison above, Ophir has to implicitly construe return as a desire for sovereignty.

All these arguments, to varying degrees, echo a long line in Zionist public discourse in which the imperative of "no return" is conceived of and articulated as foundational to the very existence of political community. In this register, Zionism is synonymous with *all and any* type of Jewish self-determination in Palestine. In other words, Jewish-Israeli political community appears content-less outside of claims for Jewish territorial sovereignty; a rejection of exclusive Jewish territorial sovereignty over Palestine becomes, *ipso facto*, a rejection of any Jewish self-determination. In contrast, it seems to me that a potential other content was precisely what Ariella Azoulay has sought to define in negative terms, in several recent works, including her essay for Ophir's *South Atlantic Quarterly* section.[14] For her, to answer the boycott call as an Israeli Jew is to exercise the right *not* to be a "citizen-perpetrator." In the state's citizenship system, Israeli Jews are, according to Azoulay, necessarily conscripted as the "preservers of the consequences of crimes committed when the country was founded."[15] The question, then, cannot be one of external solidarity. It is about how to reject one's structural complicity with a colonial polity. BDS and the return of Palestinian refugees, Azoulay insists, are not only the means by which Israeli Jews can begin to refuse perpetration, but also the condition of possibility by which a Palestinian-Israeli "we" can begin to tentatively speak. For nothing less than the total transformation of the principle that organizes the body politic can stop the "regime-made disaster" and the political regime from which it is *inseparable*.

Colonizing, or the Present Continuous

BDS and the call for return elicit another charge: moral inconsistency. What's so special about Israel, the detractors ask? "To be a nation," writes Gitlin, "is to have been conceived in sin. Virgin births may be possible in Middle Earth but not on this planet."[16] This statement (and its underlying logic) not only elides the settler-colonial history of Jewish-Israeli nationalism in a now standard but still startling homology, it also effectively brackets the question of decolonization. Return carries no moral or ethical weight because it is rendered a historically naïve response to a violence that is foundational to the political order of nation-states everywhere. Opposition to BDS appears, here, grounded in a kind of universalism of the unvirtuous. This rationale finds, as Bruce Robbins shows, a curious echo chamber in recent political theory on the Left that insists on the foundational extralegal violence of all nation-states: "Who has not nodded sagely at the idea that the state of exception reveals the truth of the norm, and that every liberal democracy has its origins in bloody atrocities that it then has to cover up?"[17] The problem is that we fail to interrogate the movement, made by people like Gitlin, between political theory and political history. That violence is foundational to most of our *notions* of polities and political orders is certainly true, but to argue that all modern states are therefore historically born in a morally analogous violence is another claim entirely. It is to move from a truism about an organizing *virtuality* of state power (its *arcana imperii* as Agamben might have it) to a claim that this is the *actuality* of all our political histories. Such homologies are necessarily premised on the disavowal of anticolonial thought, on the omission or outright dismissal of the ideas of people like Frantz Fanon or Georges Sorel who carefully parsed the political and historical differences between forms of violence across the colonial binary. In fact the very relevance of that binary (and its contradictions) to the emergence and inheritance of many of our political forms and technologies—including the nation-state, sovereignty, and international law—all but disappears. The anticolonial violence that enabled the eventual independence of, for example, Egypt, is not only historically dissociated from the imperialist order that contemporaneously enabled the ethnic cleansing of Palestine to establish Israel as a Jewish state, but as forms of foundational violence they come to inhabit the same political and ethical plane. To base a critique of BDS activism on this crude flattening of political history is not only bad argumentation; it is also an ethical non-starter. Gitlin's rhetorical move diffuses accountability in an endless and irremediable stream of collective guilt. The premise, as Robbins aptly surmises, acts as an impossible moral threshold: "You can't criticize except from a position of moral purity. You don't occupy a position of moral purity. Therefore you can't criticize." The effect is to paralyze any kind of activism: "If everyone were responsible for everything, no one would really be responsible for anything."[18]

More important than its argumentative sloppiness, the problem with Gitlin's critique is how it works to close the actuality of colonial conquest as an ongoing process. Leaving the glaring historical reductions aside—not *every* nation-state is a settler-colony founded on the ethnic cleansing of hundreds of thousands of people and not *every* nation-state builds a racial binary explicitly into its national institutions—the rhetorical force of Gitlin's argument does not lie in its claims to opposing inconsistency, but in an implicit yet assiduous temporal sleight of hand. What he underscores is the sheer *pastness* of the issue at hand. These are *settled* states, and to dredge up past injustice is to open up a moral sinkhole that might swallow us all. The rhetoric does not simply imply, "yes, of course, ethnic cleansing and dispossession happened but, well, it happened everywhere," but more insistently, "it happened *then*, this is *now*." As Robbins also notes, from Gitlin's perspective, the present is simply a matter of historical fact. Return has been "rendered obsolete by events."[19] For Palestinians, the injunction is, as it always has been, to "get over it and move on." Return is caricatured as a Sisyphean attempt to reverse the past. It appears, in Gitlin's telling denigration of BDS as "a tantrum" and "a stomping of the collective foot," as the ingenuous cry of a childlike population still clinging on to imaginary attachments; or, in the psychoanalytic terms employed by Joseph Massad, the irrational demand of a pathological subject unable to properly mourn a lost object.[20] These critiques entirely misunderstand the political significance of return in the Palestinian intersubjective world, where it signifies neither an atavistic desire for an antediluvian past nor a denial of cold historical facts but a sober recognition of the continuity of colonial violence and the grinding consistency of its relations of force. By contrast, Azoulay's notion of the "citizen-perpetrator," in its very hyphenation, insists that perpetration does not end with the formalization of the state and its regime of citizenship, but subtends the citizen as the very condition of its existence and endurance. Azoulay presents what she calls the "regime-made disaster" not as an "original sin" that might be acknowledged and symbolically sutured yet remain outside of time, but as an ongoing event that constitutes our present. The task is to recognize the colonization of Palestine not as something that has happened but as something that *is* happening, as our present continuous.

There is, nonetheless, an element of truth to the critiques of BDS I have cited above: if the stakes are the (necessarily colonial) sovereign claims of the Jewish state in Palestine, then Palestinian return indeed poses an irreducible challenge. As the historian Gabriel Piterberg makes clear, the disjuncture between Jewish "return" and Palestinian "non-return" is what the entire edifice rests on: "If this dynamic of return/ non-return were to disappear, the Zionist state would lose its identity."[21] Piterberg's observation resonates with Eyal Weizman's reflections, in the present volume, on the right of return as another word for decolonization: "Israel could *not* remain Israel if the right of return were granted. It would have to become another place completely—and that's the hope." This insight begins to approach something of the politico-temporal valence of return. Return is not restoration; it is nothing short of a future without Zionism. It is an offer to relinquish sovereign fantasies and their normative hold by recognizing that any right to self-determination can only ever be constrained by the binational reality. It is the name of a shared, if often ineffable, will to not only rectify the injuries of a still-present past but also to do so in a way that frees us all of its enduring effects. It is an invitation to a future no longer bound to the trajectories of the colonial encounter, or the antagonistic identities forged in that encounter's primal event. The future not of justice (perhaps always a vanishing point), but of cohabitation in Palestine, ultimately rests on joint struggle. That joint struggle will only open up genuine newness by connecting future redress to past dispossession, by *returning* to another time altogether.

NEOLIBERAL POLITICS, PROTECTIVE EDGE, AND BDS[1]

Joshua Simon

"Alors, comment agir sur un instrument qui vous échappe,
qui vous est adverse même?"
—Trotskyist Michel Grandville to Jewish-German refugee
Erna Wolfgang in *Stavisky* (dir. Alain Resnais, 1974)

At this moment, neither Israelis nor Palestinians are able to bring
the Israeli military occupation of Palestinian territories to an end.
The corrupting influence of the ongoing occupation leaves Israeli
society rationalizing apartheid and massacre as defensive tactics.
The Boycott, Divestment, and Sanctions (BDS) movement has
emerged as a reaction to this paralysis, strategically recognizing
how political agency has shifted from tax-paying citizens to external
investors, debtors, and bondholders. By responding to the reality
of this new, neoliberal form of sovereignty on its terms, BDS
interferes with this model and reflects some of the entaglements
of political activism in the context of neoliberal sovereignty.

1.

In many ways, the question of how to operate a device that escapes you, that resists, is the question of political power, for politics is the operation of writing with a pen that is not in your hand. The epigraph above refers to a reality of power struggles in a well-organized hierarchical party formation: Trotsky's influence on Soviet politics during his exile in the mid-1930s. But our own distinct political conditions call for a reconfiguration of power and demand that we too rethink how we are to write with a pen that is not in our hands.

For the current condition of deadlock in Israel there are many reasons. As much as it is specific to the unique regime that has been established since the occupation of Palestinian territories, this condition highlights several characteristics of contemporary sovereignty models that are widespread worldwide. Today, deprived of any macro-politics through the collapse of political parties and unions, we are left with phantom political entities such as NGOs that rely primarily on funding abilities before they are able to produce structural analysis and organizational efficiency, and generate solidarity and social change.

The two predominant economic theories on the Israeli Left saw the occupation as either costing too much money or as a money-maker. The first Oslo agreement led to a brief hopeful period but as time went by it became clear it was serving military and financial elites without local input. The Oslo Accords presented an economic logic that was critiqued by Israeli scholars Jonathan Nitzan and Shimshon Bichler as a globalized New World Order based on agreements for offshoring industries and outsourcing control; according to this logic, there was much more economic potential in "peace" than in "war."[2] But this argument was no longer relevant by the outbreak of the second intifada in the year 2000, when it became obvious that the Israeli military-financial nexus relied on the occupation for its booming information technologies. Israel's economy is today largely dependent on one product: military technologies. The occupation fosters Israel's economic advantage as it becomes the justification for high-tech R&D operations, a development that has been celebrated by Dan Senor and Saul Singer[3] and critiqued by Eyal Weizman.[4]

Jeff Halper of the Israeli Committee Against House Demolitions (ICAHD) has compared the occupation to the ancient Chinese game Go. He writes,

> Unlike the Western game of chess, where two opponents try to "defeat" each other by taking off pieces, the aim of Go is completely different. You "win" not by defeating but by immobilizing your opponent by controlling key points on the matrix. This strategy was used effectively in Vietnam, where small forces of Viet Cong were able to pin down and virtually paralyse some half-million American soldiers possessing overwhelming firepower. In effect Israel has done the same thing to the Palestinians on the West Bank, Gaza and in East Jerusalem. Since 1967 it has put into place a matrix, similar to that of the Go board that has virtually paralysed the Palestinian population. The matrix is composed of several overlapping layers.[5]

The internal dynamics of such deadlock bring to mind a possible resolution in the form of implosion. Here the idea is basically that the Israeli government, being militarily unassailable and having silenced any opposition, will dismantle itself through the internal contradictions of its own actions. For example, the Israeli movement toward the annexation of Palestinian territories, which has had a strong influence on recent Israeli governments, might actually terminate the whole project of the settlements in the West Bank. As a settler society relying on constant expansion, annexation of the West Bank might mean an end to that movement and many of them becoming ghost villages. As they are so scattered, what is now their advantage in the service of land grabbing will become redundant and useless, once they all become part of one uninterrupted space in a bordered state.

2.

Examining the 2014 military assault on Gaza more closely, we recognize a model of sovereignty which, for lack of a more precise phrase, we can call neoliberal sovereignty. While escalating the targeting of civilians in Gaza and intensifying its use of firepower,[6] Israel was operating in a seemingly contradictory manner. It initiated and accepted all ceasefire proposals throughout the fighting. This, together with the sudden withdrawal of ground troops with no clear military results, raises questions as to what exactly the fighting was about.

It seems clear that the war, though officially known as Operation Protective Edge, did not aim to ensure the security and well-being of Israelis living in towns and settlements that neighbor the Gaza Strip. It neither resulted in a decisive takeover of the Gaza Strip, nor did it help bring about an agreement with Hamas, which has governed it since 2006. In the long term, the mass killing of Palestinians effectively pushes the possibility of a negotiated peace agreement between Israelis and Palestinians at least a generation down the line. This in itself might be a reason for the settler-led Israeli government to engage in the fighting. As it sees no point in any agreement, the war is another step toward making peace an impossibility. But what could be the meaning of using unprecedented firepower against civilians on the one hand, while accepting repeated ceasefires on the other? The contradictory manner in which this was managed teaches us that the objective of the operation was neither defeating Hamas nor ensuring the safety of Israelis. It is the security and prosperity of another constituency that was in the minds of Israeli leadership throughout: bondholders. These are individuals, institutions, states, and corporations that have a stake in the external debt of a government. This war and the way it was waged were meant to ensure external investors that Israel would remain safe and stable. In this respect, strategically the biggest concern Israel faced was the fact that the U.S. Federal Aviation Administration suspended flights to Israel for twenty-four hours on July 22, 2014, after Hamas rockets fell near its main international airport. But the solution for investors is the problem for citizens.[7]

3.

Naomi Klein and Wendy Brown have both shown how the smooth functioning of neoliberalism, for those who benefit from it, is dependent on war and primitive accumulation. They use the terms "disaster capitalism" and "stealth revolution," respectively.[8] Michel Feher proposes neoliberalism as a form of governance that is different from liberal politics by that its sovereign is not tax-paying citizens but rather lenders and bondholders.[9] For him, the advent of neoliberal sovereignty is marked by a shift from the taxpaying citizen to the bondholder. Unlike the liberal social contract theorized and at least partially implemented in Europe during the eighteenth and nineteenth centuries, according to which politics is shaped by the contestation and consent that takes place between citizens and governments, neoliberal politics is concerned with the power relations between a state and holders of its external debt. Today all governments are preoccupied with this matrix of power relations surrounding their external debt.

The realization that politics takes place between government and bondholders is shared by some boycott movements, including BDS. Mapping power relations in such a way produces a form of protest that on the level of liberal politics might be deemed withdrawal or resignation, but within the logic of neoliberal sovereignty amounts to direct political engagement. These movements are resigned to operating within the economic and political coordinates that have been determined by the power structures they ostensibly oppose. The BDS movement, for example, does not have an Israeli addressee per se—it is not addressing the Israeli government, the Israeli public, or the Israeli working class. It has already come to terms with the understanding that Israeli citizens cannot influence their government and change its policies. In this respect, the analysis that undergirds BDS is extremely poignant. BDS aims to shame and intimidate potential investors and existing ones, so that they will pull their businesses out of Israel. On an economic level, the threat of BDS is that it will cause the external debt to increase, downgrading Israel's credit ratings and making the interest it pays for its debt skyrocket. This, BDS activists believe, is the pressure the Israeli government feels it needs to answer to. Such sanctions touch neoliberal sovereignty where it really hurts. In this respect BDS is a form of neoliberal protest. It is an acute symptom of post-Oslo Palestinian dependency on the international community or, better said, individuals with international stature.

If we take this form of activism under neoliberalism further and imagine how its strategy might evolve, we see that Greece's economic crisis—including its creditors' directives for restructuring—has become the model for neoliberal sovereignty. We can envision the so-called international community arriving at the conclusion that if only international economic and financial institutions exerted absolute control over the external debt of Israel, they could force policies on the country from the outside. But when applied to Israel, the Greek model of neoliberal statehood might have an opposite effect than the one intended by the BDS movement, because any external debtor would want the occupation to continue. This is because Israel, like the United States or Russia, is a war-state; its means of making money depend on maintaining a state of military occupation, siege, separation, and surveillance, with regular outbreaks of war. The occupation *is* the safe investment in a state whose best business is war. Thus, any solution based on current economic conditions is itself a problem. If we accept the political rationale of the call for BDS, we therefore find ourselves facing a dilemma similar to that posed by the Oslo Accords.

In a post-Soviet world where unfettered capitalism defines the global economic structure, economic agreements, incentives, and threats are being used to impose political solutions that defy justice, prosperity, or peace. For example, the Oslo Accords, which were supposed to bring peace, were in fact a series of agreements that benefited the settler movement, construction companies, ex-military officials, and big industrialists who were able to maintain their contracts with the Israeli military as they left Israel for cheaper labor in neighboring countries, at the expense of both the Palestinian and the Israeli working class.[10] In this respect, we should understand the basic assumption of political pressure for just cause through the current economic power structures of globalized capitalism not as an alternative, but rather as a variation of the logic.

4.

The Israeli Right has been so efficient in cracking down on opposition at home and abroad that its victory leaves it with no rivals. Now it has only enemies. The situation is such that for those wishing to act in solidarity with the Palestinians there is no available project other than to join the call for a cultural and economic boycott on Israel. As a movement, BDS relates to the activist line of engaging with politics. By that I mean that it is not a party, an organization, or a rigidly hierarchical political movement, but a movement of individuals who act directly in relation to a call for solidarity. As individuals in a neoliberal world, our main agency is consumerist. On the tactical level, boycotts may prove to be efficient (gaining media attention, getting big business to make small concessions), but on a strategic level, they have to generate a different political dynamic outside the reality of consumption as our sole agency. While liberal activism pushed for mutual-interest political action by taxpaying citizens, political struggle under neoliberal sovereignty has been converted into individual moral positions (a whole array of daily consumerist choices become our political identity). There needs to be a political project of strategizing a new formation of power. Parts of BDS already suggest new Jewish-Arab subjectivities, if mainly outside Israel-Palestine. But under the occupation, which in its current phase combines annexation with segregation, BDS reflects the tragic collapse not only of a common Jewish-Arab political project, but also of solidarity within Palestinian communities. "Gone are the days when solidarity formations worked with Palestinian communities in the diaspora, the PLO, and kindred Palestinian political parties," write Mezna Qato and Kareem Rabie. They explain:

> Instead, and in part because there is no longer a
> Palestinian representative body, Palestinian solidarity
> now almost exclusively interfaces with large civil
> society umbrella groups and NGOs in Palestine,
> and with only a few exceptions—including the

U.S. Joint Struggle Delegation to the World Social
Forum, Free Palestine in Porto Alegre, and student
collaborations with other campus movements—they
do not have a sufficiently direct relationship with
progressive formations in Palestine or Palestinian
communities in exile. Such disconnects are linked to
other problems. Increasingly, the movement seems
composed of constellations of well-known figures—
academics, artists and poets, journalists, activists,
Twitterers—who generate thinking and rhetoric
that becomes associated with them as individuals.
In the past, this kind of thinking was collectively
deliberated and determined. Such people clearly
contribute to advancing the Palestinian cause, and
there is much to laud in the decentralized work
of countless Palestine organizers. But the way the
abundance of voices maps onto the wider strategy
of public engagement here has had the unintended
consequence of crowding out collective work.[11]

5.

Occupying a similar role as the strike has in the traditions of unionism,
anarcho-syndicalism, and communism, boycotts can constitute not
only passive reaction but also a tactical production of actions. The hope
is that the strike's strategic potential to change everything as it attains
revolutionary dimensions could be obtained by BDS. Victory cannot
mean partial concessions within a reality of segregation, but only
radical change that generates new Jewish-Arab subjectivities. For this

to happen we need to consider the realities of neoliberal sovereignty and not only use them, but challenge them as well. With these various problems to consider within the current condition of helplessness, the question remains: how do we act with a tool that constantly escapes us, that opposes us? How do we write with a pen that is not in our hand?

THE UTOPIAN CONFLICT[1]

Yazan Khalili

What if BDS wasn't merely a political movement?! What if its agenda
was not purely political, hinged on the reactionary relationship
to Realpolitik? BDS along with many political parties in power
demand the end of the Israeli occupation of the '67 lands, full
rights for Palestinians living in the Israeli state, and the return
of Palestinian refugees—all of which allows the apparatus that
created the atrocities to continue existing. In a way, it is like giving
black South Africans political representation and civil rights
but keeping the apartheid system in place. Can the movement
make an ethical demand: the seizure of the oppressive apparatus?
That is to say, ending the very existence of the Zionist state?

Can an end to the injustice be achieved? Could one imagine the
end of the injustice with the continuation of the apparatus that produced
it? Haven't we learned from the history of post-colonial states that a
real end to colonialism requires an end to the colonial system altogether
rather than just a withdrawal of the direct occupation?

One of the many problems with addressing such an ethical
demand is that it creates another ethical problem: the subjects of this

apparatus—Israeli Jewish citizens—are missing from this demand.

What if we simply add another demand: In addition to emancipating the Palestinians from Israeli settler colonialism, emancipate all the Jews from Zionism! Instead of boycotting Israel in support of the Palestinians alone, what if we boycott in support of the emancipation of Jewish subjects from the Israeli state as well?

I'm not an expert on history, but it is common knowledge that the Zionist movement came about as one of the reactions to the establishment of the European nation-state, and to centuries of Christian European racism against its Jewish population. This racism first manifested itself as the systematic separation of Jews from society in the form of ghettoes, and culminated in the physical annihilation of the European Jewish population during World War II. In this sense, the establishment of Israel as the state of "the Jewish people" should be read not as the emancipation of Jews from Christo-European oppression, but as a continuation of it, which actively cleansed European society of its Jewish citizens, ghettoized them far away, and made them someone else's problem.

The creation of the Israeli state didn't only result in the Palestinian catastrophe; it also allowed for the continuation of the Jewish catastrophe, by fixing "the Jew" as a national identity. This conflation of the religious and the political subject relies on the racism that led to the destruction of Jewish existence in Europe and, after the creation of the Jewish state, the destruction of Jewish existence in Arab and North African communities.

So, the Palestinian can't be emancipated without Jewish emancipation, and the Jew can't be emancipated within the structure of the Israeli state, or the state itself, as the structures of any state can only be structures of oppression. For the boycott movement to have a radical demand, a structural one, it must call for boycotting the Israeli state until it dismantles itself as a Jewish state, meaning that the Israeli is no longer "the Jew."

The boycott movement should speak on behalf of all the victims of the Zionist state, the Palestinian and the Jew; otherwise, whatever structure will come out of such struggle will only continue the injustice.

The moral emancipation of the Palestinian and the Jew is, first, the emancipation of the state from Zionism, and later their emancipation from the state as such.

WHO SPEAKS? WHO IS SILENCED?

*Freedom of expression is widely considered a central tenet of a free,
democratic society. It is a concept that people fight for, die for, hold sacred,
and also, increasingly, question. Is free expression in the highest interest
of civil society? How do structural inequities impact who can speak?
How do we consider historical and current power dynamics in the context
of free speech? How does silence, or refusal to participate, play into this
analysis? Can privileged groups hide behind arguments of free expression
to suppress other voices? Who can speak for whom? Who determines what
must be protected as free speech, and what must be rejected as hate speech?
Does free speech advocacy need to be complemented with commitments
to "safe spaces"? Can one group's freedom incite another's self-censorship?
In this section, each author confronts a particular facet of cultural
production vis-à-vis how such freedoms are used and leveraged.*

*In a wide-ranging piece, the artist Tania Bruguera reflects on
what it has taken for her, having been born in Havana a decade after the
revolution, to evolve a complex art practice rooted in free expression and
political engagement. Inspired by artists who came to Cuba early in her life,
despite the U.S. embargo, she points to their influence on her way of thinking
as an argument for participation and the necessity for free and open exchanges*

of thought. Bruguera describes her dramatic encounters with censorship in Cuba, her response to these conditions as an artist, and her new endeavor, the Hannah Arendt Institute of Artivism, a project that has emerged in the aftermath of her detentions in Cuba.

Naeem Mohaiemen, a member of the artist collective Gulf Labor, weighs questions of artists' responsibilities in confronting unjust institutional labor practices. He describes the formation and evolution of this group of artists as they pressured the Solomon R. Guggenheim Museum to engage with and improve the conditions for workers at the Guggenheim Abu Dhabi construction site. Mohaiemen suggests that "[o]ne step toward building another kind of world must be to recognize the direct links between the art we exhibit in institutional settings and the labor of the workers who build, maintain, and operate those institutions," and therefore, that artists have particular leverage within these institutions, and should use it.

Svetlana Mintcheva, programs director at the National Coalition Against Censorship, examines the role that power and systemic bias play in the consideration of absolute freedom of expression. She unpacks legal definitions of free speech, and raises important examples of campaigns that have called for curtailing speech on the grounds that it is discriminatory—acts of protest that have often led to institutional self-censorship rather than truly transformative debate. Through this lens, Mintcheva's analysis affirms an unfettered approach to freedom of expression, if one that considers the embeddedness of inequity in society and demands deep ethical and political engagement with various forms of bias.

The anthropologist Ann Laura Stoler contributes a paper written in support of the efforts of Anthropologists for the Boycott of Israeli Academic Institutions, highlighting the growing support and justifications for the BDS movement. She asks important questions about the self-censorship surrounding the Palestinian-Israeli conflict, particularly in the field of anthropology, a field that has increasingly grappled with its colonialist legacy but has, in Stoler's view, insufficiently confronted what she sees as similar colonial conditions in Israel-Palestine today. She ends her paper with a rousing challenge, to anthropologists, but perhaps also to civil society, advocating truth-telling as "a form of fearless speech in the agora of public space—a fearless speech that can only be measured by the incivilities it embraces, the transgression of which it is accused, the displeasures it invokes, and the risks one is willing to take."

In this volume on boycott as a cultural tool, these texts address the themes of risk, self-censorship, and artists' responsibilities and points of leverage, adding new perspectives to debates surrounding freedom of expression. The authors raise crucial questions about the stakes of expression and cultural production in times of struggle for greater equity, and highlight the multivalent and increasingly complex roles artists, thinkers, activists, and philosophers must enact along this journey.

THE SHIFTING GROUNDS OF CENSORSHIP AND FREEDOM OF EXPRESSION

Tania Bruguera

When I performed *Tatlin's Whisper #6* at the Havana Biennial in 2009, I relied on the principle that an art institution can be a civic institution. Art spaces offer a platform to say what it is not possible to say in other spaces, to be the citizen you are not permitted to be in public.[1] The Havana Biennial offers a distinct opportunity to sharpen this potential, because many foreigners and journalists are present, and all eyes are on Cuban art for a moment. The government uses the biennial to position Cuba within an international art community, tempering its stricter forms of censorship to project an image of openness to the world. Aware of this recurrent exception to the rule, I wanted to do something that would not otherwise be authorized. I staged a performance that conveyed the absence of a leader—and therefore the possibility that anybody, or indeed everybody, can be a leader—but also the idea that by conquering your fears you can feel what freedom is. My hope has always been that once people experienced freedom, they would seek it in spaces where their rights have been denied; in this way, I see art as a safe space to rehearse the future.

As soon as this performance finished, I was called to the Ministry of Culture and reprimanded in meeting after meeting. I was asked to sign a paper regretting the interventions of the audience into the piece. I explained that as an artist I only set up the conditions for the work, which is ultimately made by its participants, and that I would not sign such a declaration. What I didn't understand at the time was that I would be banned from every cultural institution in Cuba. Only five years later did I realize that nobody had invited me to show in Cuba since, and it was no accident. In the summer of 2014, I met with the deputy minister of culture and asked him about my situation. He told me, "No, of course we're not going to let you do anything in our institutions after what you did." Then he asked, "Are you coming here to negotiate your new relationship with us?" And I said, "Yes, but I'm going to do things on my own terms." After that they became even more suspicious of me, and needless to say, I was kept on the blacklist.

So, when I thought about performing *Tatlin's Whisper #6* again, in December 2014, amid the new geopolitical context of restored diplomatic relations between Cuba and the United States, I knew that I wouldn't try to do it through art institutions. This time I understood that the biggest challenge would be to conquer public space, because everything happens behind closed doors in Cuba, and that is where art is supposed to stay—among one's peers, and not the people. Cuban artists, like all citizens, are trained not to see the public sphere as an option.

I believe that political art works cannot simply be repeated, but must be updated by understanding the source of the work's impact in its initial context, and analyzing how a current political state affects not only the reception but the content and the form the work takes. In the case of *Tatlin's Whisper #6*, it was important to preserve the collective memory of its first reiteration because freedom of expression had reemerged in the imagination of many Cubans, with a new valence.

People thought, if the United States and Cuba were in negotiation, surely the right to free speech was under discussion. And they were imagining a different reality for the first time in decades. I responded to this collective enthusiasm by creating a space for everyone's imagination and desires. Raúl Castro had announced the restoration of relations as a fait accompli in which Cubans had no say; the people were pronounced happy with the decision, and that was supposed to be that. It was the right moment for art to enter everyday political life. Art could help construct a civic sphere, restoring the right of everyone to imagine the society we were building, and to make sense of a state of uncertainty.

The new version of *Tatlin's Whisper #6* began with a simple, spontaneous act. I wrote a letter congratulating the Pope, President Obama, and President Raúl Castro on the historic decision to reopen relations and set in motion the process to end the U.S. embargo on our country. But the letter went on to ask Castro what would come next for Cubans. What would happen to the revolution and its aspirations for social justice? What would happen when capitalism took root in Cuba? I posed socially oriented questions that were particularly uncomfortable at this moment, when new forms of racism and classism are setting in, and Cuba is rapidly transforming into a neoliberal country with socialist propaganda. The letter went viral on Facebook, and someone made a fan page for it called #YoTambienExijo (#IAlsoDemand), which became the title of the piece. #YoTambienExijo was therefore a collective project for which I was only the spokesperson. All I did was help to create a space for Cubans of various backgrounds and political leanings to express their hopes and concerns about their country's future.

In Cuba you are labeled a dissident not for making a statement, but for asking the "wrong question." #YoTambienExijo quickly angered the government, which attacked the letter because I wrote it outside Cuba and put it on the internet. But if I had written it in Cuba,

I wouldn't have been able to finish it, let alone circulate it. Government officials would have intervened; that's how censorship works in Cuba today. Even so, it was important for me to follow through with the work by going to Cuba—by moving from the digital to the direct experience. Artists should not just be observers from afar but a presence in places where there is injustice, even if it will hurt their careers. Such are the consequences of political beliefs, and they are actually not that important when you see the effect the work has on people.

Boycotting an unjust state or institution from afar is important, in that this act works as an educational tool for people who are unaware of a situation, while showing those closer to the site of injustice how others perceive them. I will always support economic boycott as a tool against oppression, because it has proven effective no matter what the issue or target at hand is. Cutting the bottom line for corporations and governments is the surest way to change their policies. Nevertheless, there should always be a combination of tactics. One tactic that should not be neglected is witnessing. This is why, as artists, we have to go to the frontlines of a struggle and tell stories to counterbalance official propaganda and fight the status quo. We have to be present, not just engaged. This is a long tradition in our history. Artists have been correspondents from the trenches and the streets, working in the places of political upheaval where they are needed.

As for cultural boycotts, I am still waiting to see whether they can have effective results. To me, such boycotts cannot be a matter of simply saying, "I'm not participating in this." Instead I would like to see artists ask, "What is the most effective way we can change this situation?" We should not settle for the most popular response to this question, but rather think hard about whom a cultural boycott will impact and how. It is important to recognize, too, that it is not the same for a popular musician or athlete to boycott an event or country as it is for a visual artist or scholar. It can be very effective to boycott as a celebrity, as most of one's fans will likely learn about the political situation in question through one's withdrawal. By contrast, if a pop musician plays a concert as usual in a place s/he has been asked to boycott, it will only validate the status quo.

For visual artists, however, I don't like the idea of *remaining* afar when you are engaging with the politics of another community. It's too comfortable. It's much easier to stand in New York with a placard that reads "Free speech for Cubans" than it is to be in Cuba and not even finish writing on your poster board by the time you are detained. If you want to fight for the Cuban people, go to Cuba; if you want to fight for Palestinian rights, go to Israel-Palestine. But do not go only to mount another show of your "best" work, assuming it will magically change people. Go to make work addressing the uncomfortable facts of the place, to make the institutions that invited you confront their complicity—even if it means you will not be invited back. If you have privileged access to these institutions as an outsider, then make sure that before any act of yours, you speak with local artists and activists so you are informed not only by your own impressions or research from a distance, but by people who live the unjust situation as their daily reality. Above all, know that you will have to keep these conversations going in the long term, dedicating yourself to putting pressure on institutions to change—and boycotting them if they don't—and to staying in touch with the people most affected by the political situation. Never get seduced by the access those in power will give you in exchange for your collaboration with them; you are not there for yourself but for a cause.

As someone who grew up in Cuba, I am the person I am now in part because of people who came to Cuba despite the sanctions, despite the embargo, despite all the obstacles. They showed us another reality, other aspirations. I remember the conversations I had, as an art student, with people who came from the United States and Europe. They talked to us as if we were free people, and the contradiction between those encounters and our daily reality instilled a desire for more of these experiences. We wanted to fight to be as free as we were when we were talking to these people.

In Cuba, censorship has taken many forms over the years. During the first years of Castro's rule, Cuba didn't have to censor anyone because people were so happy about the great achievements brought about by the revolution. There were amazing social advancements that people hadn't even dared to dream of, so there was legitimate enthusiasm among artists of all kinds, and no need for censorship. But toward the end of the '60s, artists began to show some of the contradictions of the revolution, and the government came to understand the power of cultural propaganda. Officials began to "suggest" to artists what they should be working on, and whoever didn't follow their advice was isolated until eventually they could find no venues to release their music, print their books, or show their paintings. Of course censorship was never framed as political. Government officials would criticize your art, or they'd call you depraved and denigrate your character in whatever way they thought would demoralize you. Political censorship was expressed as moral or aesthetic censorship. This was hard on the artist, because if you claimed persecution, you were essentially told, "No, it's not that; it's just because you're a bad artist."

Then in the '70s and '80s a new figure emerged: the official artist. These artists did not complain, defended government decisions in gatherings where other artists expressed their political frustrations, and sometimes snitched on their peers when they became "dangerous." Many of these men (they were almost all men) were trustworthy enough to those in power that they could incorporate a bit of social critique into their work, but only as long as it was mild, and pointed to the symptoms rather than the sources of the problems.

During the late '80s, Fidel himself said for the first time, "We have made mistakes." This admission caused huge turmoil because he had never recognized that he had done wrong—he was the Revolution. There followed a very special moment in culture, with art aiming to address the people, not just the art world. Women came into positions of power in major cultural institutions and created more openness. Artists began to make more critical work, sometimes featuring Fidel, and one artist defecated into a national newspaper as a performance.[2] It was all very performative: artists understood and used the power of the gesture. The gesture was changing visual art, even if there were still many objects being made. It was a renaissance for Cuban art, similar to the first years after the revolution. Soon after, the government got scared and started censoring these artists. Backlash to the government's actions generated more awareness of censorship among the public, and stirred discussion among artists, but that only led to more severe censorship. Many artists emigrated because their shows were closed and they had nothing left to do. That's when the Cuban government came up with its amazingly effective strategy of controlling artists through the market.

In the '90s, Cuban officials put aside the socialist model of censorship for the capitalist model—success on the "free market." It was around this time that they started opening state galleries, so if you wanted to be a successful artist, you had to be in a state gallery, which would take your work to art fairs and show it to collectors. Still, in the '90s there were virtually no Cuban collectors, because there were few Cubans rich enough to buy art. There was no market, but all the critics talked about the market. I remember thinking, "What are they talking about? Nobody is selling anything!" Later I realized it was all in preparation for the moment to come; they were projecting the parameters of success they wanted people to respect, the forms of art they wanted people to desire.

Today we are seeing the self-censorship that follows twenty years of institutional policy, driven by the Ministry of Culture, positioning the art market as the index of what makes good art. A comfortable life making art: what artist can resist that? But to be a "good" artist, you have to be extremely subtle in your critiques, or become entirely apolitical. All those who make critical art lose access to collectors and institutions, so they slowly descend the social scale until they are regarded as total failures—and examples of where artists will end up if they don't tow the line. Meanwhile those who hold back their critiques of the government get rich quick. Now many of these artists are part of the 1 percent of Cuba—something unheard of elsewhere, that so many visual artists are ultra-wealthy relative to other professionals. As a result of their socio-economic position, they are reactionary on many political issues, and they never push for change, because they are comfortable with things as they are. Self-censorship is their currency.

Another recent development is how government officials have learned to censor earlier in the process. In the past, when a show opened and they saw something wrong, they'd close the show and ask the artist to take down the work. Then they realized this was not effective because it created a scandal. So they started to come by the gallery while the show was being installed, and they negotiated with the artist: "Take this down or your work will not be shown." And some artists agreed while others refused. Since it wasn't working with everybody, they started to enter the process of production. They would come to the artist's studio (or send a trusted artist to do it for them) and complain that one work or another was not aesthetically strong, or might create political conflict, and then advise them not to show it.

Government censors have now become so afraid that they may even try to pre-emptively censor an artwork. One day, when I asked people to come to my house so I could give my version of what happened during #YoTambienExijo, since the government was propagating a version that was not true, people from the local government came to me and said, "We know you have a meeting today. We are not going to allow you to go out and march on the street." I told them, "Thank you for the idea." I hadn't even thought about marching. Now they censor you before you even have an idea; they're thinking for you. I think that's the one specialty Cuban censors have that nobody else has: imagining an artist's work before she imagines it, and censoring it before it even exists.

Unfortunately, although I've never seen this fantastic form of pre-emptive censorship in other countries, I've experienced similar strategies of censorship everywhere I've worked. The difference between Cuba and places like Europe or the United States is that, whatever censorship you face, you can discuss it in the public sphere. Even if you have right-wing politicians shutting down a show, you can have a conversation in the open, and this is how you push perceptions and policies forward. You can make cultural change by challenging censorship. In Cuba the government works so hard to instill fear in people, and to make it impossible to imagine change coming from the people, by labeling any dissent a national security issue. And recognition never comes later, because the same people who censored you remain in power for decades. They never say, "We were mistaken." They just pretend nothing happened. Only when well-known artists die will they proclaim their importance—after framing their work so that it appears to be in favor of the revolution, or at least, not critical of it.

On the other hand I was actually shocked when I first came to the United States and saw how much power the market had. Back then many artists separated their art from their activism, distinguishing what they did in their spare time or their civic life from what they did in their professional lives as artists. That's why I claimed and defended the idea of "artivism"—to unite the two activities. I believe it is important to be an artist-citizen, to be both of these things together, and to think of aesthetics and ethics as conjoined—aesth-ethics.

I believe that artists are losing their fear. In Cuba today there are many artists who do believe in making political art, like the graffiti artist El Sexto, who has been arrested many times, or the duo consisting of the critic Yanelys Nuñez Leyva and the artist Luis Manuel Otero Alcantara, who created an online Museum of Cuban Dissent. They started with Hatuey, who was the first Indian to famously rebel against the Spaniards, and they even included Fidel as a dissenter during the Batista regime, but they were censored nonetheless. Nuñez Leyva was fired from her job and Otero Alcantara has been discredited as an artist and isolated.

Still, I am certain that we're going to have freedom of expression in Cuba. It's hard to see it, and people think I'm utopian for saying this, but I know it will happen. The real problem is not to have freedom of expression—it's what to do with it. Before we have this right, we need to discuss how we will express ourselves, how we will make our desires for our society into reality. That's why I'm starting the Hannah Arendt Institute of Artivism at my home in Havana.

As the last Havana Biennial unfolded, I decided to do a four-day, twenty-four-hour-a-day marathon reading of Arendt's *The Origins of Totalitarianism*. It was a kind of defense mechanism. I knew that they were going to accuse me of doing something wrong because they were so eager to portray me as a disrupter, or insane, or desperate for attention, to empty my gestures of political meaning. I wanted to tell the government, in a way that would be difficult to stop, that we're a totalitarian society that does not allow freedom of expression. So I thought, how better to do this than to read Arendt with the people around me and discuss the state of Cuba today?

When one of my neighbors came over and started reading, he looked at me and said, "Tania, you're crazy. You're going to get into trouble because of this text. Why are you reading it? This is really subversive." That was when I realized I had to turn this moment into an ongoing process, because Arendt was clear and pertinent, but it would take more than a single gesture to make sustainable change. I thought, let's make an institute carrying Arendt's ideas forward—let's take her ideas, and the discussions we are having about civic literacy and education, and facilitate a long-term conversation.

In addition to freedom of expression, what we need now in Cuba is social responsibility. I have seen in other formerly socialist countries how the idea of collectivity transforms into a fierce individualism, where even doing socially engaged art is not possible because people have become cynical and are fed up with social commitment. I think that is very dangerous, because you can end up with an extreme right-wing society. My hope is that we can transition from an authoritarian form of socialism to something that is not capitalism but a new way to bring about and uphold social justice.

THE LONELINESS OF THE LONG-DISTANCE CAMPAIGN[1]

Naeem Mohaiemen

2011: the Arab Spring had just started, and its winter not yet
arrived. A contagious sense of optimism radiated in all directions,
spilling over into the formation of a new group, the Gulf Labor
Coalition (GLC). By itself, the formation of an artist collective to
make demands of a cultural institution, in this case the planned
Guggenheim Abu Dhabi, was not unprecedented. The withdrawal
of artwork from a museum, meanwhile, is not usually cause for
optimism. But the signals that global shifts toward social justice
were underway, as well as the configuration of this particular group,
pointed to the possibility that our demands would have traction.

    Looking around at fellow GLC members as we first visited an
Abu Dhabi work camp, I noted their longstanding involvement in both
the MENASA (Middle East/North Africa/South Asia) region and the
Guggenheim Museum in New York. Among the initiators of the GLC
were two artist collectives that had done extensive work in the Gulf
region; a recipient of, as well as a finalist for, the Guggenheim's Hugo
Boss Prize; and artists who had participated in projects at the museum

and in the region over the years. It was not, therefore, an appeal from outside the museum walls, nor an intervention by interlopers. During that first site visit six years ago, conversations focused on the Guggenheim setting a "higher standard" for labor rights for all new museum construction. We were energized by the possibility that there would be parity of influence between artists with commitments to the region and a museum that was extending its lens beyond North America and Europe.

Artists can cause tremendous discomfort and upset equilibrium by challenging the conditions under which their work is shown. Institutions have often countered the threat of such moves by painting artists' activism as "misguided." This charge seems to adhere especially to artist collectives, perhaps because artists are stereotyped as disconnected dreamers who nurture their practices in splendid isolation. Some may point to the failure of negotiations between the Guggenheim and the GLC[2] as evidence such stereotypes are rooted in reality, in order to foreclose the potential for future activism inside the museum. Some may even think that the GLC was undertaking research and negotiations purely as a performative gesture, without a tangible aim in mind. Replaying the film of those first optimistic moments, in the shadow of the Arab Spring, is one way to counter retrospective readings that can demoralize future artist-run initiatives.

One of the radical moves artists can make is to challenge the conditions under which institutions exhibit their work. But why are such tangible demands dismissed as posturing, while metaphoric confrontations are celebrated? Defiance is welcomed when it is sanctioned and staged *as art*. Drill a crater in the floor, flood a gallery, smash an object, stage a pitiful death—critics hail these gestures as having the power to "shape worlds." But when artists sit down at a conference table with museum administrators and read from a list of demands for labor rights, this work—involving conversation, negotiation, research, protest—suddenly becomes illegible to the same museum. The artists whose projects were previously praised as stretching boundaries are now tagged as maverick spoilers.

How did it all start? Back in 2010, there had been months of meetings with the Guggenheim, led by Walid Raad, to resolve the issues raised by a Human Rights Watch report on migrant labor conditions on Saadiyat, "The Island of Happiness."[3] Eventually the talks stalled, and so the GLC was formed to press for the rights of workers on Saadiyat. Given how immovable large institutions tend to be, we were pleasantly surprised when TDIC, the Abu Dhabi national firm managing construction on Saadiyat, immediately responded to the GLC with an invitation to visit the work site. During a guided tour, we found an orderly facility with new accoutrements. The visit did not, however, address our core concerns: reducing exorbitant "recruitment fees" that cause worker debt, preventing wage theft by intermediaries and subcontractors, implementing a living wage, and creating avenues for worker self-representation.

We returned to New York, and here the long haul of the work began. We had already heard criticism that artists did not know the "realities on the ground." It was now crucial to become experts, by reading all the secondary material we could find and by talking to rights organizations that had years of experience in these matters. Within the GLC, Ashok Sukumaran, Ayreen Anastas, Paula Chakravartty, Rene Gabri, and Shaina Anand had already done in-depth research on the movement of South Asian labor in the Gulf. For the rest of the group, the economics of migrant labor was something we needed to study quickly. In this process, months of field research led by Nitasha Dhillon and others produced primary data from India (Telangana, Bihar, Uttar Pradesh, and Kerala) and Abu Dhabi, which complemented information gathered by NGOs.

Each time the Guggenheim agreed to a meeting, we knew we needed to study and prepare. Our planning sessions prior to the meetings would go on for hours, and GLC members picked up new skills in parsing legal jargon in a thicket of reports. Although meetings between the GLC and Guggenheim management continued until 2016, it was usually press coverage of a protest action that would result in the institution of reforms. Paradoxically, we did not always receive recognition for those milestones. The significant revisions to TDIC's Employment Practices Policy (EPP),[4] and the appointment of PricewaterhouseCoopers (PwC) as an independent monitor,[5] all came about as a result of pressure applied by the GLC. Yet, because the revision of TDIC's EPP stopped short of addressing our key demands (recruitment fees, living wage, and worker self-representation), and because PwC was selected in lieu of the monitors we had recommended due to their lack of conflicts of interest in the region, the GLC considered the majority of our work incomplete. This meant that what tangible reforms were implemented, even if inadequate, were not clearly understood in the media or in the museum world as the accomplishment of the GLC.

As the negotiations with the Guggenheim continued over the years, the enervating impact of time made itself felt. Doug Ashford was an old union hand, involved in the successful attempt to unionize Cooper Union School of Art teachers, and Doris Bittar was involved in union struggles in Connecticut and California. They both cautioned us that reaching a full agreement with the museum through consensus would be challenging. Debates regarding strategy went on for hours, and one issue that troubled us was whether direct action at the museum (by the GLC or allies) would be seen as "bad faith" negotiation on our part. As a way to address this dilemma, a group of GLC allies formed a separate coalition, G.U.L.F. (Global Ultra Luxury Faction), which carried out several actions inside the New York branch of the Guggenheim. G.U.L.F. was not officially part of the GLC, so our negotiations were not directly affected by the Guggenheim's reactions to their more confrontational tactics.[6] G.U.L.F.'s instincts about shifting public perceptions were borne out by events, as many concessions from the Guggenheim (including restarting stalled negotiation meetings) usually came after a round of events and protests.

G.U.L.F.'s protests were sporadic and unannounced, irregular and yet highly effective. By contrast, the longevity of the GLC's own work (research, analysis, advocacy, meetings) around labor conditions on Saadiyat posed a different challenge because a volunteer group still had ongoing expenses, a fact we felt sharply after receiving an invitation from Okwui Enwezor to present at the 2015 Venice Biennale. Andrew Ross and Gregory Sholette fundraised extensively to send members on research trips to India and the Gulf, organize plenary sessions in Venice with various NGOs, and finally publish a book, *The Gulf: High Culture / Hard Labor*.[7] One afternoon, after a particularly long meeting, Noah Fischer walked with me to a subway stop in Chinatown. Then he stopped his bicycle for a moment, leaned on it, and said: "I just became a father. I need to look for work. There are jobs that may take me out of New York, away from Gulf Labor." I stood there absorbing the organizational impact of this life change. Noah was the flamboyantly costumed, hyper-visible "human coin" to whom Sujani Reddy[8] had introduced me during the first week of Occupy Wall Street. I had never seen his face during Occupy, so total was his commitment to being an anonymous figure in Zuccotti Park. But we had all been animated by the energy he brought to Occupy-related activist projects, including Occupy Museums (tactics of which later spilled into G.U.L.F.). That same indefatigable Noah was now a father, worried about raising his family, and unable to give his days over to the GLC (as he had to Occupy, for months). We were all starting to get gray hairs from this long-running campaign. Few had anticipated how long it would take, or prepared for all the challenges it would throw our way.

The passage of time shifted our composition, bringing new members in as others left. In a New York that has become a money parking spot for the elite, and a laboratory for some extreme forms of racialized gentrification, it is a sharp uphill struggle for artists to stay grounded in their neighborhoods. Many of our members are artists in their thirties and forties, and city changes and new jobs took them away from here. Beth Stryker moved to Cairo, Emily Jacir to Rome, Haig Aivazian to Beirut, Rana Jaleel to California; Mariam Ghani took a temporary teaching position in St. Petersburg; Tania Bruguera faced a travel ban inside Cuba. This is par for the course for the "precariat," but it made research especially challenging. We looked to those with a long-term presence in New York City (Andrew Ross, Greg Sholette, Hans Haacke, Walid Raad) to be anchors, while at the same time extending the network to Paris (Elisabeth Lebovici, Eric Baudelaire, Nataša Petrešin-Bachelez), Mumbai (Ashok Sukumaran, Shaina Anand), Los Angeles (Doris Bittar, Sam Durant), Ithaca, NY (Todd Ayoung), Chicago (Michael Rakowitz), London (Guy Mannes-Abbott), and Berlin (Natascha Sadr Haghighian), as well as to affinity groups Who Builds Your Architecture?, Gulf Labor West, the Illuminator, the Precarious Workers Pageant, the Aaron Burr Society, the Workers Art Coalition, Occupy Museums, and the Guerrilla Girls.

After one arduous meeting at the Guggenheim on the eve of its UBS Latin America show (we usually had more leverage before a show), a museum representative asked us to do further research on the issue of worker debt. By then we had already introduced the Guggenheim to the International Labor Organization (ILO) and other groups so they could work together to pursue this same research. Amin Husain replied:

"You have to understand, we are artists struggling to survive in this city. But you get paid to do this, you should do the research." Later, in an internal discussion, Rene Gabri argued against this characterization: "The notion of 'volunteering' is already fully on board with the capitalist subject endowed with a profession, [consisting of] things one does for money, versus things one does for love or atonement, as a volunteer. I prefer to destroy this split in life, which is not far from the split between political life and biological life." I admire Rene's commitment—and he and Ayreen Anastas put this into practice in the long-running 16 Beaver space—but I also worry about the grinding life in the neoliberal city. Integrating multiple, long-term struggles into one's daily life is a huge challenge in cities that are designed to make communities come apart. Museums may imagine artists as energized on protest adrenaline, but keeping a coalition operational and active in the face of both institutional intransigence and economic punishment is intensely arduous.

The lengthy process of negotiations has not been kind to the Guggenheim, either. The dynamics of refusal that underpin the closure of negotiations has eroded goodwill for this once cutting-edge institution. This manifests itself in who is tasked to speak for the institution, something that has changed more rapidly than on the side of artists. Every time the GLC nurtured a contact at TDIC (Bassem Terkawi, Rita Aoun Abdo, et al.) who pushed for positive movement, we soon found that person shifted away from her role. At the Guggenheim, curators Suzanne Cotter and Nancy Spector left for other museums; Fawz Kabra and Reem Fadda left for other projects. Two PR heads also left quietly, perhaps the fallout from missteps that included an email exchange with Molly Crabapple that came out in the press. In November 2016, Finnish lawmakers voted not to fund the Guggenheim Helsinki, signalling that models of global museums need rethinking. One evening, a Guggenheim staff member posted a picture of a beautiful sculpture in the museum patio. I remembered it as one of my favorites—but we both may find it harder to spend an afternoon admiring this piece, located inside a museum mired in discord with artists.

The question of a consistent stance troubles any boycott. While the dreaded phrase "it's complicated" is often a tactic of obfuscation that tries to take the wind out of a campaign, it also points to real dilemmas. The GLC was often asked why we were only speaking about the Gulf, when labor exploitation is a problem at building sites around the world (including in my own country, Bangladesh, which is one of the largest suppliers of labor for the Middle East). Of course, artists will focus their energies on places where they feel they can be heard. I know that I have more cultural leverage with a New York museum than with a Dhaka museum, even though I grew up in the latter city. The same is perhaps true for many other GLC members. But I also wonder whether a boycott targeting a Middle Eastern project, rather than one in the United States or Europe, was "easier" for people to sign on to.

Furthermore, the Guggenheim was initially responsive to our protests, inviting us to meet; this traction encouraged activists to focus their efforts on the museum that was open to conversation. Conversely, the Louvre, which has a much bigger financial stake in its Abu Dhabi branch, and a construction phase that is half complete, has been relatively unscathed by protests. The GLC's position was that an initiative targeting the Louvre had to come from French artists, but such an initiative never materialized. In Finland, it was local artists who launched an initiative opposing the Guggenheim Helsinki, and members of the GLC became involved as allies at a secondary stage. Similarly, GLC members learned from the tactics of Liberate Tate, an artist collective that protested BP's sponsorship of the Tate museums, with evident success.[9] As the Louvre Abu Dhabi nears completion, the absence of major debates among French artists concerning the rights of workers building the museum opens the question of troubling situations where shared solidarities do not coalesce. The necessity of widening the conversation is signaled in the GLC's October 2016 statement: "we are also committed to struggling for these rights in Asia, Latin and South America, Africa, North America, and Europe."[10]

When the Guggenheim Abu Dhabi project was still at a very early blueprint stage, artists' non-participation was primarily symbolic. However, as time passed and the Guggenheim (as well as other Western museums) began rolling out related global expansion plans, GLC members had to make difficult choices. When the Guggenheim launched its UBS MAP Global Art Initiative, signatories to the boycott were approached for exhibitions, acquisition, and events. We debated whether we, as signatories, should withdraw from actual sites, or only from a site that does not yet exist. Individual artists have adopted different strategies, including attaching a rider to participation agreements specifying that their work cannot be shown in Abu Dhabi until the boycott ends. The GLC has ultimately welcomed various methods of participation in the boycott, not wishing to enforce a uniform rule. These decisions were influenced by, and refracted through, debates unfolding elsewhere over whether it is more effective to "stay outside and boycott" or "participate and protest from inside"—most recently in the boycott of the Jaipur Literary Festival, sponsored by the environmentally and socially destructive mining company Vedanta.[11]

The question of participation came up again in 2016, when the exhibition *But a Storm Is Blowing from Paradise: Contemporary Art from the Middle East and North Africa* opened at the Guggenheim just weeks after negotiations between the Guggenheim and the GLC were terminated. Many of the artists in the exhibition (Abbas Akhavan, Ahmad Mater, Ali Cherri, Hassan Khan, Iman Issa, Joana Hadjithomas, Kader Attia, Khalil Joreige, Mariam Ghani, Zineb Sedira), and related film program

(Azin Feizabadi, Jayce Salloum, Jumana Manna, Mounira al-Solh, Sille Storihle) signed a statement asking the Guggenheim to resume negotiations with the GLC. The securing of artists from the Middle East, and the ending of talks with the GLC, seemed to divide the artist community of the region. Indeed, artists participating in "But a Storm Is Blowing from Paradise" received a letter seeking to assure them that the proximity of the show to the cutting off of talks was coincidental. Regardless of the timing, should a museum expand to include art from a nascent local scene while remaining unwilling to adjust its plans in response to the political demands of artists linked to that context?

Reflecting on the way people within the visual arts community get divided along the axis of participation/withdrawal, the Lebanese artist Tony Chakar wrote: "Is this what we—contemporary artists—have been reduced to? Wandering nomads eagerly waiting for visibility, for approval, for the spotlight? I'm writing this so we can think together about this infernal structure that we call the 'contemporary art world' that is bullying us all, that is forcing us to stray away from everything that made us want to be artists in the first place."[12] It is both artists and institutions that are straying in the way that Tony laments. The current art world, under the suffocating pressure of speculative capital, is losing its potential as a space where utopian concepts can be dreamed and voiced. One step toward building another kind of world must be to recognize the direct links between the art we exhibit in institutional settings and the labor of the workers who build, maintain, and operate those institutions. As the world heads into new dark waters of globalized xenophobia, it is urgent to engage with artists not as "content providers" or a "nice" social presence,[13] but as political actors who must have some say regarding the rights of those who construct the conditions under which artwork is shown.

STRUCTURES OF POWER AND THE ETHICAL LIMITS OF SPEECH

Svetlana Mintcheva

Shortly after the salvos in support of free speech that followed the 2015 massacre of *Charlie Hebdo* cartoonists and editors in Paris, critical voices—while condemning the violence—started to question the binary opposition according to which unfettered speech is always heroic and suppression of speech always bad. Writers and artists have the right to work without fearing for their life, but should we be *celebrating* a publication, these critics asked, which stereotypes already marginalized minorities?[1] Contrary to misperceptions of this debate as a polarized battle between those who support free speech and those who stand against it, critics were neither siding with the violent murderers nor advocating for more censorship. Instead, they were posing an ethical question: Can free speech be isolated as an absolute value when any practice of freedom is inevitably affected by the social and political context of today's unequal power relations?

With the maturing of a generation shielded from overt government censorship and concerned about social justice, questions about the ethics and social effects of symbolic expression are gaining traction in the United States and other liberal democracies at the expense of an absolutist defense of free speech. It is increasingly recognized that the equal *right* to free expression has unequal value for unequal actors in the public sphere. Inevitably, the social position from which you speak determines not only who hears you, but also how they hear you—how they interpret your words and how much value they attribute to them. But what does all this mean when it comes to specific, practical decisions about censorship and self-censorship?

Both U.S. and, to a lesser degree, international law protect all sorts of hateful speech from government intervention. It is a popular misperception that there is a line to be drawn between prohibited "hate speech" and protected "free speech": in the U.S. there is no law banning "hate speech" and, hence, no legal definition of what constitutes such speech. As a result, unless they directly incite to immediate violence, all manner of offensive opinions can be freely expressed in this country.[2] Broad constitutional protections mean that, when it comes to artistic expression, direct government censorship is limited and declining. In contrast, private constraints on expression are on the rise: they range from the limits set by social media platforms (which often do prohibit "hate speech") and the self-censorship resulting from market demands to programmatic decisions (and excisions) made in response to political pressure exercised by ad hoc civil society groups.

How do these pressures affect American cultural institutions, which are increasingly supported by private foundations and donors and thus outside the reach of First Amendment law, even as they claim commitment to free speech principles? When deciding whether to persist with potentially controversial programming, cultural institutions—both private and public—take into account far more than the limits of the law: there are questions of responsibility to a community, the need to welcome diverse audiences, and the imperative to keep funding streams flowing. And this may appear as a good thing, until one finds that, in practice, there is no consensus on what is offensive or hateful speech and what responsibility demands.[3]

Private funding kept many U.S. institutions sheltered from the political ire of the culture wars. In the 1990s, culture warriors from the religious right focused on public funds going to "offensive art" and rarely targeted work supported by private funds. Today, however, campaigns against cultural institutions do not make a distinction between public and private, and are increasingly coming from communities that are, in the broad sense, on the same side ideologically: groups concerned about racial and economic privilege, social inequality, or various forms of discrimination. Behind an institution's stated social-justice commitments, such groups detect practices of persistent institutional racism and discrimination. As a result, the battles are fought not through open ideological disagreement, but over the implications of certain practices: about how artifacts from different cultural traditions are displayed, about who participates in museum programs, about intentional—but even more frequently unintentional—inclusions and exclusions. Activist groups use social media to spread their message and sometimes force institutions to cancel programing. Private cultural institutions, which are not compelled under the Constitution to protect freedom of speech, are vulnerable targets of such campaigns.

In summer 2015, responding to a wave of complaints, Boston's Museum of Fine Arts abruptly canceled "Kimono Wednesdays," an interactive weekly event in which audience members were invited to wear a replica of the *Uchikake* (overcoat) worn by Camille Doncieux in Claude Monet's iconic 1876 painting *La Japonaise*. The event had been a hit in Japan, but once imported to the United States it sparked outrage and was condemned as "Orientalist." The MFA Boston was criticized for its presumably uncritical support of "archaic values and belief systems that promote racism by way of cultural appropriation and cultural insensitivity."[4] Initially resisting, the MFA eventually bowed to the protesters and canceled "Kimono Wednesdays."

In a similar situation, a few months earlier, complaints from indigenous students led to the removal of a student art project at Santa Barbara City College (SBCC): a teepee built to fulfill a time-based performance assignment in which the students intended to bring people together and offer a space for connectivity, engagement, and reflection. Some indigenous SBCC students were offended by the way in which the teepee, an architectural form developed by Native American peoples of the Great Plains, was used as material in an art project. They protested what they saw as "negative stereotyping"[5] and were joined by others who called the use of the structure "disgusting and racist," an "insult," and an example of "white privilege."[6]

Cultural appropriation, the potentially racist adoption or use of elements of one culture by members of a different (usually dominant) culture, something that has been practiced widely throughout cultural history, has recently become an area of highly exacerbated sensitivity and a justification for censorship. As often happens the pendulum has swung from unquestioning acceptance of the practice and blindness toward its colonial and violent implications to the other extreme of routine and automatic condemnation—and suppression.

In a globally connected world, often referred to as post-colonial, cultural institutions in the West are increasingly aware that representations of the cultural "other" are often a representation of our own fantasy of the other, and that cultures should be approached as complex systems rather than boutiques of exoticism offering ideas and practices ripped out of their cultural and historical context. But what does such recognition mean in practice? Without attempting to answer a question that calls for a complex process of negotiation rather than a miracle formula, all I would venture to claim here is that we have a serious problem if the awareness of the pitfalls of trans-cultural borrowing is used to demand its absolute prohibition. The exoticizing practices of past cultural appropriation do not justify the erection of an impenetrable fence around cultural traditions (nor would such a feat be possible).

The reuse of materials, traditions, and philosophies from other cultures may raise many ethical questions. Yet, cultural give and take has always been the fuel of human creativity and imagination. In today's mash-up culture, this is truer than ever. And we can learn more—and accomplish change more effectively—through a vigorous critique and examination of the social effects of trans-cultural borrowing than through suppression. The quick removal of a project the moment somebody claims offense is much more likely to reduce the conversation to a rehearsal of familiar (op)positions, rather than bring out shades of complexity and deepen understanding.

One need not privilege artists' intentions over viewers' interpretations to consider the immediate suppression of "offensive" work a questionable resolution to any conflict. The SBCC protest by Native American students was an unexpected, but potentially productive response to the piece. These students pointed out how deeply embedded and naturalized structures of power are and how often they remain invisible. Yet, there was disagreement about the connotations of using the structure even among Native Americans: though hardly representative, comments in the media discussion that accompanied the controversy were far from univocally condemning.[7] The protest could have opened the possibility for an exploration of contexts, perceptions, and histories. In the course of that exploration, the protesters themselves may have had to face the fact that not all Native Americans objected to the work. But none of this happened: the lines of opposition were quickly and bluntly drawn, the college issued an apology, and the art students were pressured to remove the teepee before any nuanced discussion had a chance to develop. While an open discussion on cultural appropriation[8] was eventually held, the conclusion was predetermined as it followed upon what could well be seen as an admission of guilt, and excluded professors that had vocally supported the work.

Faced with charges of institutional racism, cultural institutions like the MFA and SBCC—whose predominantly white staffing makes them extremely vulnerable to such accusations—are quick to cancel a project or encourage students to do so. The conversation about the complexities of intercultural borrowing and appropriation usually comes as a coda, following the shamed removal. At best there is a belated nod toward the value of free and open debate.

The suppression of a campus art project and a museum event may not seem so significant, but such incidents—watched closely by other cultural actors—are likely to have long-term effects: peer ostracism, or the threat of ostracism, works very efficiently in chilling speech. Criticism is an essential part of cultural production; what is of concern are campaigns against cultural institutions that do not intend to generate a considered conversation around a project, but simply seek to silence it. Such attack campaigns do not present arguments to counter an artist's concept or debate its implications. They aim to exclude, silence, and blacklist a participant; they present an ultimatum and a demand to censor. And these ultimatums are gaining traction, especially as a result of social media activism.

In June 2015, one such social media campaign led to the cancellation of the Berkeley Poetry Conference, a gathering of poets for five scheduled days of seminars, readings, and panel discussions, as well as of a public program planned at the Whitney Museum in New York. In both cases the reason for the cancellation was the controversy generated around the participation of conceptual poet Vanessa Place, who had also been removed from a committee of the Association of Writers & Writing Programs (AWP) the previous month. Place's long-running project about property—intellectual and otherwise—and race, which consisted in tweeting the full text of Margaret Mitchell's novel *Gone with the Wind*, had become the object of attack, mostly conducted through social media.[9] Most of those protesting expressed little interest in engaging in a debate about Place's work or responding to the detailed statement of intent she issued; they called her a racist, labeled those supporting her "white supremacists," and set as their goal her complete banishment from cultural institutions.

Social media activism, for all its groundbreaking contributions to the Arab Spring or the Occupy movement, is increasingly playing a much more ambiguous role. While social media successfully amplifies the voices of protesters, it is not congenial to any subtlety: Twitter's 140 characters are supremely unsuited to the expression of complexity. Radically simplified and effortlessly joined, campaigns quickly turn from expressions of active democracy to the rule of unthinking mobocracy. As technology critic Evgeny Morozov presciently noted in *The Net Delusion*, his pointed critique of cyber-utopianism, "Tweets will not dissolve all of our national, cultural, and religious differences; they may actually accentuate them."[10]

Even activism for a good cause is not always democratic, and its results not necessarily in the service of the public good. What do the numbers of easily collected clicks, whether petition signatures or "Likes" and retweets, really tell us? How many of those who clicked to condemn Vanessa Place had bothered to read and think about her rather densely theoretical statement? It's hard to tell, but whatever the case, cyber mobs have obviously proved effective in intimidating institutions. The Whitney didn't even have to receive direct pressure before canceling its public program: apparently made aware of the raging online controversy at the last minute, the organizers were unable to assure the other participants that the integrity of the program (whose subject, the death penalty, had nothing to do with the controversial project) would be preserved.

None of the institutions embroiled in these controversies—MFA, SBCC, or the Whitney—expressed agreement with the claims of protesters. They cancelled the programs simply because of a failure to manage controversy. Resisting (self-) censorship in the name of protecting historically victimized minorities appears to be harder than opposing censorship in the name of a dominant religion.[11] And liberal cultural institutions seem especially unprepared to handle dissent when it comes from within the ranks of those who share many of the ideological values endorsed by their administration, curatorial teams, and teaching staff.

Those protesting Place's presence at a poetry conference, or the teepee student art project, would argue that institutional self-censorship, in such cases, is a good thing—that free speech in an uneven playing field can only give more advantage to the privileged and further marginalize minority voices. Paradoxically, it is precisely in the name of creating welcoming spaces for participants coming from divergent backgrounds that these groups advocate the banishment of controversial participants and projects. But if a welcoming space is defined by exclusion, by its isolation from the clamor of heterodox voices, there is no end to the demands for censorship that institutions will face.[12]

The assumption behind demands for censorship in the name of social justice is that social problems can be ameliorated on the level of the symbolic. If symbolic expressions give voice to and reinforce inequalities, the logic goes, changing the terms of the conversation and creating taboos around opinions, or even people, we disagree with will help overcome such inequalities. Call it the symbolic turn in left politics.

However, for better or worse, language and thought control goes only so far, as the propaganda departments of many a repressive regime have found out. Action on the level of the symbolic, through which a social media campaign or an ad hoc group of activists succeeds in getting an art project to be removed or a poet banished from a cultural venue, carries emotional satisfaction, but hardly resolves the underlying social problems.

The suppression of speech in the name of social justice risks a token substitution of work on the symbolic level for the political work of creating economic opportunities, diversifying institutions, or addressing racial discrimination in the criminal justice system. Indeed, it is worth remembering that the suppression of speech has never contributed to the cause of social justice; throughout history, censorship has invariably been on the side of totalitarianism and repression. The coercive power of group pressure on cultural institutions—which have precarious funding sources and which are, as the examples above have shown, not well prepared to handle controversy, especially when it concerns race or ethnicity—is certainly effective in forcing them to self-censor, but it does not bode well for the future of complex critical discussion.

Cultural institutions play a crucial role in maintaining the openness of social and political debate. That role is threatened if those institutions fail to take on real controversies around difficult and emotionally charged subject matter because some of that subject matter may be offensive or even traumatic. Unless they are prepared to welcome genuine conflict and disagreement, cultural institutions will operate as echo chambers under the pall of a fearful consensus, rather than leaders in a vibrant and agonistic public sphere.

The deep social problems that are fueling protests—the lack of diversity in cultural institutions, racial violence, disparities in educational opportunities or in political and economic power—will not be resolved by pointing out perceived racism in art projects intended as anti-racist and punishing their creators. Condemning artists and institutions for alleged complicity with dominant racist structures may serve as a weak substitute for the work needed to change material circumstances. Worse, it may lead artists and institutions to avoid engaging with the complexities—and complicities—of racism altogether. There is always the fear of being "called out" for saying the wrong thing because, no matter how deep and sincere the soul-searching of the well-intentioned, who can ever be sure of having achieved a state entirely free of complicity with dominant structures of thinking? The resulting self-censorship is already producing, in the culture at large, a backlash of "un-politically correct" populism lauding racist speech as heroic free speech.

While we do need to think about free speech in a more complex way, as a value that cannot be seen in isolation from its political context and as an ethical rather than merely legal issue, the response to systemic disparities should not be to limit speech. Instead, we must cultivate diversity within institutions, together with social equality outside them, as a primary condition of possibility for a genuine democratic exchange of ideas.

BY COLONIAL DESIGN, OR: WHY WE SAY WE DON'T KNOW ENOUGH

Ann Laura Stoler

Stoler presented this paper at the Annual Meeting of the American Anthropological Association (AAA) on December 4, 2014, on a panel entitled "Anthropologists and Controversial Engagements: The Boycott of Israeli Academic Institutions," which also featured Nadia Abu El-Haj, Lara Deeb, Ghassan Hage, Lisa Rofel, Magid Shihade, and Jessica Winegar. The text was subsequently published online by Jadaliyya. *For the present volume, Stoler has written a brief update regarding the AAA's June 2016 vote on the boycott of Israeli academic institutions, which follows the original article. We are grateful to* Jadaliyya *co-editor Noura Erakat, also a contributor to this volume, for permitting us to reprint Stoler's essay.*

I am honored to be here and to have been asked to speak in this forum today. I do so at once eagerly and with discomfort and dis-ease, and I doubt I'm alone with those sensibilities, knowing on the one hand that there is too much to say in fifteen minutes and, on the other, that nothing need be added to what has been said so many times before. Discomfort also in knowing that our usual protocols may be strained, giving way to further inquiry, disparate starting points, challenges, and conclusions that don't necessarily align. And given the current explosion of conferences, special sessions (even at the American Historical Association next month), teach-ins, and coverage of the Steven Salaita "affair," it would seem we are perhaps neither as untimely nor as vanguard as one might expect anthropologists to be as we consider and think aloud about where and how we position ourselves with respect to the Palestinian-Israeli situation. If an ethics of discomfort is one definition of effective critique, we are plunged deeply within it.

Controversial sites have long been at the center of anthropology's engagements and conversations. We have taken brazen pride in our capacities to disclose, to dissect, to make uncommon sense of the common-senses that go without saying because they so obviously need to be said, may not be said, or are removed from the ready repertoire of conceptual convention or censored to speech by politics. We are schooled and school our students to challenge what evades scrutiny and doggedly pursue why and how that is made so. In that process, we have taken positions individually and collectively that call into question our own cherished political investments, their epistemic valence, and affective implications.

This is business as usual in a critical anthropology—however defined—for decades: with respect to the Vietnam War, exported/offshore drug-testing, drone targeting, decimation of forest preserves, Department of Defense deployment of "strategic culture" in warfare, and not least with respect to the privations and disenfranchisements that earlier imperial and colonial formations have cast and continue to cast across the lives of so many of the people with whom we've been privileged to work. These sorts of engagements, however, have for the most part pitted some portion of an ever-changing "we" that makes up our discipline against multinationals, government policy makers, and more recently the goodwill of humanitarianism's advocates. (These are commitments that join us and make us feel better about our collective edginess and disobedience, and thus about our insubordinately fashioned selves.)

But for many of the same reasons, the dispossession of Palestinians and the colonial nature of the Israeli state have stayed on the outer fringes of anthropology for too long. It seems to me that to consider the situation in Israel-Palestine as a site of "controversial engagement" (our topic today) is perhaps to understate and bypass what makes this site of contest and governance so charged and seemingly unlike the rest: inordinately discomforting, rendered until so recently at once impolitic to broach and impolite, tactless to raise in collegial company with whom we might otherwise avidly engage and find common ground. Our critical anthropology follows in the amorphous tradition of respecting differences but here in uncharacteristic ways, as if a sizeable contingent among us has drawn a protective shield around Israel, U.S. government backing, and the Israeli lobby in the United States in ways we would otherwise neither abide by nor have submitted to before.

The question is, why this is so. Is it that it traces an invisible corridor, a wide berth around some of our own intimate affiliations and family alliances, cultural heritages, and semi-sacred sites—notably, initially (or is it fundamentally?) around guarding the memory of the Holocaust? (As if equal Palestinian rights would somehow betray and negate that memory.) These issues are not only not to be touched, but so sensitive that we have devised carefully guarded, implicitly agreed-upon protocols (in both private and public conversation) that ensure that the issues don't "need" to be raised. Being labeled anti-Semitic or a self-hating Jew, or interpellating our colleagues as such are the epithets we disdain, the domain of Campus Watch and zealots of whatever persuasion, but hover unarticulated over conversations. Among some colleagues, even such thoughts are unseemly, uttered or not, no matter where or how one was raised.

It seems to me that support for Israel or for the Palestinian right to have rights raises a red flag indicating that self-censorship is more civil and appropriate despite the disciplinary norm that so values challenges to convention. One could hazard something rarely stated: namely that anthropologists of Jewish background cannot see themselves desecrating their own family's memories of gas chambers, or the fiction that Zionism as originally conceived was a liberal and liberatory project, only later to warp into a surrogate colonialism (as Scott Atran called it some thirty years ago), that kibbutzim pioneering the wastelands outside Jerusalem were intrepid freedom fighters made up of family, fellow students of another generation, and family friends rather than the blue-eyed labor power of settler expansion.

This may be part of the issue—one rarely discussed—but I think it misconstrues how deeply support for Israel and its survival as a special Jewish state pervades a much broader geopolitical field and Euro-American imaginary. Israel has stood as a buttress of much more than an imagined utopian homeland freed of anti-Semitism. Israel has stood as the bulwark of a Euro-American colonial civilizing mission against Islam, woven into the fabric of European imperial pursuits, and U.S. "foreign policy" for a much longer time. It is not my case to make nor do I have time to do so. It has been made, traced in more documents than any one person could read or name. Ahmad Sa'di's recent study describing the genesis and unfolding of a systematic Israel policy in the 1940s (and many would argue Zionism's project earlier) to manage, surveil, and control Palestinians, to ensure that they would be reduced to a minority, is only the last installment of what is so extensively documented again and again.

Why have those of us, so otherwise attuned to the severed histories that have laid bare the connectivities tying imperial formations to the distribution of inequalities in so much of the world, for so long refused to make the connections between U.S. and Israeli investments, shared technological infrastructure, and media monopoly where we would otherwise find these deeply embedded political collusions and financial arrangements the very meat of our inquiries? How can we abide by accounts that position Israel as a democracy, when we would otherwise scathingly indict any other polity that has expanded and continues to expand at the expense of a population and a people— Palestinians—who have been so boldly and blatantly disenfranchised over decades of dispossession? How does the notion of apartheid not fit (and this is not to say that every feature of South African apartheid and that of Israel is the same)?

Given this, it is difficult to comprehend any argument that one did not and could not know. It also almost renders repetition superfluous, and makes unclear even *what kind* of things one needs to say. Do we really need to say again that Israel has only been a democracy in the most distorted sense of the term, *for some*, not for roughly 4.5 million Palestinians subject to its rule—some precarious residents of Jerusalem, others living under occupation and siege, often in camps, dispersed and pressed outside its borders? Ignorance and ignoring, as I have argued for some time, share a nefarious wedded political etymology. Contrived ignorance is an achieved state in which colonial governance invests. "Learned ignorance," as Pierre Bourdieu once put it, is what people hide from themselves—but as much at issue is *how* they/we do so. And it is more than that: ignorance and ignoring are intimately bound to an ongoing operation, a labored effect that makes knowing and not knowing, regard and disregard conjoined and easier to achieve.

I signed the BDS statement in 2010 and as I wrote at the time, I did so from a specific location—steeped for some thirty years teaching, studying, uncomprehending, and attempting to understand again colonial governance and the intimate consequences and enduring duress of imperial effects.

It was a measured decision, but also a visceral one, a response to an uncanny shock of recognition that reasserted itself with each stay in the Armenian quarter of Jerusalem and in Ramallah, each trip to Hebron, Nazareth, Haifa, Jaffa, Nablus, to refugee camps squeezed on their borders, to village homes cut off from their own working fields by the "security" wall, to Al-Quds University on a morning and the plush Van Leer Institute in the afternoon, and to Beit Sahour outside Bethlehem. It was accentuated at Israeli checkpoints that could appear and disappear in a day. These were not those (much more publicized) fixed structures between the occupied territories and Israel but the makeshift bottlenecks constructed of massive boulders placed and displaced at the entrances to Palestinian villages. It struck me as I watched other bus passengers quickly pull scarves over their noses as I gasped unprepared at the stench of settler waste dumped in the lower village of a Palestinian colleague, or at the account of a Birzeit colleague arriving late to our seminar because her car was awash with excrement thrown on her by Israeli settlers outraged that she drove a car on their Sabbath. And then there was the shock of recognition that was more deeply wed to what I had studied for so many years, when I found myself jolted in Tel Aviv, by that bastion of well-heeled European comforts, where one could imagine that nothing was happening at all.

My Israeli friendships are as strong as ever, and since that time I have returned to Palestine to teach mini-courses at Birzeit, to partake in a project on "Archiving Palestine," to stand with Palestinian villagers (and, yes, Japanese tourists) at Bil'in outside Ramallah, to be part of and witness a staged choreography of Israeli soldiers who shoot tear gas pellets at the hilltop crowd while the family members of a man slain by Israeli fire several years earlier pose every Friday afternoon for international newspapers.

These are poor credentials. I am not a Middle East specialist and can only barely make out some of the letters in the Arabic alphabet to the chagrin of my able teachers. This is merely to say that I am here for three reasons: first, because I signed on to the BDS campaign; secondly, because I have felt compelled to be in Palestine as often as I can over the last five years; thirdly, and more importantly, because so much of what I have studied for decades about colonial security regimes, their technologies of rule, gradations of sovereignty, and degradations of rights underscores by the year, the day, and the hour that expansionist settlements, confiscation of land, secondary citizenship, discrimination on the streets, ransacking of homes—as well as the privations that come when schools are policed, infrastructure is denied, water resources are confiscated—are all part and parcel of, and constitutive of, colonial situations.

I have no interest in proselytizing or suggesting that the rightness of my choices impels others to my position (an unfortunate tactic in this discussion on both sides). I do not want to make the case that a boycott of Israeli institutions is unconditionally the only course of action that makes sense. I take it to be both a choice with material effect and symbolic weight. Noam Chomsky's speech this July, parsed as unequivocally against BDS and a cautionary tale against equating South Africa's apartheid regime with Israel's, went viral, to the glee of those who still felt they should not or could not sign. But Chomsky's message was much more subtle and well conceived than this takeaway from it. As he said a month later, in an interview with Amy Goodman, "Far from being critical of BDS, I was strongly supportive of it....That article strongly supported these tactics. In fact I was involved in them and supporting them before the BDS movement even existed. They're the right tactics."[1]

Chomsky may not be the last word for all of us, but what is important is to see how swiftly and easily he was misconstrued. Many would argue that BDS does not stand a chance and that it plays into Netanyahu's hands. I see it differently. I see it as a call to attunement and a call to attend, *not the choice of committing an act so much as committing to a set of practices and priorities that creates in itself a political space, that puts demands on oneself, to know, to look, to discern, to question the comparisons relinquished and those refused to be made, to marshal one's resources, to account for oneself, and to know better what the consequences of those choices are.*

But there is something else I wanted to talk about today: to consider what is so troubling around the issue of Israel-Palestine—the elisions that are its effect, the suspension of those analytic tools we have honed in our craft, to question the conditions that have made Israel's commitment to decimation and dispossession so off our radar and out of bounds.

There is something strange about it. We certainly do not come early to this conversation. We are not close to the forefront in asking about "freedom of speech" and censorship in and outside the academy. But something is afoot vis-à-vis Palestine. It is not only Salaita's case that has made this evident, nor the cascade of European states finally recognizing Palestine, nor the latest call by Netanyahu for enforcing what has de facto been the rule in Israel, a nationality law that further inscribes those who are Palestinian as second-class citizens. I am not alone in noting that there is probably no issue that has been more radically avoided in the allegedly collegial world we inhabit than the colonial situation of Palestinians vis-à-vis the Jewish, allegedly democratic state of Israel. Not for the first time, freedom of speech in the academy is on the line: the consequences of not supporting Israel are real if still in a minor register. But they are there: where fellowships for our students, jobs and promotions for ourselves, invitations to speak may be and are rescinded if one disobeys the respectable boundaries of civil disagreement, appropriate for a well-mannered dissension.

Let me end (or just begin) by outlining what I see as a set of queries that demand attention:

Among those who have signed for support of a boycott as well as those who have uncomfortably refrained, there is a common, almost whispered comment that goes something like, "I'm not sure I really know enough." "Do I know enough?" "I should know more." Why is it that in the case of Israel's incursions, many of us feel we don't know enough? What protection does this offer? Would we claim not knowing enough in other contexts and at other times? I know I don't know enough. But there are facts on the ground and they are not Golda Meir's "facts on the ground"—and they are hard to miss.

Taking considered positions on controversial issues in the public domain has been, if not our raison d'être, at the very least what continues to beckon a fearless new generation of anthropologists in the making to zones of damage and hope and regeneration. I would hope that my generation could join with them to embrace the challenge of pursuing what Foucault learned from ancient Greeks and what we might, too; namely, that *parrhesia*, truth, must be a form of fearless speech in the agora of public space—a fearless speech that can only be measured by the incivilities it embraces, the transgression of which it is accused, the displeasures it invokes, and the risks one is willing to take.

—

The day after this paper was delivered at the 2014 American Anthropological Association meeting, AAA members resoundingly defeated a resolution against a boycott of Israeli academic institutions.[2] In June 2016, when votes were cast on a resolution to boycott Israeli universities, those favoring the boycott lost by less than one percent, a mere 39 votes: 2,432 members opposed the resolution, while 2,384 supported it. What became increasingly clear during the lead-up to the vote was that "pro-Israel organizations devoted considerable resources to defeating the AAA boycott."[3]

One could see the bottle as half-empty. But I would argue that we should see it as half-full. Rarely if ever have the mechanics and practices of Israeli policy been so minutely described and discussed in such prominent academic and media spheres within the United States. It is no longer possible to claim we don't know enough about the incessant expansion of Israeli settlements in Palestine, the widespread evictions in the South Hebron Hills, or, as one legal scholar puts it, the "room-by-room" evacuations of Palestinians in East Jerusalem. Nor can we say that we do not know about the blacklisting and harassing of Palestine solidarity activists. This year the Modern Language Association (MLA) will vote on a similar resolution to support the boycott of Israeli academic institutions. With nearly 25,000 members, the MLA is one of the largest academic organizations in the world. Thus the very fact of the vote, and the careful delineation of arguments for it, should place "ignorance" and one might call the "will to ignore" further out of reach for us all.

DIS/ENGAGEMENT FROM AFAR

This concluding section examines specific cases of boycott under the rubric of "distance"—geographical, political, cultural, even temporal distance. Each of the contributions underscores consciousness-raising as a core principle of the particular engagement this book advocates, and asserts the potential of a global (as well as local) audience for every iteration of boycott. While there is little doubt that the increasing number of calls for cultural boycotts enacts global connections that already underpin the economic and information exchanges of hyper-capitalism, including those of the art market, the contributions to this section provoke an additional question: Are the various ways that cultural workers apply strategies of withdrawal or refusal also indicative of shifts in the art-making process itself? It has been a long time since the artwork was considered a discrete object shorn of the context of its making. But can we posit that our engagement with disengagement, especially as it transcends the local and covers distances, is not only a response to global capitalism but also a reflection of newly emerging artistic practices? And are these newly articulated practices politically viable in ways earlier forms were not, because they declare ethical considerations a foundational part of art making?

Art historian Chelsea Haines critically dissects the claim that art "in itself—as a special ontological category"—is not only inherently political but also largely progressive in its politics, and traces it back to philosophers of the Frankfurt School, raising doubts about the political efficacy of such "trickle-down liberalism." In its stead, she proposes a reformulation of a politics of seeing that seeks to understand as part of the artwork itself the historical, cultural, and political context of its production and exhibition. Haines argues that such an approach, when informed by recent critiques of human rights discourse, challenges inequalities at a structural level, for instance by complicating the binary between oppressor and oppressed.

Artists Mariam Ghani and Haig Aivazian propose to dispose of another misleading dichotomy, that of engagement versus disengagement. As members of Gulf Labor, the artist coalition that advocates for the labor rights of workers constructing museums, especially the Guggenheim Museum in Abu Dhabi, they declare that "cultural boycott [can] open a parallel space for a different kind of engagement of ideas and issues behind and around the boycott itself." Ghani and Aivazian point to 52 Weeks, Gulf Labor's yearlong online platform, which resulted in fifty-two distinct but interrelated art projects that connected to other social issues and parallel activist work throughout the world. An artwork here is deployed in its strategic role in both a trans-local economic system and an aesthetic regime in order to use its leverage, apply pressure to this system, effect positive change, and renegotiate ethical demands every day afresh.

Artists Nathan Gray and Ahmet Öğüt zoom in on the 2014 Sydney Biennale boycott—a "conditional withdrawal," as they emphasize. It was initiated by Australian artists four weeks before the exhibition's opening on March 21, 2014, in protest against the transfer of the controversial Australian refugee detention camp on Manus Island to Transfield, a core funder of the Biennale. As Gray and Öğüt disentangle the corporate, political, and cultural threads intersecting in the Sydney Biennale, it emerges as a particularly relevant case study for understanding the ecology of many large-scale art events today. Implicitly, Gray and Öğüt also deliver the purest argument for a cultural boycott: as the Biennale's governing body urged the artists to consider the financial foundation of the event before deciding to boycott or not, the organizers themselves, perhaps inadvertently, declared ethics part of any viable contemporary artistic practice. In such a situation, when artists are invited to take on this responsibility—regardless of whether they are local or not—"distance" dissolves as a relevant criteria for (or against) boycott. Here, Gulf Labor's professed love of the museum meets the sense of ownership artists are expected to harbor toward the institutions of art.

The closing contribution by anthropologist Radhika Subramaniam reveals rich material in seemingly paradoxical pairings. Using "intimate distance" or "remote sensing" as metaphors for connecting across various kinds of distances, she asserts that the difficult work of translation required in these situations must entail the journey as much as the destination. Further, Subramaniam ascertains, such work will not result in a leveling of differences, nor will it enable the insertion of a distinct project into a distant situation as in staid forms of temporary cultural exchange. Instead, it provides the opportunity for a politics that seeks the intimate in the distant in order to be effective. Such a counter-topographic politics, she continues, "entails more than just connecting a here with an over there in a transnational alliance in which two place-based imaginaries are constructed. Rather, the politics itself must take on the global challenge[s] even while its specific grounds are local."

Taken together, the four contributions that follow offer a rich register for nuanced engagement with unfamiliar economic, political, and social conditions that impact the presentation of art. But they go further, and delineate how such engagement can materially affect the artwork regardless of how far the distance traveled may be—or rather because of it. Engagement from afar presents itself as a moment of both practice and research, a perspective particularly fitting for a compendium intended to enhance teaching and learning.

THE DISTANT IMAGE

Chelsea Haines

On September 2, 2015, at a press conference for the 14th Istanbul
Biennial, artistic director Carolyn Christov-Bakargiev was asked to
comment on a letter by biennial artists Pelin Tan and Anton Vidokle
being circulated to their fellow participants in the exhibition. In the
letter, Tan and Vidokle asked their colleagues to temporarily "disrupt"
the biennial's opening by collectively removing or turning off their
works for fifteen minutes.[1] This temporary suspension of the exhibition
was intended to raise awareness of deadly clashes in Silopi between the
Turkish military and the separatist Kurdistan Workers Party (PKK), and
to call for a return to peace negotiations. Christov-Bakargiev responded
that she was fine with the gesture—with two reservations. The first was
with regards to the action's possible political efficacy ("I'm a skeptic");
the second called on a rather murky relationship between art, politics,
and well, everything else ("Politics starts with how we eat, what we
do, how we make love.... Politics is everywhere, it's in all of us").[2]

I start with this anecdote because it reflects recent tensions
between large art institutions and their curators, on the one hand,
and, on the other, international artists who use their cultural cachet to

intervene in the local political, social, and economic contexts in which these institutions operate, often through acts of boycott or withdrawal. These tensions—between action and inaction, art and politics—have been identified by the editors of this volume as the politics of (dis)engagement from afar. In the last few years, artist-initiated protests and boycotts have become almost commonplace at international art events. For example, in spring 2014, a group of artists invited to show work in the Sydney Biennale refused to participate in the exhibition until the biennial cut its sponsorship ties with Transfield Holdings, a company that manages offshore detention centers for the Australian government, which has a stringent national policy of mandatory (and often indefinite) detention for all migrants and asylum seekers who enter the country without a valid visa.[3] Just a few months later, sixty-one artists and collectives out of sixty-nine included in the 31st São Paulo Biennial signed a letter threatening to remove their work from the exhibition unless the biennial disavowed its sponsorship from the Israeli Consulate.

Such events are not just happening in faraway places with regards to far-off issues (nearby, for me, is New York). In 2014, the artist collective HowDoYouSayYaminAfrican? pulled out of the Whitney Biennial following repeated complaints of institutional racism[4] in an exceptionally white exhibition.[5] In summer 2015, the New York public art agency No Longer Empty was criticized for programs held during the group exhibition "When You Cut Into the Present the Future Leaks Out" at the abandoned old Bronx Borough Courthouse. A private party for real estate brokers held in the exhibition space angered both community organizers and some featured artists who felt the project was being used as a springboard for gentrification.[6] In November 2015, a group of artists and activists protested the Brooklyn Museum's hosting of the 6th Annual Brooklyn Real Estate Summit. This protest has developed into a longer-term anti-gentrification initiative that has been in dialogue with the museum to assess its responsibilities to its surrounding neighborhoods and communities.[7] The list goes on.

In light of these events, we have been presented with two phenomena well worth examining. The first is the extraordinary rise of artist-initiated boycotts and protest movements in recent years, which is the overall subject of this book. It is apparent to me that the widespread social movements and political revolutions of 2011 have had a deep effect on the ways that many artists understand the political impact of their work as it makes its way into the world. These events have inspired many artists to collectively redouble their efforts toward social justice in ways that have not been seen by visual artists, on the whole, since the end of the 1980s.[8] The second phenomenon, which I will examine more closely here, is the way in which art institutions and their intellectual gatekeepers—curators—have responded to these protests and uprisings, on a spectrum that ranges from quiet approval to outright hostility, with a few exceptions.[9] Let's take Christov-Bakargiev's reservations, which are not at all uncommon, regarding the intention of the Istanbul Biennial artists to temporarily shut down the exhibition. The first is that artist-led boycotts are not politically effective tools for social change. This is not an unreasonable argument, although, of course, history tells us that the conditions for effective political or social change are rarely, if ever, determined in advance.

The second argument is far more complex, and far more embedded in the ways in which we tend think about art today: the idea that art in itself—as a special ontological category—is both inherently political and largely progressive in its politics. Boycotting seems anathema from this perspective because it is art itself that can effect social change. Take, for example, an argument leveled against the Palestinian-led Boycott, Divestment, and Sanctions (BDS) movement. In an open letter published in 2014, a group of artists, curators, and scholars wrote that "believ[ing] in the ability of art to tackle complex situations and political questions in a progressive manner...we ask spaces of art and cultural production to deal actively with contradictions rather than ignoring them."[10] For the signatories of this letter, boycotting merely avoids, or worse, exacerbates an existing problem while collaboration "deals actively" with conflict through dialogue, however ambiguously defined.

This position is grounded in two interlinked assumptions: that the relationship between art and progressive politics is a natural one and that art has a special power independent of its contexts of production and reception. The particular power of art, in this view, is the cultivation of an individual subjectivity that, in an indirect way, produces informed, socially responsible citizens capable of critical judgment and collective social action. This is the line of thinking that inspired Herbert Marcuse, in one of his last texts, to declare, "the political potential of art lies only in its aesthetic dimension."[11] Although Marcuse strongly supported student revolutionaries at the University of California San Diego (where he taught from 1965–1976), he also advocated separation between the realms of art and activism. The idea that art could or should be employed as a means to an end—as a political bargaining chip or a form of social capital that can be released or withheld to negotiate more favorable political, social, or economic conditions for oneself or others—is antithetical to Marcuse's understanding of the inherent value of art, as well as that of his Frankfurt School compatriots. Marcuse's colleague Theodor Adorno went even further, excoriating activism writ large. In a letter to Marcuse, Adorno complained that the late '60s actions of the Socialist German Student Union "confuses regression with revolution [and emphasizes] the blind primacy of action."[12] The notion that art should transcend the instrumental while at the same time maintain the capability to influence politics has had powerful influence on the machinations of the art world, sometimes progressive and oftentimes not. Today, this line of thinking has frequently been instrumentalized itself (undoubtedly to the chagrin of Adorno and Marcuse): as a primary means of defense by art institutions that find themselves subject to potential boycott.[13]

In response to artist-led boycotts, many institutional gatekeepers have attempted to separate and contain art (and its unlocked liberatory political potential) on one side, and activism (Adorno's "blind primacy of action") on another. This rhetorical division keeps art apart from and in many ways "above" the material conditions of its exhibition (such as corporate sponsorship, labor conditions, or political censorship). Arguably in no other recent instance has any institution invoked this rhetoric as much as the Solomon R. Guggenheim Foundation, with regard to its proposals for the Guggenheim Abu Dhabi in the Saadiyat Island Cultural District.[14] The Guggenheim Foundation announced plans for a museum franchise in Abu Dhabi in late 2007, around the same time the British Museum, the Louvre, and New York University reported the start of their satellite projects on Saadiyat Island; its press release described a 450,000-square-foot museum of international and Middle Eastern modern and contemporary art to be designed by architect Frank Gehry.

In spring 2009, Human Rights Watch published a detailed report on the abhorrent labor conditions, substandard housing, poor wages, and exorbitant recruiting fees for migrant workers (mostly from South Asia) on Saadiyat Island, raising serious questions about the conditions under which the Guggenheim Abu Dhabi would be built.[15] Following conversations with Human Rights Watch in 2010, a group of concerned artists (later to be named Gulf Labor) sent a letter to the Guggenheim, opening discussions about these labor issues with the museum. Unsatisfied with the Guggenheim's response, the artists made the letter public on March 16, 2011. Signed by over 130 artists, it demanded that the Guggenheim leadership "take steps to safeguard the rights of the workers" at the Saadiyat Island site, including reasonable compensation, sanitary housing conditions, access to adequate food and water, and exemption from onerous and predatory recruitment fees.[16] The artists concluded with their intention to boycott the Guggenheim Abu Dhabi by refusing to allow the museum to show their work until their demands were met. A response from the Guggenheim took the form of a letter signed by the museum's director, Richard Armstrong, and deputy director and chief curator, Nancy Spector, which chided the artists for their "inaccurate picture" of working conditions on the museum site that "portrays the Guggenheim as a passive agent with little consciousness of the issues at hand," instead of active agents negotiating better conditions for the workers. They conclude their letter by stating their belief that the museum can work toward social change *through* its presence in Abu Dhabi: "We strongly believe that the Guggenheim Museum Abu Dhabi, with its future program of transnational contemporary art and thought, can serve as a beacon for important intellectual activity, cultural exchange, and, ultimately, critical shifts in social practice."[17] In 2013, Armstrong reiterated his belief that the Guggenheim is a beacon for progress, this time deploying the rhetoric of artistic freedom.[18] In a letter to the editor published in the *New York Times* in 2015, Armstrong argues, "[t]he Guggenheim Foundation has a long history of international cultural exchange and open debate…we remain committed to the transformative potential of the Guggenheim Abu Dhabi."[19]

The Guggenheim has habitually deflected criticism of poor labor conditions at the project site by repeating canned statements about cultural exchange, artistic freedom, and open debate that conform to the view that art and museums in themselves are indisputably good things for society, and that any human rights violations that occur in building the museum are simply unfortunate occurrences to be corrected rather than symptoms of a structural system of economic and social injustice of which the Guggenheim Museum is a part. Perhaps most revealingly, in a 2014 interview, Guggenheim adjunct curator Sandhini Poddar stated that the Abu Dhabi project "is not just entertainment and spectacle but art, education, beauty, and it will take a while to feel internalized and natural."[20] Poddar subtly acknowledges criticism that Gehry's mega-museum, designed as a major tourist attraction and placed on an artificial "Happiness Island," epitomizes Rosalind Krauss's late capitalist museum, defined as a museum in which the sublime experience of space trumps the intellectual or historical value of any art contained within its walls.[21] Yet, following a brief caveat regarding the spectacle of the museum, Poddar shares a familiar, vague but fervent belief that the Guggenheim will over time subtly permeate Abu Dhabi with Enlightenment ideals as a kind of trickle-down liberalism.[22]

The labor conditions in the rapidly growing United Arab Emirates have been repeatedly critiqued as violations of human rights, while the barring of Gulf Labor members Andrew Ross and Walid Raad (among other scholars and cultural producers) from entering the country have seriously undermined the claims of free expression and open debate promoted by the UAE's American collaborators. When the rhetorical power of art's liberatory potential seems to falter in the face of coercive political realities, language shifts to respect for the real and metaphorical distances between the UAE and the Western centers of the art world, such as New York. In a 2013 talk, Guggenheim Abu Dhabi associate curator Reem Fadda argued with an audience member who asked about the abuse of laborers on the museum site. Her response called for understanding cultural specificity:

> Regardless of the way other artists from the outside
> world view what is happening within the UAE,

> the UAE itself has these questions....And I think
> that is something we also have to ask ourselves,
> that kind of ethical positionality, about what is
> the society itself looking and introspecting and
> commenting and criticizing on its own. Criticism is
> not imposed. Let's look at labor here in New York.[23]

As Mostafa Heddaya argues, this kind of thinking preempts any kind of response from outside; the foreign critic is summarily and immediately dismissed, even when what is up for debate is an internationally acknowledged set of human rights.[24] It is unclear who is capable of discussing the labor conditions under scrutiny according to Fadda; she intimates that artists from the UAE may be qualified, but perhaps only them, while overlooking the many members of Gulf Labor from the Middle East and South Asia, and furthermore, ignoring the voices of the workers themselves. Ironically, the director of the Guggenheim himself is either unable or unwilling to discuss labor law in the Emirates. In a 2015 interview, Armstrong stated that he was ill equipped to answer questions regarding whether workers on the Guggenheim's construction site currently have "the right of assembly to express grievances and to strike."[25]

Fadda's call for a better understanding of cultural difference is not entirely unwarranted, particularly in the United States and Europe, where much of the public debate over the construction of the Guggenheim Abu Dhabi has been shaped. Certainly, the UAE, along with the broader region, remains unfamiliar for many cultural workers, despite a booming art scene. And it is potentially always a problem to speak on behalf of others, especially when their experiences and conditions in life are very dissimilar to your own. Amplifying the voice of individuals who are politically restricted from speaking for themselves is a delicate and difficult task. Well-intentioned individuals and groups who want to engage with, or through their work are implicated in, political situations in faraway places often risk charges of ignorance, hypocrisy, paternalism, and in some cases, even opportunism.[26] When we start to think about these events in the frameworks of geographic distance and cultural incommensurability, we can be engulfed in a gap so wide that we feel we can't say or do anything except look, and possibly point out injustices when they arise. Fadda's point, then, bears consideration; but ultimately, it contradicts both the realities of Gulf Labor's multinational member base and the Guggenheim's own prevailing rhetoric of art as a catalyst for mutual understanding.

It seems to me that what is required to productively analyze these recent boycotts, and institutional responses to them, includes nothing less than a reformulation of the politics of seeing as framed both in the fields of art and human rights. As we understand from Marcuse, art requires disinterested, critical viewing. Despite almost fifty years between the time of Marcuse's writing and today, quiet contemplation of the solitary art object remains the default display mode. As much as solitary contemplation can serve as a consciousness-raising device, it can also lead to uncritical reverence, even fetishization, of objects. Just as an artwork may open minds, it may also be employed to conceal inequality and injustice. What is needed now from all cultural workers is to focus anew on the relationship between the work of art and the historical, cultural, and political contexts of a work's production and exhibition.

Ariella Azoulay has cogently argued that human rights discourse since the end of World War II assumes, as its theoretical basis, a distance between subject (bystander or witness) and object (victim).[27] This way of seeing focuses on the ability of witnesses to recognize the plight of victims, often in faraway places, giving the witness the responsibility of recognizing atrocities when they happen, and implicitly distinguishing witness from victim, self from other. The perpetrator almost always remains outside of the frame. Azoulay proposes to reveal the flip side of this formula, choosing to give a human face to the perpetrators that produce conditions of inequality and victimization. The perpetrator is not necessarily an active evildoer, a kind of stock villain easily identified and dispatched with. Rather, victims, perpetrators, and witnesses are structural categories that need to be both understood and reframed. If the dominant way of looking in both art and human rights discourse has been rooted in a politics of distance, Azoulay's proposal for us to move closer and turn inward marks a radical reversal of thinking, not just theoretically, but methodologically, as artists and other cultural workers reconsider their individual roles and ethical responsibilities in the face of institutional complicity in human rights violations.

When individuals and groups boycott events or organizations, such as the Guggenheim Abu Dhabi, they are not just singling out a particular institution for critique and condemnation; they are exercising what Azoulay has called "the right not to be a perpetrator."[28] Azoulay's formulation is simple yet radical, and probably seen as a provocation to some who, trained to think of perpetrators as those who actively harm others, would rather not think of their passive acceptance of injustice and inequality on the same terms. Powerfully, Azoulay's right not to be a perpetrator flips the emphasis of human rights discourse from identifying victims over *there* to understanding our collusion in systems of abuse and inequality right *here*. By recognizing the mundane complicity many of us have in crimes against our fellow humans, we start to be able to articulate a new language of rights premised on an ethics of equality. This articulation is at first an awkward and somewhat risky process, as it reframes human rights discourse to center on the one who *inflicts* harm either through specific acts of violence or latent and pervasive structural privilege. Perpetrators, by definition, violate the rights of victims. To grant a new right to a group that has violated the rights of others seems to be, at first glance, another injustice of a system rigged for those in power. Yet this right offers those who are structurally positioned with oppressors, and able to influence others, a chance to refuse the binary category designed to separate and contain populations into oppressors and oppressed. This repudiation of the status quo is the very starting point of a new political imaginary. Such acts of refusal are necessary to grapple with our increasingly interdependent relations with unfamiliar and unknown people and places across the world, and to challenge the structural inequalities that inevitably pervade our life and work.

52 WEEKS, AND ENGAGING BY DISENGAGING[1]

Mariam Ghani with Haig Aivazian

Most people know of Gulf Labor from our cultural boycott of the Guggenheim Abu Dhabi, which is now entering its fourth year. But others first learned about us through the 2013–2014 campaign *52 Weeks*, which marked an important tactical shift for the group. Every week for an entire year, Gulf Labor published one or more artist's projects calling attention to some aspect of workers' conditions on Saadiyat Island, the political context of their plight, and the problematic compact between the Western cultural institutions and their Abu Dhabi partners. Gulf Labor used this campaign to apply regular and constant pressure on these institutions to seek uniform and enforceable human rights protections for all workers on their construction sites.

While Gulf Labor's position may appear from the outside to be a straightforward staging of refusal, the overall campaign has unfolded as a series of engagements, disengagements, and reengagements. By this we mean that the group has used refusal strategically, in order to open negotiations that previously seemed impossible, to change the tenor of those negotiations when they began to seem untenable or insincere, and to try to negotiate real changes and concessions. The group has also attempted a strategy that we might call *engaging by disengaging*: that is, to use the cultural boycott to open a parallel space for a different kind of engagement of ideas and issues behind and around the boycott itself.

The *52 Weeks* campaign presents the clearest example of this tactic. Since each week of the campaign was produced by a different artist, *52 Weeks* allowed Gulf Labor's central call—to boycott the Guggenheim Abu Dhabi—to be connected to and amplified by multiple voices each with things to say about related issues and struggles, not only on Saadiyat Island and the United Arab Emirates, but also in the Gulf, in the workers' home countries, and across the world. These additional layers of detail, meaning, byplay, and analysis accumulated over its yearlong duration. By the end of the year, *52 Weeks* had not only succeeded as a pressure tactic, but also provoked Gulf Labor organizers like ourselves to reconsider how art-driven campaigns could be used most productively and deliberately to boost public attention, as a supplement to other, more introverted and administrative forms of organizing.

Like most long-term boycotts, our campaign strategy has shifted over time, as we came to deploy different tactics. At certain moments, the group has engaged in intensive behind-the-scenes dialogue with both the Guggenheim and their partners in Abu Dhabi, even making recommendations to them with regards to resolving their own employment policies. We have read, dissected, and responded to monitoring reports by PwC, as well as Human Rights Watch reports. We have conducted our own monitoring missions on Saadiyat as well as in other labor camps, and have, in consultation with rights groups, journalists, activists, and United Nations agencies like the International Labor Organization, drafted reports setting out our own assessments of working conditions, along with recommendations for remedying the situation on Saadiyat and elsewhere. In order to formulate these recommendations, we have had to conduct research and look to other case studies while thinking creatively about finding solutions to complex problems, not least of which is the particularly complicated issue of recruitment fees. Besides our public statements, articles written by our members, and some interviews granted here and there, the bulk of our work has been conducted out of the public eye, and produced little that could be addressed to a public that may be mildly interested but not invested enough to decode the tedious legalese of monitor reports and legislative reforms.

The launch of *52 Weeks* in the fall of 2013 represented a distinct shift in strategy for Gulf Labor. From the outset, the boycott was premised on using artworks strategically, either by withholding them from the Guggenheim's acquisition plans, or by imposing conditions on particular sales, commissions, and exhibitions. *52 Weeks* inverted the tactic, by producing and circulating artworks that directly addressed or enacted the ideas behind the boycott, while bypassing the museum and market systems altogether.

52 Weeks was able to maintain a prolonged (if somewhat one-sided) conversation in public with the Guggenheim, its chief Emirati partner TDIC (Tourism Development & Investment Company), and the other Western institutions active on Saadiyat. But *52 Weeks* also allowed Gulf Labor to connect our efforts vis-à-vis Saadiyat Island to relevant issues and parallel activist projects—from the construction of stadiums for the World Cup in Qatar, to the globalization and aggressive corporatization of university campuses, to the struggles of migrant tomato pickers in Florida—through the projects produced by a diverse group of artists and writers from outside the core working group. In addition, *52 Weeks* created an occasion for direct actions to be performed as part of the campaign, giving birth to the Gulf Labor spinoff Global Ultra Luxury Faction (G.U.L.F.), which assailed the Guggenheim Museum officials and trustees in a more confrontational way.

While some contributions to the *52 Weeks* project created space for direct action, others took more laconic, analytical, or abstracted approaches to highlighting the ironies and contradictions of the grand project of Saadiyat Island. Examples include: Week 15 (by WBYA), which proposed new architectural standards to be added to the AIA Code of Ethics and Professional Conduct; the launch, through Week 34, of an activist Twitterbot programmed to alert prolific tweeters about the Guggenheim and Louvre Abu Dhabi's disregard for human rights; Week 18's reflection on the absence of migrant labor encyclopedias from the sunset of the British Empire; and Week 11's presentation of an entry on 50° Celsius for a new Emirati encyclopedia, reflecting on the dangers of working in extreme temperatures. These examples illustrate the projects' tonal range, from playful to elegiac, from meditative to sardonic.

Overall, the *52 Weeks* campaign, with its many brilliant contributors, helped to reimagine what a group like Gulf Labor can be and do, moving us beyond the declaration and maintenance of the boycott, and the more tactical and bureaucratic aspects of pressuring our target institutions. *52 Weeks*, which succeeded in bringing labor to the very center of art world discourse, was a reminder that a boycott can and should be the beginning of a larger conversation, rather than a means to shut down dialogue around an issue. The organizers of a cultural boycott in particular have the leeway to highlight practices like unfair labor, or apartheid, as objects for debate, not simply as candidates for taboo.

In "My Guggenheim Dilemma," the text published for the second week of *52 Weeks*, Thomas Hirschhorn asserts that the real dilemma of a cultural boycott lies in the contradiction between the "politics of 'good intentions' that guides 'the engagement of the artist'…and my belief and conviction that Art, as Art, has to keep completely out of any daily political cause in order to maintain its power, its artistic power, its real political power." If, in Hirschhorn's formulation, the real political power of art lies in maintaining a space that can resist the simplifications of political idealism and realism, then why use art to enact real-world politics? One response is that when culture is deployed for overtly political purposes—as it often is by autocratic regimes who want to cloak that autocracy with performances of freedom—the weave between aesthetics and politics becomes so complex that the space of art is required to pick it apart.

The conversation around cultural boycotts in the art world and in academia appears to be approaching a critical threshold. This development owes, in part, to a resurgence of a particular kind of institutional critique, or to be more precise, a growing interest by artists in questioning the conditions under which they produce, exhibit, and circulate art. Artists engaged in this critique are most often not producing works about the institutional conditions of art, but rather have mobilized into activist entities that directly intervene in the realities on the ground, confronting tedious technicalities that often exceed their professional expertise. While there is a long history of such collective mobilizations and their alignments with experts in the fields on which they touch, the most recent examples address issues ranging from the working conditions of art handlers who hang artworks in art fairs and auction houses and the endemic exploitation of interns in the gallery system to censorship and other improper institutional conduct, just to name a few.

But more often than not, when artists are moved to action by injustice in the art world, their activism quickly exceeds both the confines of the art world and the confines of their own art practices. Renewed media attention around Gulf Labor's boycott followed the *52 Weeks* launch, but it was also buoyed by G.U.L.F.'s occupations of the Guggenheim Museum and by front-page *New York Times* revelations about labor abuse in the construction of NYU's Abu Dhabi campus. The carefully negotiated artist withdrawals from the Sydney Biennale in protest of main sponsor Transfield's involvement with widely criticized migrant detention camps resulted in the withdrawal of Transfield's chairman from the Biennale board and the return of the boycotting artists to the show. The most recent edition of *Manifesta* was also the target of a call to boycott, due to its Saint Petersburg location and the manifold challenges to free expression in the current political and cultural climate of Russia, including the so-called "homosexual propaganda" laws. Accordingly, the public program of *Manifesta* included self-reflective discussions on the distinctions between "making art politically" and "making political art."

The Boycott, Divestment, and Sanctions (BDS) campaign against Israeli companies and institutions complicit in the violation of Palestinian rights received a fresh jolt of publicity when the American Studies Association voted to endorse it in the fall of 2013, and American politicians seized the opportunity to denounce professors who dare to take public and professional stands against Israeli policies. Shortly prior to the opening of the 2014 São Paulo Biennial, a group of sixty-one participating artists published a collective letter outlining the grave risks that the prominent Israeli funding of the event posed for Arab artists. Threatening to withdraw from the biennial, the signatories of the letter asked for the Biennial's foundation to return the Israeli funding. Instead, a strategic compromise was reached, whereby all materials made very clear that Israeli funding was being used exclusively to support works of those artists not opposed to such an association, as opposed to crediting Israel as a general sponsor of the entire event.

When the Creative Time exhibition *Living as Form*—a survey of socially engaged art practices—was being toured by Independent Curators International, it traveled to Israeli venues that are deeply embedded in the country's military-industrial-settlement complex without prior notification of participating artists, some of whom are BDS signatories. Creative Time and ICI have both announced that they do not participate in any cultural boycotts, because they believe it is more important to engage—to try to shift the limits and possibilities of the discourse by participating in it—than to disengage—to try to shift the discourse entirely by withdrawing from it.

Notwithstanding the limited definition of boycott implied by this formulation, the question raised by Creative Time is a strategic dilemma at the heart of every boycott. Can a given predicament be changed more by engaging, or by disengaging? The answer is certainly different for every person, for every government, for every institution, and for every situation. For some, "boycott" will always be a dirty word—whether because of a reflexive stance against blanket prohibitions, or because of harsh experience at the wrong end of economic sanctions. For others, the boycott is just another bit in the activist tool kit, or really, just an ordinary fact of life: part of the endless, everyday struggle to negotiate our personal ethics.

Thomas Hirschhorn raised another pressing question in the last line of his *52 Weeks* text, when he declared that "my signature for the boycott of Guggenheim Abu Dhabi will make sense if I have to pay a price for it." Since his text was originally a letter sent from Hirschhorn to Guggenheim deputy director and chief curator Nancy Spector and director Richard Armstrong about a proposed exhibition of his at the Guggenheim Bilbao, the allusion to paying a price was quite apposite. Yet the reality of paying a real, personal price for participation in a cultural boycott is not often acknowledged. It is more typical for us to join what Hirschhorn himself calls a "fancy artists' boycott," either as an all-but-routine gesture of solidarity—just another e-signature on a petition—or, for the organizers, as some sort of esoteric career move. But for a boycott to make a maximal impact, there ought to be a real price—lost income, frayed relationships, a certain reputation for troublemaking—and signing on must mean that you are willing to accept that price. Garnering a lesser number of signatories who have seriously weighed what it means to sign is more valuable than collecting a greater number who sign without having to bear any real consequences.

Ultimately, our experience in Gulf Labor has brought us to the following conclusions. A boycott (like a strike) should be a tactic of last, rather than first, resort. Public boycotts should be called only when negotiation proves either impossible or fruitless. Moreover, a boycott should be launched only when it is likely to produce results: that is to say, a cultural boycott will work only if the creative work being withheld has significant and immediate value to the institution or government being boycotted. If that government or institution does not in fact need cultural products for a specific purpose in that specific moment, then cultural workers have no leverage with them, and so the boycott is unlikely to succeed. Likewise, if the boycott does not include a significant portion of the most visible cultural workers necessary to the immediate purpose or project of the government or institution, then it is also likely to fail. A public boycott should not be called until enough organizing has been done to ensure a minimum of consensus around the goal and necessity of the boycott in the community most important to its success. If the demand behind a boycott is vague or diffuse, it is also unlikely to work. In a long-term boycott, however, it is possible that goals may develop over time as the situation and relationships change, from one central demand into a series of more specific or interrelated demands.

Thus far, the Gulf Labor experience suggests that the boycott dilemma, as formulated by Creative Time, is something of a false dichotomy. Describing participation in a cultural boycott as disengagement, and refusal to participate in a boycott as engagement, can be a misleading oversimplification. A long-term boycott like ours involves a good deal of dialogue with the targeted institution about the conditions under which a boycott can be lifted. So, too, many people in the coalition became involved with Gulf Labor after first producing art in the region, including long-term research-based projects. As a result, artists initiating such projects were already directly engaging with, and thus becoming implicated in, the ethical dilemmas at hand. But most of all, the dilemma of engagement versus disengagement is a false one because of the potential for a cultural boycott that, while enacting physical or economic withdrawal from a particular institution, simultaneously opens a parallel space for critical engagement with the issues motivating the boycott, as well as dialogue with all the players involved. This is precisely what *52 Weeks* achieved.

Gulf autocrats' massive investment in cultural projects does hold out a sort of promise, both to artists across the Middle East who need more support and exposure for their work, and to inhabitants of Gulf countries who might imagine that freedom of expression granted to artists within museum walls could eventually lead to greater freedom of expression in other sectors of life. But if this promise is to be more than a desert mirage, or a whitewash of dubious human rights practices, the institutions charged with realizing these cultural projects must be constructed in a truly equitable way, and held to high standards. Gulf Labor has said that it is not enough for a satellite museum, or a college campus, to function as a zone of exception, where the prohibitory norms and rules are bent for certain actors to operate within a sequestered, showpiece site. Gulf Labor thinks these institutions can be more, and should do more. By being held accountable for their openly expansionist agendas, they can be turned into levers to generate wider change across the whole region.

Saadiyat has become a particular flashpoint for at least two reasons. First, because the Western institutions loaning their names and institutional cachet to Abu Dhabi's new "culture zone" have brands to protect, and reputations that project images entirely incompatible with the unsavory image of the labor camp. These institutions have significant leverage, and Gulf Labor, along with groups like Human Rights Watch, have argued that they are refusing to use it. Consequently, Gulf Labor has had no alternative but to apply its own leverage to force these institutions to confront their responsibilities in illiberal countries where they choose to operate. Second, Abu Dhabi's sovereign wealth fund is among the largest in the world. The annual interest income from the fund alone nets the Emirate an average of 43.47 billion USD per year. Clearly Abu Dhabi does not lack the funds to resolve the problems identified by Gulf Labor, along with countless investigative journalists, rights groups, and even the state's own appointed labor monitor (PwC) on Saadiyat Island. What it lacks is the will to put its resources to this particular use. To put it even more clearly: the Abu Dhabi authorities could easily improve the living and working standards of these workers, but they visibly do not want to do so. The distinction is crucial, because it points to the global importance of this local struggle. The rulers of Abu Dhabi do not want to require better conditions for their migrant workforce because doing so would set a precedent that would spread to other countries.

Gulf Labor believes we should not be asked to overlook how our museums are being built simply out of gratitude that they are being "provided" in the first place. We don't think art has to enter the portals of the museum before the museum can become an agent of change; we think change should be demanded from the moment the museum is first imagined. We think it is just to ask more of these institutions, not because we think so little of them, but rather because we value their function and potential more highly than perhaps even their executive officers do. We are boycotting, perhaps in a funny way, out of our love and care for these institutions, because we want them to be their best possible selves.

Gulf Labor fully recognizes that the predicament of migrant workers is not limited to the Guggenheim/Louvre Abu Dhabi, to Saadiyat Island, the Emirates, or even to the Gulf region. While it is engaged in what is undoubtedly a worldwide struggle, the group had chosen to focus its energies on this particular battle because we believe it is winnable. We are asking the Guggenheim, the Louvre, and the British Museum to either halt on the brink, or, in the case of NYU, commit their resources to bettering the human rights environment in which global outposts are established in locations like the Gulf. When corporations made the same move into globalized production and distribution, the anti-sweatshop movement emerged to hold them accountable for their deliberate negligence overseas. But Nike and the Gap were not claiming to be protectors of our culture or standard-bearers for our educational methods; they were clearly seeking to maximize their profits while expanding their global presence. When museums and universities go offshore, but hold on to their claims about their cultural standing, this struggle takes on a new importance. More than any dispute over which objects end up on the walls or plinths and which names are included in the curricula, the questions of where and how museums and universities choose to expand, and which compromises they are willing to make along the way, will determine how culture is preserved, distributed, and extended. If we are to have any say in this debate, the workers who provide the currency for this sector of cultural trade and services must hold our institutions accountable, and we must begin now.

NOT WALKING AWAY: PARTICIPATION AND WITHDRAWAL IN THE 2014 SYDNEY BIENNALE

Nathan Gray and Ahmet Öğüt

Ahmet Öğüt: Nearly three years have passed since we took part in a conditional withdrawal from the 19th Biennale of Sydney, in February 2014. The Biennial was the site of a weeks-long controversy regarding the connections between the art event and its founding sponsor, Transfield, an Australian multinational corporation profiting from the country's migrant detention centers. How did you first get engaged with this issue? When did you first hear that Transfield had secured a $1.22 billion contract to work on the offshore detention facilities on Manus Island and Nauru? And how was Transfield known within the cultural scene of Australia before that?

Nathan Gray: First, let me point out your use of the term "conditional withdrawal," rather than boycott, which is what was actually being requested of us by the Australian advocacy organization RISE: Refugees, Survivors, and Ex-detainees, and the Sydney-based arts educator Matthew Kiem. I usually speak of what we undertook as political action without using the term boycott, and I think that these expressions indicate how both of us were uncomfortable with the idea of simply walking away from the Biennale and drawing a line between us and the artists who remained within its structure. We were rejecting tactics of division and shaming, and keeping open lines of communication to preserve the possibilities of continued collaboration on this issue with other artists in the exhibition.

A.Ö.: I agree, and since you say "we," I would like to mention the role of the working group that you were part of.

N.G.: The initial letter and to some extent the action itself was initially organized by the Australian artists Gabrielle de Vietri, Bianca Hester, and Charlie Sofo, while I played an early but lesser role. We formed in response to the situation as it unfolded, during the installation period for the Biennale, and referred to ourselves collectively as the Artists Working Group.

I think there is a general awareness among Australians about the injustice of our country's migrant and refugee policies, but there is also a sense of powerlessness. I first became involved with refugee advocacy while working for the Australian Greens, which is the only political party in the Australian Parliament advocating for the closure of the offshore detention centers. Thus, even though the Greens only hold about 10 percent of the seats in parliament, they play an important role in keeping the issue visible, and standing out as a clear force of opposition.

At the start of 2014 Transfield was already somewhat involved in the detention center on Nauru, and as we saw above calls to boycott had come from various activists. In the weeks before the Biennale, however, several events made the call to act more urgent. On February 17, 2014, during a disturbance in the center on Manus Island, local Papuan police and civilians entered the compound and beat many of the refugees there. Seventy-seven people were injured, some of them severely, and a young Iranian refugee named Reza Barati was killed. Two Papuan men, both employees of the center, were sentenced for the murder. (Australian

employees may also have been involved, but Australian authorities were
uncooperative in supplying them for questioning by Papuan police.) On
February 24 it was announced that Transfield Services would take over
the contract for Manus Island—the $1.22 billion contract you refer to—
just one month before the opening of the Biennale.

*A.Ö.: Yes, those dramatic events escalated the urgency around the same
time we found out about Transfield's connection to the center. At first we were
puzzled by the relationship of the Biennale chairman to the center, because we
were not sure if Transfield Foundation, Transfield Holdings, and Transfield
Services were the same thing. Can you explain this in historical and local
context?*

N.G.: The Sydney Biennale was founded by Franco Belgiorno-
Nettis, who also founded Transfield. His son Luca was chairman of
the Biennale board and his son Guido was chairman of the Art Gallery
of New South Wales, a key venue for the Biennale. The Biennale was
funded by the Transfield Foundation, a partnership between Transfield
Holdings—which the Belgiorno-Nettis family retained control of—
and Transfield Services, which ran the detention centers. This type of
structure is typical of the way companies and shareholders distribute risk
and avoid responsibility.

Transfield is a large infrastructure company that often contracts
with the government on public works. The company has contracts to
supply public transport, for instance. There are strong ties between its
current and previous board members and the conservative party that is
currently in power, the Liberal Party of Australia. Former Transfield
CEO Tony Shepard assumed the role of head of the government's
Commission of Audit immediately after resigning his role with
Transfield, which has donated money to both major political parties
in Australia. What this complex picture shows is that Transfield was
enmeshed in large arts organizations, the infrastructure of major

Australian cities, the conservative government, and the detention system. Government policymaking at state and federal levels has been thoroughly intertwined with Transfield's corporate interests.

Here I'll pose a question for you, Ahmet. I must say that I was surprised that you, Libia Castro and Ólafur Ólafsson, Nicoline van Harskamp, and Agnieszka Polska and Sara van der Heide thought the issue was significant enough to withdraw from the Biennale. To an Australian audience, I think it was important that non-Australians mobilized around this issue. I was wondering how organizing from afar felt to you, what the difficulties were, and how you became acquainted with the Australian political context?

A.Ö.: I've spent time in Sydney because I exhibited at the city's Artspace Visual Arts Center in 2010, so I was quickly able to get different opinions from my Sydney-based friends, like Zanny Begg and later Brisbane-based curator Reuben Keehan, Melbourne-based artist Nicholas Mangan, and many others. The main trigger for me was the misleading email that the Biennale's press department sent to featured artists shortly after Matthew Kiem's public letter appeared. The rushed Q&A document attached to that email made me feel very suspicious. We started to exchange emails with other Biennale artists in order to get this sensitive issue right. The working group you were part of was impressively organized to keep us updated and well informed.

On February 19, 2014, forty-six participating artists issued an open letter calling for the board to "act in the interests of asylum-seekers" and "withdraw from the current sponsorship arrangements with Transfield." The board's response was intransigent: "Without Transfield," it explained, "the Biennale of Sydney would cease to exist." We were pushed to act politically while thinking the institution's existence cannot be envisioned without cultural workers and its public. Eventually nine of us withdrew from the Biennial. Exhibition installers Diego Bonetto and Peter Nelson walked off the job over the issue.

On March 4, the issue was raised in the Australian Parliament, with Green Party Senator Lee Rhiannon making a motion in support of the artists. The motion was defeated by the two major parties. Perhaps in response to the ongoing controversy, Transfield shares dropped 9 percent that week, after an initial 21 percent rise when the contracts were first announced. On March 7, just fourteen days before the opening, Luca Belgiorno-Nettis made the decision to step down as chair of the Biennial (a position he had held for over fourteen years) and the board announced that it was severing its forty-four-year-old ties with Transfield, which had founded the Biennial in 1973.

At that moment, now that our demand had been met, seven of the nine of us who had withdrawn from the Biennale reentered. There has been a chain of consequences. First, Senator George Brandis threatened to withdraw government funding from arts organizations that reject corporate sponsorship. After that came a roughly 70 percent drop in Australia Council grants for individual artists and federal funding cuts for sixty-two arts organizations.

N.G.: Exactly. The current government, and in particular the former arts minister, George Brandis, who presided over the cuts, eliminated $100 million from the arts budget in 2014, and diverted $104.8 million into a program that was put under ministerial control in 2015. The portfolio has now changed hands but the policy has remained the same. Brandis had long had a problem with the peer-reviewed arts funding body, the Australia Council, and had repeatedly sought control over particular funding decisions. He was highly critical of the Biennale for severing ties with Transfield—as was the current prime minister, Malcolm Turnbull, who accused the artists of "vicious ingratitude"— and demanded that the Australia Council deny funding to bodies that rejected corporate sponsorship. Many people saw the cuts as retribution for artists' actions against the government's policies vis-à-vis the refugees; however, it is important to realize that this agenda predates the Biennale withdrawal.

Today, the government plays down the cuts, as a large proportion of the money has been reallocated to a fund originally called the National Program for Excellence in the Arts, now called Catalyst, which is directly administered by the government. The original name of the program reveals the ideological gulf between Brandis and the wider arts community; his given examples of great Australian art include Shakespeare companies and chamber orchestras, which to my mind are dubiously Australian in character. The clear aim with these cuts is to bring critical art into the service of governmental and conservative agendas.

At the time, these cuts were implemented as part of a larger program of false austerity—false because the Australian economy was not hit by the 2008 financial crisis but in fact had an economic boom. Given the billions of dollars the government allots to detaining refugees and subsidizing mining companies, these funding decisions are clearly political. The cuts were aimed at implementing a neoliberal program of withdrawing government services, cutting science and research, health, and education, as well as the arts.

A.Ö.: Those are some of the unfortunate events that followed our political action. What about the effects the action had on Australia's refugee policies? Under Australian law, any asylum seeker arriving in the country without a visa can be detained indefinitely, a policy that contradicts the UN Refugee Convention of 1951. Is there any movement to change this law after what happened in 2014? Do you think our pressuring Transfield through the Biennale withdrawal had a long-term impact, together with the political actions of advocacy organizations and the detained refugees themselves, considering the recent closure of the Manus Island detention center?

N.G.: First, I should note that opposition to government policy is first expressed by refugees themselves, in the offshore camps and detention centers within Australia alike. Refugees live in tents, have limited use of water despite extremely hot conditions, face restricted access to doctors and medicine, and often queue for hours for meals. There are constant fears for safety, with multiple cases of sexual abuse reported, and several deaths due to inappropriate or inadequate medical treatment. Refugees have resisted these conditions in a variety of ways: organized protests, hunger strikes, civil disobedience, and calls for action from the wider Australian community. Refugees also resist on a personal level, in less organized ways that involve self-harm or suicide, including a recent wave of self-immolations. However, the main way that the people in the camps resist is through their resolve not to leave despite the fact that many of them have been in detention now for more than three years with no end in sight, in conditions that the United Nations has described as systematically violating its convention on torture. They have been offered resettlement in Papua New Guinea and Cambodia, or to be returned to the countries from which they are fleeing because of persecution. These offers have largely been turned down because there are major safety concerns in Papua New Guinea and Cambodia (not to mention the nations they left), but the government continually attempts to wear down their resolve.

Since the Biennale political action we have seen a wider movement aimed at shutting down detention centers by pressuring investors. This has had some success, with several pension funds divesting. There have also been challenges to deportation, lawyers have sought intervention orders, doctors in hospitals have refused to discharge children that were being returned to camps after visiting Australia for treatment, and flights deporting refugees have been disrupted by activists. Divestment and disruption seem to be increasingly embraced as protest and other forms have proved to be ineffectual.

Specifically, we have seen legal challenges move through the Papua New Guinea judicial system, and pressure from divestment campaigns are bearing fruit. The Manus Island camp, which is the larger of the two, was recently declared illegal by the Papua New Guinea government and ordered to cease operating. This was followed by a further Supreme Court decision, in August 2016, that indicated that both Australia and Papua New Guinea were responsible for closing the camp and resettling the refugees despite Australia's claims to the contrary. This effectively paves the way for lawyers representing the refugees and asylum seekers on Manus to pursue enforcement applications for their release, and to have them returned to Australia as well as to seek compensation.

The effect of the Papua New Guinea Supreme Court's decision on Broadspectrum (the name Transfield was given after the Belgiorno-Nettis family sold their shares in September 2014) was dramatic. Its stocks went into free fall during the case, and the company advised its shareholders not to sell their stock to Ferrovial, a Spanish company that was attempting a hostile takeover. As soon as the verdict was issued, they changed this advice and delisted themselves from the stock exchange to prevent a further slump in stock prices. Ferrovial owns 90 percent of shares in Broadspectrum as of June 7, 2016 and has stated it will not be retendering for the detention center contracts. More recently, the security contractor at the camps, Wilson Security, also stated that it would not be retendering for the contract, citing activism as one of the main reasons. This is a remarkable reflection of the financial impact concerted political action has had on Broadspectrum. Detention contracts will be far less attractive to other companies that might consider taking them on. The government's response has been to extend the current contracts, which would have been due for renewal in 2016, until October 2017.

So it took a while but I see the artists' threat to withdraw from the Sydney Biennale as an early high-profile action that concentrated attention on the companies that were carrying out the government's unethical policies. I think this shift proved effective, so it's heartening to know that we played a part in the collapse of Broadspectrum, and that the system is undergoing major changes as a result. This also indicates to me that many contemporary art events are the results of collaboration between governments, institutions, and corporations, a fact that presents both difficulties and opportunities for activism.

A.Ö.: The latest edition of the Sydney Biennale closed in June 2016. Was there any productive discussion around what happened during the previous edition? Or did the Biennale organizers strategically avoid the topic?

N.G.: I did not attend the Biennale but went to a talk delivered by its curator, Stephanie Rosenthal, largely to make sure that the history of the action was acknowledged. I was surprised that this was done, not through a mere hint but by naming Transfield and talking about the policy of mandatory detention. The framing of this year's Biennale is in itself interesting, with the different venues being referred to as embassies, and many of those engaged with the Biennale termed ambassadors. This diplomatic framework seems to be acknowledging that the Biennale, once so central to the cultural life of Sydney, now needed to re-establish itself.

A.Ö.: Do you feel like there is more organized solidarity among Australian artists, curators, and art workers these days? Or has fear taken over individual and collective positions?

N.G.: The arts cuts started a movement of advocacy for the arts. Organizations that were previously averse to making any sort of political comment were forced to speak out against the government's plans. The Senate Inquiry into the cuts received 2,719 submissions, from individuals, small-to-medium organizations, and even some larger organizations that were not subject to cuts themselves, almost all critical of the cuts and their consequences. However, it was completely ignored by the government.

The cuts forced a recognition of the arts ecology that allows less established artists to develop careers in smaller institutions before going on to larger ones. I am hopeful that arts institutions might develop a more cooperative network of support in order to overcome these cuts. If the cuts continue, it may be that small organizations are forced to find alternative models outside of government funding.

Even after the National Day of Action for the Arts in May 2016, in an interview, it became quite apparent that the prime minister had little idea about the widespread opposition to the cuts and seemed to be unfamiliar with them or how they were being applied. He even stated on national television that "the Australia Council is getting more funding now than it did under the Labor government," which is clearly untrue.

The Labor Party has promised to axe the Catalyst funding body and return $150 million to the arts sector, which is $20 million more than before the cuts but less than the Labor Party's previous commitments to increases in funding.

For the moment these cuts seem to have united artists and arts organizations against current government policy. I hope this unity can be maintained as these austerity measures start to bite.

LOOSE CONNECTIONS

Radhika Subramaniam

Loose Contacts

It has been decades now since one could snicker at someone caught out
by the lack of loose connections. In the India in which I grew up, it was
taken as a reasonable excuse for not being in touch to say you "couldn't get
through" on the phone. Telephones went periodically dead. Sometimes
you could call out but didn't receive calls, and at other times, you would get
calls but couldn't make them (prompting you to enlist the very first caller in
making a complaint to the repair line); if you did get connected, it might be
to an exasperated "wrong number," and the very few pay phones that were
around gave no guarantee of a voice in return for one's rupee. In any case,
most of the country's residents had no phone at all. In the late eighties,
PCOs—public call offices—completely revolutionized communication
across the country, cropping up at every other corner, providing local
and long-distance telephonic access to the ordinary person. However,
there was still a chance that the connection would be fitful or poor.

When someone raised within this wheezy infrastructure was
suddenly transplanted into the firm sonorities of first-world technologies,

the results were often amusing. The scenario would go something like this: As an excuse for not having been in contact, the person would casually proffer, "I couldn't get through." This explanation would meet with a puzzled response: "What time did you call? Did you have the right number? Didn't you get the machine?" As the questions bored in with great sincerity, the squirming addressee might weakly suggest, "It was engaged…?" meaning what Americans more often refer to as "busy" or "getting a busy signal."

The disengagement facilitated by this temperamental telephony made comrades of procrastination, delay tactics, rebelliousness, oversights, the need to switch off, a brush-off, or deliberate withdrawal. It went hand in hand with other manifestations of discontinuous engagement that were part of the common vocabulary. There was "loose contact," which meant, as elsewhere, unstable electrical connections and faulty wiring, although the consistency with which this looseness manifested itself strongly seemed to suggest either a faulty diagnosis or the perception of its value. The inaugural flicker of a fluorescent light tube lent itself to the epithet "tube light," still used to refer to anyone who is either slow on the uptake or a bit behind the times.

And who would want to be anything but with the times and well connected? So completely have connectivity and immediacy become fused with a sense of being au courant that few of us would advocate for anything otherwise. We want to be *with it*, not to have *missed the moment*, and mostly, we believe that being in touch keeps our fingers on the pulse of things in a way that enables both informed and timely civic participation. To be connected is to be part of a community, ideally one of choice, and not to be so embraced is often taken to imply that one has been politically forsaken—because of socioeconomic or cultural barriers and by extension, a lack of infrastructural provisions.

In India, the advent of mobile phone technology put paid to the kind of expansive disengagement that was once an option for some and mandated for the rest. Inaugurated about twenty years ago, it brought contact to the humblest fingertip, ensuring that so many who were otherwise denied access to private or independent communication—working classes, rural peasantry, women domestic workers—could conduct their own businesses and relationships both near and far. Insofar as "not getting through" had been what anthropologist James Scott elsewhere calls a weapon of the weak[1]—the small act of resistance of the relatively powerless—that arsenal was now diminished. What is available now by way of excuses are protestations of "no charge," meaning that the phone battery is running low, or if circumstances such as travel make it plausible, claims of being "out of range."

Remote Sensing

To be physically here and mentally out of range is a familiar experience of the cell phone age. The experiential leap between a basic cell phone and the retronymous landline isn't altogether unimaginable, even as the former has intensified and expanded people's sense of connection across distance. However, smartphone technologies and the internet have catapulted people across spaces in ways that appear radically different from television, a medium that was always, as the term would suggest, conceived of as "far-seeing." Television's flickering images themselves brought other worlds into living rooms in substantially different ways from earlier modes of media representation such as newspapers. The sudden and surprising ways in which global media events on television could erupt into everyday experience created what McKenzie Wark, in an early analysis, called "virtual geographies"—connections not predicated on propinquity but encouraged by a peculiar "telesthesia" or perception at a distance.[2] Even when places and people appeared in one's living room, they were confidently asserting their reality elsewhere. Home on a wide range indeed.

Home was always a remote affair for members of immigrant communities engaged in "long-distance nationalism," a phenomenon identified early on by Benedict Anderson, ever attentive to the work of media and technology in constructing imagined communities.[3] Aided by communication technologies, immigrants and exiles actively follow the news and politics of their countries of origin and create cross-boundary ethno-cultural and political networks that often intervene with considerable impact in national affairs. Today's complex media world facilitates more immediate and affective modes of transnational connection than the "email nationalism" of which Anderson wrote, and thereby supports emergent forms of political alliance that expand well beyond national diasporas.

Smartphones and their various platforms and applications have made connection a relentlessly addictive and intimate affair. Few of us are unfamiliar with the percussive-thumb, head-down stance that is the first position of connectivity today. Flipping channels on television was done with a mixture of inertia and ennui, but the distraction produced by smartphone "multitasking" has quite a different charge. With dozens of discrete communications unfolding on a variety of platforms, the smartphone is far from a broadcast medium. Receiving an email or a text message with news is qualitatively different from picking up the morning paper or hearing someone speak on television. Direct, intimate, charged, the information that floods into the palms of our hands grabs us with the illusion of immediate, personal address, blurring any trace of its journey or the distance traveled.

What's happening in this environment of multiple direct communications? With every new communication technology and

platform, from email to smartphones and social media, we're told that
the world has grown smaller—and yet, it seems that in our effort to
bring things up close to take a good look, we've overlooked the fact
that some things always remain at a distance, or out of sight, even
if they are just next door. Distance goes beyond simple geographies,
and new cartographies of connection must be drawn. But couldn't
this mean that the old geographical imagination that gave us the
dark continents, terrae incognitae, black holes, and the Orient, along
with their variously savage, brutal, primitive, vulnerable, noble, or
even absent inhabitants, can no longer work in the same way—that is,
predicated on little direct observation but plentifully fueled by self-
reinforcing imagery?

Some years ago, students in a class I taught on urban poetics
surprised me with their old-fashioned bewilderment: "How can we
say anything about places we haven't been to?" The question seemed to
hark back to a conception of local knowledge that flew in the face of
contemporary notions of networked social connectivity. It shifted my
attention from the analyses of images and other representations that tend
to take priority in the study of media to the socio-technical systems and
infrastructures that mediate the perception of a here and an elsewhere.
How do we now understand the ways in which we're tweeted at, poked,
and pinged for attention from people, particularly from afar? Could the
sense of intimate distance created by these technologies be said to change
the "rules of engagement," a term whose military antecedents we would
do well to remember? Can this remote sensing, in fact, stand in for
direct contact effectively enough to propel new forms of solidarity across
distance and difference?

The immediacy of today's tele-technologies tends to downplay
the significance of translation in making conditions and demands
originating elsewhere matter. The work of contextualization hasn't

vanished but its labor and effects are increasingly obscured. When cultural exchange was the currency of an internationalizing world, contextualization was the passport with which cultures traveled, even if it wasn't always apparent that the passport itself—that is, the contextual framework—was responsible for creating the cultures that could step onto a global stage. Today, exchange, a term that implies an extractive, appropriative, pleasurable, and consumable form of contact, has given way to engagement, a term that conveys the fuzzy tactility of our present connections—immediate and intimate yet not close at all.[4] The histories of exchange already demonstrated a preference for encountering foreign artifacts over strangers—think of the museum displays, lively circuits of sound and music, bodywork and food crazes, accompanied by wall texts, liner notes, and background articles, that have contributed to the circulation of avowedly cosmopolitan milieux. Traveling culture of this sort was frequently packaged for the palate such that it began to create the shorthand of cultural representation. Often functioning in parallel with political structures that strongly regulate the movement of associated bodies, they provide the reasons why explanatory notes often stand in for actual, perhaps difficult, translation that, in turn, tells us the story of how engagement is put in place—and in its place. Today, places, people, their practices and their politics present themselves no more directly to the world than they ever did, but the awareness of mediation has receded into the background.

The question posed by my students could be interpreted or extended another way—not as expressing reservations or confessing a lack of familiarity, but as asking *in what way* they might be able to speak on behalf of and in solidarity with people at a remove. Under what circumstances and in what ways should we engage in far-flung politics in which we are undoubtedly implicated but whose effects we may not feel? Taking our cue from activists, campaigners, and cultural workers on the ground is a first step, but the politics of our own context will still necessarily inflect our actions.

If the eclipse of distance means that the faraway can be brought into the palm of one's hand, it does not mean a future without places; rather, this tactility can reveal the contours of sites linked through a topography, and open up possibilities for a "counter-topographic politics."[5] This is the tool Cindi Katz offers for conceptualizing engagement across space and scale in her eloquent discussion of feminist political strategies in a globalizing world. Topography accounts for how the specific histories and geographies of a given location shape its social relations of power and production. It is sensitive to the local while aware of its enlistment in global processes. A counter-topographic politics entails more than just connecting a here with an over there in a transnational alliance in which two place-based imaginaries are constructed. Rather, the politics itself must take on the global challenge even while its specific grounds are local. There are those for whom the so-called "elsewhere" is actually right here and for whom the stakes are high—they are personally connected to the issues, affected by its outcomes, vulnerable to oppositional authorities—and there are others for whom the issue may be a larger question of justice and solidarity. But the socio-technical mechanisms through which we are *touched* by political acts and global movements are as critical to the story of how we are called to political engagement (or disengagement) as is the ethical imperative to act.

Neither Here Nor There

There is little question in my mind of the validity of targeted forms of disobedience, withdrawal, and repudiation aimed at more just political ends. What I have been trying to explore is how today's media technologies create connections across time and space in ways that obscure the circumstances of their creation.

These days, the engagement summoned forth by so-called global citizenship is typically twinned to connectivity. This implies that we can swiftly act or be called to action—and the relentless tumble of exhortations and appeals that appear in email inboxes testifies not only to how quickly political orientations are identified, sometimes by algorithm, but also to how solidarities are experienced and indeed engaged in these virtual landscapes. In fact, the "global village" makes persistent and steady claims upon us from which we can never rightfully profess to be "otherwise engaged." The promise of immediate, worldwide action on shared concerns is out there, and that is thrilling—that is, if we contribute through swift, decisive responses rather than detachment, inaction, and passivity.

But what forms of contact are assumed in this conception of engagement? Is it predicated on the notion that in a networked world of continuous information flow, we are actually free of the burden of trying to understand how connection is manufactured and felt? If the rapid, simultaneous, stable, personalized communications that come through our glowing devices prompt us to believe that those far away are close enough to us to matter, we can surely be thankful for the work they do. And yet, the memory of loose contacts provides a salutary reminder of how distance might persist between the closest points—a distance whose topographies incorporate differences in beliefs, demands, practices, values, lived experiences, and material circumstances. Who among the "politically engaged" hasn't at some point posted, tweeted, or digitally signed one's name not because of the trustworthiness of the source so much as a sympathetic acceptance of its claims, or alternately, saved an online petition indefinitely, meaning to learn more about the issue? Learning more is indeed the heart of the matter. Every instance at which the possibility of acting in solidarity presents itself is a moment for research—a moment that does not drop the call but actually secures the connection.

To participate conscientiously in these transnational public spheres is difficult. It requires a particularly energetic attentiveness to keep oneself informed, not only of the issues but also of the effects of one's actions; despite our notional immediacy, these often occur at a remove, brought into view only by prostheses. Why do such incommensurate and intransigent conceptions of places such as Kashmir, Baghdad, and Palestine-Israel persist despite new skeins of global connective tissue? We don't actually stand shoulder to shoulder with those afar even when we see ourselves as their allies, and the mistranslations and tensions of our alliances and alignments demand continual critical reflexivity. Do we boycott the effort altogether? No! Disconnection is not the easy way out. Nor is this a cautionary tale. All those years of asynchronous connectivity remind me that disengaged lines were assiduously kept open, and losing touch only meant repair before reconnection. Yet, as we each practice our own forms of remote sensing, we would do well to be vigilant that the spurious security of tight connections does not foreclose the recognition of what ultimately "couldn't get through."

Acknowledgments: Many thanks to Kareem Estefan, Victoria Hattam, and Laura Liu for their feedback on various versions of this essay. All loose connections remain mine.

CONTRIBUTOR BIOGRAPHIES

Nasser Abourahme is a writer and doctoral candidate at Columbia University, where he works between political theory, urban studies, and postcolonial critique. He has published widely on colonial urbanism, Palestinian political history, camps and refugeehood, revolt and revolution in the Arab world, and aesthetics in contemporary Palestinian politics. He is currently the Special Features editor of the journal *CITY*, where many of his publications appear.

Haig Aivazian is an artist living in Beirut. Working across a wide range of media, he delves into the ways in which ideologies embed, affect, and move people, objects, and architecture. Often departing from known events, and weaving in lesser known narratives, he has explored apparatuses of control and sovereignty at work in sports, finance, museums, and music. His work has been presented at FRAC Aquitaine, Marrakech Biennial (2016), the Istanbul Biennial, the Armenian Pavilion in Venice, the Museum of Modern Art Warsaw (2015), Asia Society New York, the Kölnischer Kunstverein (2014), VideoBrasil São Paulo, Homeworks Beirut (2013), FID Marseille (2012), and Mercer Union Toronto (2011). He curated *Roads Were Open/*

Roads Were Closed, the Third Line Dubai (2008), and was Associate Curator of the Sharjah Biennial (2011). He has written for *Afterall*, *Manifesta Journal*, *Bidoun*, and *Makhzin*, and has taught at the American University of Beirut and the Ashkal Alwan HomeWorks Program.

Ariella Azoulay is a professor of Modern Culture and Media and Comparative Literature, Brown University, curator, and documentary filmmaker. Her recent publications include *From Palestine to Israel: A Photographic Record of Destruction and State Formation, 1947-1950* (Pluto Press, 2011), *Civil Imagination: The Political Ontology of Photography* (Verso, 2012) and *The Civil Contract of Photography* (Zone Books, 2008); and, co-authored with Adi Ophir, *The One State Condition: Occupation and Democracy between the Sea and the River* (Stanford University Press, 2012). Among her exhibitions are *Time Machine: Stereoscopic Views, Palestine 1900* (co-curated with Issam Nassar), Pembroke Hall, Brown University; *The Natural History of Rape*, F/Stop Photography festival, Leipzig; *When The Body Politic Ceases To Be An Idea*, Exhibition Room; *Manifesta Journal Around Curatorial Practices* No 16 (folded format in Hebrew), MOBY, Bat Yam; *Potential History*, Stuk / Artefact, Louven, *Untaken Photographs* (2010, Igor Zabel Award, The Moderna galerija, Lubliana; Zochrot, Tel Aviv), *Architecture of Destruction* (Zochrot, Tel Aviv) and *Everything Could Be Seen* (Um El Fahem Gallery of Art). She has also directed several documentary films including *Civil Alliances, Palestine, 47-48* (2012), *I Also Dwell Among Your Own People: Conversations with Azmi Bishara* (2004) and *The Food Chain* (2004).

Tania Bruguera is an artist who creates socially-engaged performances and installations that examine the nature of political power structures and their effect on the lives of society's most vulnerable individuals and groups. Her research focuses on ways in which art can be applied to the everyday political life; on the transformation of social affect into political effectiveness. Her long-term projects are intensive interventions on the institutional structure of collective memory, education and politics. By creating proposals and aesthetic models for others to use and adapt, she defines herself as an initiator rather than an author, and often collaborates with multiple institutions as well as many individuals so that the full realization of her artwork occurs when others adopt it. Awarded an Honoris Causa by The School of the Art Institute of Chicago, she was selected one of the 100 Leading Global Thinkers by *Foreign Policy* magazine, shortlisted for the #Index100 Freedom of Expression Award, a Herb Alpert Award winner, a Guggenheim, Radcliffe and Yale World Fellow, and the first artist-in-residence in the New York City Mayor's Office of Immigrant Affairs.

Noura Erakat is an assistant professor at George Mason University, where she teaches in the legal studies, international studies, and human rights/social justice studies concentrations. Her scholarly interests include humanitarian law, human rights law, refugee law, and national security law. She earned her BA and JD from Berkeley Law School and her LLM in National Security from the Georgetown University Law Center. She is a co-Founder/editor of *Jadaliyya* e-zine. Prior to beginning her appointment at GMU, Erakat was a Freedman Teaching Fellow at Temple Law School and has taught International Human Rights Law and the Middle East at Georgetown University since 2009.

Mariam Ghani is an artist, writer, filmmaker, and member of the Gulf Labor Working Group. Her work looks at places and moments where social, political, and cultural structures take on visible forms. Solo exhibitions include the Queens Museum of Art, the Saint Louis Art Museum, the Indianapolis Museum of Art, the Rogaland Kunstsenter, and the Gatchina Museum. Notable group exhibitions and screenings include dOCUMENTA 13, the Liverpool Biennial, the Sharjah Biennial, the Dhaka Art Summit, the National Gallery in Washington, DC, the Secession in Vienna, the CCCB in Barcelona, and the Met Breuer in New York. Recent texts have been anthologized in *Critical Writing Ensembles*, *Dissonant Archives*, *Utopian Pulse*, and *Social Medium: Artists Writing 2000–2015*. Ghani holds a BA in Comparative Literature from New York University and an MFA from the School of Visual Arts, and has received a number of awards, grants, and fellowships, most recently from Creative Capital. She teaches at Queens College, CUNY, and the Cooper Union.

Nathan Gray is an Australian artist and experimental musician based in Berlin. His continued interest is in the restrictions and rules within which improvisation happens. His work employs a variety of strategies to make visible and disrupt the various structures within which we co-exist. Gray's work *Species of Spaces* (2014) was the winner of both the Substation Contemporary Art Prize and is now part of the permanent collection of the National Gallery of Victoria. He curated the exhibition *The Object as Score* that was based on his 2014 Master's thesis. Gray has also shown at the 19th Biennale of Sydney and the 2012 Tarrawarra Biennale. He has performed for more than a decade in the duo Snawklor and in various other improvised music ensembles.

Chelsea Haines is an independent curator and doctoral candidate in art history at the Graduate Center, City University of New York. She is currently a Presidential Research Fellow at the Center for the Humanities, where she recently curated *Christian Palestinian Archive: A Project by Dor Guez* at the James Gallery. Since 2009, she has organized exhibitions and public programs for institutions such as Independent Curators International, Museum of Contemporary Art Detroit, and the Vera List Center for Art and Politics at The New School. She is currently adjunct lecturer in the Spitzer School of Architecture, the City College of New York.

Sean Jacobs is an associate professor of International Affairs at The New School and editor and founder of *Africa Is a Country*. He was born and grew up in apartheid South Africa where he also finished college at the University of Cape Town. He holds a PhD in Politics from the University of London and a MA in Political Science from Northwestern University. He has been a Fulbright Fellow, Commonwealth Scholar, and held fellowships at Harvard, New York University, and The New School. Previously he worked as a journalist and political researcher in South Africa. He has published op-eds in, among others, the *New York Times*, *Volkskrant*, *Brasil de Fato*, *The Guardian*, *The Nation*, Fusion.net, *Jacobin Magazine*, and *The National*.

Yazan Khalili lives and works in and out of Palestine. He is an architect, artist, and cultural producer. His work has been seen in numerous exhibitions including the Shanghai Biennial 2016, the Jerusalem Show (2011 and 2016), *In Search for a Present* at EMMA, Finland (2016), and the XII Baltic Triennial, Krakow, Poland (2015). His writings and photographs have been featured in several publications including, among others, *WDW Magazine*, *Kalamon*, *Manifesta Journal*, *Frieze*, *Race & Class*, *C-Print*, *Ibraaz*, *Contemporary Art: World Currents*, and *Subjective Atlas of Palestine*. Khalili currently runs the Khalil Sakakini Cultural Centre, Ramallah, and is a visiting lecturer at the Media Studies department, AlQuds Bard College, Palestine.

Svetlana Mintcheva is director of programs at the National Coalition Against Censorship, a forty-two-year-old alliance of U.S. national nonprofit organizations. She is the founding director of NCAC's Arts Advocacy Program, the only U.S. national initiative devoted to the arts and free expression today. Mintcheva has written on emerging trends in censorship, organized public discussions, and mobilized support for individual artists. She is the co-editor of *Censoring Culture: Contemporary Threats to Free Expression* (New Press, 2006). An academic as well as an activist, Mintcheva has taught at the University of Sofia, Bulgaria, at Duke University, from which she received her PhD in Critical Theory in 1999, and at New York University. Her current research interests are in the area of "soft censorship" and self-censorship in neoliberal democracies.

Naeem Mohaiemen is currently working on *The Young Man Was*, a series of films, installations, and essays exploring the 1970s revolutionary left. The protagonists of his projects often display misrecognition, ending up as "accidental Trojan horses" that carry tragic results to the countries in question, ranging from Japanese hijackers commandeering Dhaka airport for "solidarity" to migrant labor pipelines transformed into PLO "volunteers." In spite of its failures, Mohaiemen's reading of the potential of international left solidarity is still, always, one of hope. Various chapters of *The Young Man Was* premiered at the Sharjah Biennial (2011), the Museum of Modern Art, New York (2014), the Venice Biennale (2015), and Berlinale (2016). Historian Afsan Chowdhury (whose diary entry inspired *The Young Man Was* project) has spoken of a "second wave of history writing about Asia," defined by the work of Mohaimen as well as that of Jasmine Saikia, Dina Siddiqi, Nayanika Mookherjee, and Bina D'Costa. Mohaimen is a PhD candidate at Columbia University and a 2014 John Simon Guggenheim Fellow (film-video).

Hlonipha Mokoena received her PhD from the University of Cape Town in 2005. She is currently an associate professor and researcher at WiSER (Wits Institute for Social and Economic Research) at the University of the Witwatersrand, Johannesburg. Her articles have been published in *Journal of Natal and Zulu History*, *Journal of Religion in Africa*, *Journal of Southern African Studies*, *Scrutiny2: Issues in English Studies in Southern Africa*, and *Baobab: South African Journal of New Writing*. She has contributed opinion pieces and book reviews to *African Studies Review*, *History & Theory*, *The Politics of Jacob Zuma*, ACAS Bulletin No. 84, the blog *Africa Is a Country*, and the exhibition *PASS-AGES: References & Footnotes*. Entitled *Magema Fuze: The Making of a Kholwa Intellectual*, Mokoena's first book focuses on South African intellectual Magema M. Fuze, author of *Abantu Abamnyama Lapa Bavela Ngakona* (1922)/*The Black People and Whence They Came* (1979), and the emergence and arrested development of a black intelligentsia and literati in nineteenth- and early twentieth-century South Africa. Fuze's life and writings reveal his goal to forge a literary career—under adverse cultural, political, and social conditions—while participating in the constitution of a discourse community or a public sphere of Zulu-speaking intellectuals.

Ahmet Öğüt, born in 1981 in Diyarbakır, is a sociocultural initiator, artist, and lecturer who lives and works in Berlin and Amsterdam. He is the initiator of The Silent University, which is an autonomous knowledge exchange platform by refugees and asylum seekers. Working across a variety of media, Öğüt's institutional solo exhibitions include *Round-the-clock*, Alt Art Space Istanbul (2016); *Forward!*, Van Abbemuseum, Eindhoven (2015); *Happy Together: Collaborators Collaborating*, Chisenhale Gallery, London (2015); the MATRIX Program at the UC Berkeley Art Museum (2010); and Kunsthalle Basel (2008). He has also participated in numerous group exhibitions, including the *British Art Show 8* (2015–2017); *Okayama Art Summit*;

11th Gwangju Biennale; *Museum On/OFF*, Centre Pompidou, Paris, (2016), the 13th Biennale de Lyon (2015); 8th Shenzhen Sculpture Biennale (2014); Performa 13, the Fifth Biennial of Visual Art Performance, New York (2013); the 7th Liverpool Biennial (2012); the 12th Istanbul Biennial (2011); the New Museum Triennial, New York (2009); and the 5th Berlin Biennial for Contemporary Art (2008). He has taught at the Dutch Art Institute, Netherlands (2012); the Finnish Academy of Fine Arts, Finland (2011–ongoing); and Yildiz Teknik University, Turkey (2004–2006), among others. Öğüt was awarded the Visible Award for The Silent University (2013); the special prize of the Future Generation Art Prize, Pinchuk Art Centre, Ukraine (2012); the De Volkskrant Beeldende Kunst Prijs 2011, Netherlands; and the Kunstpreis Europas Zukunft, Museum of Contemporary Art, Germany (2010). He co-represented Turkey at the 53rd Venice Biennale (2009). He is currently working on a duo exhibition with Goshka Macuga at at Witte de With Center for Contemporary Art (2017).

John Peffer is a specialist in modern African art and photography and associate professor of Art History at Ramapo College in New Jersey. His research has examined the historiography of African Art History, art and visual culture in South Africa during apartheid, and general issues of global modernity and human rights in art, photography, and visuality. Recent publications include "Vernacular Recollections and Popular Photography in South Africa" in Morton and Newbury (eds.), *The African Photographic Archive* (Bloomsbury, 2015); and "Notes on Cuts on Censored Records," *Afrikadaa* 10 (2016). He is currently working on a book project, *Colored Photographs and White Weddings: A Study of Reception in South Africa*, which examines the vernacular experience of photography in South Africa with special emphasis on hand-colored wedding photographs in Soweto from the 1950s. During

2013–2015 he conducted research toward that project in South Africa on Fulbright CIES and National Endowment for the Humanities grants.

Joshua Simon is director and chief curator at MoBY-Museums of Bat Yam, Israel and a co-founding editor of the Tel Aviv-Jaffa based *Maayan* magazine. A Vera List Center for Art and Politics Fellow (2011–2013), he is the author of *Neomaterialism* (Sternberg Press, 2013) and editor of *Ruti Sela: For The Record* (Archive Books, 2015). Recent curatorial projects include *Factory Fetish* (Westspace, Melbourne, co-curated with Liang Luscombe), *Roee Rosen: Group Exhibition* (Tel Aviv Museum of Art, co-curated with Gilad Melzer), and *The Kids Want Communism* (yearlong project at MoBY in collaboration with State of Concept, Athens; Tranzit, Prague; Skuc gallery, Ljubljana; Free/Slow University of Warsaw; VCRC, Kiev). Simon holds a PhD from Goldsmiths College, University of London.

Radhika Subramaniam is a curator and writer interested in urban crises and surprises, particularly crowds, cultures of catastrophe, and human-animal relationships. She is director/chief curator of the Sheila C. Johnson Design Center (SJDC) at Parsons School of Design/The New School where she teaches. Previously director of cultural programs at the Lower Manhattan Cultural Council, she was also founding executive editor of an interdisciplinary journal, *Connect: Art.Politics. Theory.Practice.* She has had a SEED Foundation teaching fellowship in urban studies at the San Francisco Art Institute (2012) and was artist-in-residence at the Banff Centre (2014). She has a Masters in Anthropology and a PhD in Performance Studies. Recent writing includes "In Search of the Indian Cow" (in Laura Gustafsson and Terike Haapoja (eds.), *History According to Cattle*, Punctum Books, 2015), "Wild Tales, Cosmic Waters" (catalogue entry for Vibha Galhotra's exhibition *Absur-city-pity-dity*, 2015), and "Small Acts, Forlorn Practices" (in Sheryl Oring (ed), *Activating Democracy*, Intellect, 2016).

Ann Laura Stoler is the Willy Brandt Distinguished University Professor of Anthropology and Historical Studies at The New School for Social Research, New York. She received her PhD in Anthropology from Columbia University in 1983. Stoler has taught at the University of Michigan from 1989 to 2003 and has since been at The New School for Social Research. She has worked for some thirty-five years on the politics of knowledge, colonial governance, racial epistemologies, the sexual politics of empire, and ethnography of the archives. She has been a visiting professor at the École des Hautes Études en Sciences Sociales, Paris VIII, and at the École Normale Supérieure in Paris, the School of Criticism and Theory at Cornell, Birzeit University in Ramallah, the Goethe University in Frankfurt, and the Johannesburg Workshop in Theory and Criticism. She is recipient of SSRC, NEH, NSF, Fulbright, and Simon Guggenheim fellowships. Her commitment to joining conceptual and historical research has led to collaborative work with historians, literary scholars, and philosophers, and to the creation of the journal, *Political Concepts: A Critical Lexicon*, of which she is one of the founding editors. She is founding director of the Institute of Critical Social Inquiry (http://www.criticalsocialinquiry.org) devoted to bringing together fellows from around the world with the work of major thinkers who have shaped the course of social inquiry. Stoler's most recent book is *Duress: Imperial Durabilities in Our Times* (Duke University Press, 2016).

Eyal Weizman is an architect, professor of Spatial and Visual Cultures and director of the Centre for Research Architecture at Goldsmiths, University of London. In 2011 he set up Forensic Architecture, a research agency that provides architectural evidence in human rights cases and war crimes trials. This work was a subject of a forthcoming exhibition at MACBA, Barcelona, and a book by the same title coming out with Zone. In 2007 he set up, with Sandi Hilal and Alessandro Petti, the architectural collective DAAR in Beit Sahour/ Palestine. He is a director at the Centre for Investigative Journalism.

Frank B. Wilderson III is professor in the departments of African American Studies and Drama at the University of California, Irvine. He is also the director of the Culture & Theory PhD program. Wilderson spent five and a half years in South Africa where he was one of two Americans to have held elected office in the African National Congress during the apartheid era. He also worked as a psychological warfare, secret propaganda, and covert operations cadre for the ANC's armed wing Umkhonto We Sizwe. Wilderson's books include *Incognegro: A Memoir of Exile and Apartheid* and *Red, White, & Black: Cinema and the Structure of U.S. Antagonisms*. In addition to being an activist and scholar, Wilderson is also a creative writer and is the recipient of numerous awards, among them a National Endowment for the Arts Literature Fellowship, the Maya Angelou Award for Best Fiction Portraying the Black Experience in America, the Zora Neale Hurston/Richard Wright Legacy Award, the Eisner Prize for Creative Achievement of the Highest Order, the Judith Stronach Award for Poetry, and the American Book Award.

ENDNOTES

Introduction

1 Andrea Fraser, "From the Critique of Institutions to an Institution of Critique," *Artforum* Vol. 4, No. 1, September 2005.

2 Negar Azimi, "Good Intentions," *Frieze* 137, March 2011: http://www.frieze.com/article/good-intentions/.

3 A full account of significant artist-led protests and boycott campaigns of recent years, as well as their precedents, is beyond the scope of this introduction. In addition to the articles included in this volume, and other texts cited here, see especially: Yates McKee, *Strike Art: Contemporary Art and the Post-Occupy Condition* (New York: Verso Books, 2016); Andrew Ross, ed., *The Gulf: High Culture/Hard Labor* (New York/London: OR Books, 2015); and Tirdad Zolghadr, "Shades of No," *WdW Review*, June 2014: http://wdwreview.org/desks/shades-of-no/.

4 An anthology of texts by artists and curators that focuses on boycotts of biennials—in particular, those in Sydney, São Paulo, and St. Petersburg, plus a fourth in Istanbul in 2013—is forthcoming as of this writing. See Joanna Warsza, *I Can't Work Like This: A Reader on Recent Boycotts and Contemporary Art* (Berlin: Sternberg Press, 2017).

5 Formed in 2009, Working Artists and the Greater Economy (W.A.G.E.) is an important influence on these post-Occupy groups. Defining itself as an "activist organization focused on regulating the payment of artist

fees by nonprofit art institutions and establishing a sustainable labor relation between artists and the institutions that contract our work," W.A.G.E. holds arts institutions accountable through a certification system that recognizes those organizations that pay artists what it defines as a minimum payment standard. See: http://www.wageforwork.com/.

6   The artist-activist collective MTL, whose core members Nitasha Dhillon and Amin Husain were deeply involved in Occupy, is especially focused on highlighting the intersections of various social movements and political struggles, drawing connections between the causes of labor rights, student debt, migrant rights, #BlackLivesMatter, indigenous rights, and Palestinian liberation, most recently through its campaign #DecolonizeThisPlace, which started as a protest of a Brooklyn Museum show of photography from Israel-Palestine and recently took the form of an Artists Space exhibition that became a platform to launch creative direct actions.

7   Vittoria Martini, "A brief history of *I Giardini*: Or a brief history of the Venice Biennale seen from the Giardini," *Art & Education*: http://www.artandeducation.net/paper/a-brief-history-of-i-giardini-or-a-brief-history-of-the-venice-biennale-seen-from-the-giardini/. Subsequently, an offshoot of the Art Workers' Coalition, the Emergency Cultural Government, organized a boycott of the American Pavilion at the 1970 Venice Biennale in protest of the U.S. war in Vietnam. See Julia Bryan-Wilson, *Robert Morris* (Cambridge, MA: MIT Press, 2013), 198.

8   Ahmet Öğüt, "CCC: Currency of Collective Consciousness," *e-flux journal* #62 (February 2015): http://www.e-flux.com/journal/62/60952/ccc-currency-of-collective-consciousness/.

9   Azimi, "Good Intentions."

10   *Assuming Boycott* contributor Sean Jacobs has co-edited (with Jon Soske) an anthology of essays, *Apartheid Israel: The Politics of an Analogy*, reflecting on the analogy between apartheid South Africa and present-day Israel. For information about the book, which is available in full online, see: http://www.africasacountry.com/2014/11/the-apartheid-analogy/.

11   Information about the history, strategy, and composition of
the BDS movement, as well as a more thorough account of its
demands, is available at: http://www.bdsmovement.net.

12   Representative of disagreement on BDS within a left-leaning
publication is a debate between BDS activists Omar Barghouti
and Lizzy Ratner and anti-BDS commentators Eric Alterman
and Bernard Avishai published in *The Nation* in 2012: http://www
.thenation.com/article/opinionnation-forum-boycott-divestment-
sanctions-bds/. See Nasser Abourahme's contribution to this volume
for a critical analysis of the anti-occupation, anti-BDS position.

13   The African Literature Association, the Association for Asian American
Studies, the Critical Ethnic Studies Association, the National
Association of Chicana and Chicano Studies, and the Native American
and Indigenous Studies Association are among the other academic
associations to collectively endorse the academic boycott. Most recently
the American Anthropological Association and the Modern Language
Association both narrowly voted against the academic boycott. For
incisive discussions of BDS and the academic boycott, see the philosopher
Adi Ophir's edited selection of essays, "Israeli Jews Address the
Palestinian Boycott Call," *South Atlantic Quarterly* Vol. 114, No. 3 (July
2015): 652–693; a November 2016 online dossier of texts, "The Academic
Boycott," published by *Social Text*: http://www.socialtextjournal
.org/periscope_topic/the-academic-boycott-movement/; and the
ongoing blog maintained by Anthropologists for the Boycott of Israeli
Academic Institutions at: http://www.anthroboycott.wordpress.com/.

14   For an account of BDS' impact on visual art in particular, see Chen
Tamir, "A Report on the Cultural Boycott of Israel," *Hyperallergic*,
February 3, 2015: http://www.hyperallergic.com/179655/a-report-
on-the-cultural-boycott-of-israel/. For a statement of opposition
to BDS within the visual art community, on the grounds that it
forecloses dialogue (and targets Israel disproportionately relative to
other countries with poor human rights records), see the collective

letter "Challenging Double Standards: A Call Against the Boycott of Israeli Art and Society": http://www.cds-call.tumblr.com/.

15   Nato Thompson, "Engagement or Disengagement? A Conversation About Manifesta 10 with Joanna Warsza," *Creative Time Reports*, June 26, 2014: http://www.creativetimereports.org/2014/06/26/engagement-or-disengagement-manifesta-10-nato-thompson-joanna-warsza/.

16   Not all the curatorial team supported the cultural boycott of Israel, but all expressed their support for the artists' right to protest. Two of the curators were Israeli, and one, Galit Eilat, is a vocal supporter of BDS. See: Kareem Estefan, "When Artists Boycott," *Art in America*, December 2014, 37–38; Mostafa Heddaya, "São Paulo Biennial Curators Join Artists in Repudiating Israeli Sponsorship," *Hyperallergic*, August 29, 2014: http://www.hyperallergic.com/146308/sao-paulo-biennial-curators-join-artists-in-repudiating-israeli-sponsorship/.

17   Creative Time's response to artists' boycott of the exhibition "Living as Form" as mounted at Technion University, the Israel Institute of Technology, is emblematic: "For more than 40 years, free speech has been fundamental to our mission and hence we do not participate in cultural boycotts. Instead, we believe that art can play a powerful role in addressing, even advancing, social change." The letter is available in full at: http://www.creativetime.org/blog/2014/06/13/creative-time-responds-to-bds-arts-coalition-petition/.

18   Chelsea Haines' contribution to this volume, "The Distant Image," explores the theoretical premises of these assumptions in greater depth.

19   Öğüt, "CCC: Currency of Collective Consciousness."

I. The Cultural Boycott of Apartheid South Africa
The Legacy of the Cultural Boycott Against South Africa

1   This essay draws on conversations and discussions with a number of interlocutors, most notably Jessica Blatt, Dan Magaziner, Lily Saint, Percy Zvomuya, Nicol Hammond, Peter Limb, Benjamin Fogel, Herman Wasserman, and Achal Prabhala.

2   "The treatment of Indians in the Union of South Africa,"
    resolution adopted on the joint first and sixth committee,
    General Assembly, United Nations, December 8, 1946.

3   "General Assembly resolution: The question of race conflict
    in South Africa resulting from the policies of apartheid of the
    Government of the Union of South Africa," December 5, 1952.

4   That arms embargo was made mandatory on November 4, 1977.
    Historical information in this paragraph sourced from UN.org.
    "The United Nations: Partner in the Struggle against Apartheid,"
    http://www.un.org/en/events/mandeladay/apartheid.shtml.

5   "Boycott" as a political strategy was not just central to the ANC's
    diplomatic offensive, but was a very common tactic in resistance
    politics even inside South Africa, whether consumer boycotts, rent or
    service boycotts, bus boycotts, school boycotts, or electoral boycotts.

6   Steve Davis, "The ANC: From Freedom Radio to Radio Freedom,"
    *Southern African Liberation Struggles. New Local, Regional and
    Global Perspectives*, UCT (2013): 117–142; Shirli Gilbert, "Singing
    Against Apartheid: ANC Cultural Groups and the International
    Anti-Apartheid Struggle," *Journal of Southern African Studies* 33.2
    (2007): 421–441; Sekibakiba Peter Lekgoathi, "The African National
    Congress's Radio Freedom and its audiences in apartheid South Africa,
    1963–1991," *Journal of African Media Studies* 2.2 (2010): 139–153.

7   Rob Nixon, *Homelands, Harlem and Hollywood* (New York: Routledge,
    1994): 155–156.

8   Nixon, *Homelands*, 157.

9   Some of those who signed included Harry Belafonte, Leonard Bernstein,
    Sammy Davis Jr., Arthur Miller, Sidney Poitier, and Nina Simone.

10 Information from ANC.org.za.

11 UN.org.

12 Steven Van Zandt, et al., "Sun City" (Manhattan Records, 1985).

13 John M. Wilson, "UN's 'Register' of Performers Raises Blacklist
    Spectre in S. Africa Boycott," *Chicago Tribune*, May 19, 1985.

14 These include, for example, Hugh Masekela and Miriam Makeba, who later joined Paul Simon on his *Graceland* tour, and who, in numerous interviews, questioned the need for a cultural boycott.

15 Some black South African artists would not turn down the possibility of lucrative work in a depressed economic environment and in contexts where, for the most part, they were not properly remunerated. A number of locally based black South African artists who performed with Paul Simon resented being asked "to suffer more." Examples include the influential bandleader and guitarist Ray Phiri.

16 Nixon, *Homelands,* 156.

17 Wilson, "UN's 'Register'," 1985.

18 See for example the film *Under African Skies* (dir: Joe Berlinger, 2012), which revisits the events around the recording of *Graceland* on the album's 25th anniversary. Also, Dave Marsh, "Talking Sun City with Steven Van Zandt," Backstreets.com, January 14, 2014; Robin Densilow, "Paul Simon's Graceland: The acclaim and the outrage," TheGuardian.com, April 19, 2012. Simon's main defense is captured by Densilow (2012): "Personally, I feel I'm with the musicians. I'm with the artists. I didn't ask the permission of the ANC. I didn't ask permission of Buthelezi [a notorious Bantustan leader], or Desmond Tutu [an activist priest and Nobel Peace Prize winner], or the Pretoria government. And to tell you the truth, I have a feeling that when there are radical transfers of power on either the left or the right, the artists always get screwed. The guys with the guns say, 'This is important,' and the guys with guitars don't have a chance."

19 Thanks to Lily Saint for this point.

20 See Omar Barghouti, "Israel vs. South Africa: Reflecting on cultural boycott," ElectronicIntifada.com, May 8, 2008; see also various statements by Palestinian Campaign for the Academic and Cultural Boycott of Israel (PACBI.org); Jon Soske and Sean Jacobs (eds.), *Apartheid Israel: The Politics of Analogy* (Chicago: Haymarket Books, 2015).

21 "Tutu urges Cape Town Opera to call off Israel tour," Timeslive.co.za, October 26, 2010.

22   "Letter: Over 100 artists announce a cultural boycott of Israel,"
      TheGuardian.com, February 13, 2015.

23   Nixon, *Homelands*, 156.

24   Russia Today, "'Show Israel red card!' Pro-Palestine protests at European
      Championships qualifier," September 15, 2015; Rob Nixon, "Apartheid on
      the Run: The South African Sports Boycott," *Transition* 58 (1992): 68–88.

Art, Resistance, and Community in 1980s South Africa

1   This essay combines sections of chapters 3 and 5 from John Peffer, *Art and
      the End of Apartheid* (Minneapolis: University of Minnesota Press, 2009),
      and is reprinted here with kind permission of the author and publisher.

2   United Nations General Assembly, *General Assembly Official Record*,
      23rd session, supplement No. 18, resolution no. 2396, 1968, 19–21.

3   All UN sanctions were ended in 1994, though the cultural boycott was
      significantly relaxed in 1991. See: http://www.sahistory.org.za/topic/
      united-nations-and-apartheid-timeline-1946-1994. On December 13,
      1991, "the General Assembly adopted seven resolutions, three of them
      by consensus, on the 'Policies of Apartheid of the Government of South
      Africa.' It called upon the international community to resume academic,
      scientific and cultural links with democratic anti-apartheid organisations
      and sport links with unified non-racial sporting organisations, as well
      as to review existing restrictive measures as warranted by positive
      developments." And on May 25, 1994, "The Security Council adopted
      a resolution lifting its 1977 Arms Embargo and other restrictive
      measures against South Africa, thus removing the remaining United
      Nations sanctions against South Africa. [Resolution 919(1994)]."

4   Gavin Cawthra, *Policing South Africa: The SAP and the Transition
      from Apartheid* (London: Zed Books, 1993), 20–24.

5   The Freedom Charter signed in 1955 in Kliptown, Soweto at the Congress of
      the People, is a list of basic human rights demands and nonracial principles
      that became the foundational document of the anti-apartheid movement
      broadly, including the ANC and the broad-based UDF during the 1980s.

6   South African History Online, "Medu and the Culture of Liberation":
      http://www.sahistory.org.za/article/medu-and-culture-liberation, n.d.

7   Ibid. Junction Avenue was founded in the mid-1970s by William
      Kentridge and Malcolm Purkey, the Community Arts Project was
      established in Cape Town in 1977 by Gavin Younge, and *Staffrider*
      magazine was founded in 1978 in Johannesburg by Mike Kirkwood.

8   The Poster Book Collective, *Images of Defiance: South African Resistance
      Posters of the 1980s* (Johannesburg: Raven Press, 1991), 3.

9   Keorapetse Kgositsile, "Culture and Resistance in South
      Africa," *MEDU Art Ensemble Newsletter* 5, 1 (1983): 23–24.

10   Ibid., 29–30.

11   See Peffer, *Art and the End of Apartheid*, xxi, 34–40, et passim.

12   This section paraphrases generously from Keith Gottschalk, "United
      Democratic Front, 1983-1991: Rise, Impact and Consequences," in Ian
      Liebenberg, Bobby Nel, Fiona Lortan, and Gert van der Westhuizen,
      eds., *The Long March: The Struggle for Liberation in South Africa*
      (Pretoria: Kagiso-HAUM, 1991), 187–188, 191, 194, et passim.

13   According to Thupelo records, the participants included Bill
      Ainslie, Peter Bradley, Peter Clarke, Garth Erasmus, Kay Hassan,
      David Koloane, Dumisani Mabaso, Philip Malumise, Patrick
      Kagiso Mautloa, David Mogano, Sam Nhlengethwa, Tony
      Nkotsi, Madi Phala, Durant Sihlali, and Kenneth Thabo.

14   "Thupelo Art Project," promotional brochure, Johannesburg: USSALEP,
      1987.

15   If one were to attempt the designation of a "school" of artists
      emanating from Thupelo during the 1980s, these names would
      head the list: Koloane, Ainslie, Sotiriades, and Bongiwe Dhlomo
      organized the workshops and attended every year; Kay Hassan
      attended in 1985 and 1989; Lionel Davis participated in 1986, 1987,
      and 1988; Durant Sihlali attended every workshop except when
      he was abroad in 1986; Patrick Mautloa, Sam Nhlengethwa, and
      Dumisani Mabaso attended every year; and Madi Phala attended

the first five workshops. Mmakgabo Sebidi was also a prominent participant. This is just a partial list of the Thupelo regulars.

16   After a hiatus from 1992–94, Thupelo moved to Cape Town in 1995 and became more international in terms of the numbers of annual attendees.

17   "Thupelo Art Project," 2. See also Elizabeth Rankin, *Images of Metal* (Johannesburg: Witwatersrand University Press, 1994), 39.

18   There is no record of any international visitor for 1988. American sculptor Willard Boepple is shown in the group picture for Thupelo in 1989, but he was not listed on the official roster. That year Boepple was the leader of a Thupelo spin-off workshop in Zimbabwe. Robert Loder (personal communication, January 9, 2007) recalled that the project was unable to invite international guests because of financial difficulties, since in 1987 USSALEP had cut off funding for the visiting artist program. In 1987, partly to save expenses, the workshop was held at the Johannesburg Art Foundation. The following year Thupelo "squatted" in an unfinished portion of the Africana Museum behind the Market Theatre in Newtown.

19   David Koloane and Ivor Powell, "In Conversation," in Clémentine Deliss, ed., *Seven Stories about Modern Art in Africa* (London: Whitechapel Art Gallery, 1995), 265.

20   Owen Kelly, *Community Art and the State: Storming the Citadels* (London: Comedia, 1984), 50–51.

21   See Peffer, *Art and the End of Apartheid*, 140–151.

22   Ibid., 153–167.

23   David Koloane, personal communication, July 24, 2001.

24   In addition to Koloane, several artists had participated (either in person or with artwork) at both Culture and Resistance and Thupelo, including Bongiwe Dhlomo, Peter Clarke, David Mogano, Sydney Kumalo, and Lionel Davis.

25   Conny Braam and Fons Geerling, "Towards New Cultural Relations," in *Culture in Another South Africa*, Willem Campschreur and Joost Divendal, eds. (New York: Olive Branch Press, 1989).

26   "ANC Cultural Boycott Policy, Adopted by the National Executive Committee of the ANC" (Lusaka: ANC, 1989). Accessible online via: http://www.sahistory.org.za/archive/anc-cultural-boycott-policy.

27   Ivor Powell, "Corner of the cultural blanket lifted," *Weekly Mail* June 30–July 6, 1989: 21.

28   Sachs' essay is reprinted in Ingrid de Kok and Karen Press, eds., *Spring Is Rebellious: Arguments about Cultural Freedom by Albie Sachs and Respondents* (Cape Town: Buchu Books, 1990).

Kwaito: The Revolution Was Not Televised; It Announced Itself in Song

1   The American Committee on Africa (ACOA) was founded in 1953 and based in New York. The organization provided continuous, decades-long support for African struggles against colonialism and apartheid. ACOA grew out of the ad hoc Americans for South African Resistance (AFSAR), which was set up in 1952 to support the African National Congress's Campaign of Defiance Against Unjust Laws. In 1966, ACOA founded the Africa Fund, which was registered under U.S. tax law as a charitable and educational organization. For more information about ACOA and to search the online database of their archived documents, see: http://www.aluka.org/struggles/collection/ACOA.

2   "Cultural Boycott of South Africa—Percy Sledge Sells Soul," American Committee on Africa press release, July 16, 1970: http://www.aluka.org/action/showMetadata?doi=10.5555/AL.SFF.DOCUMENT.acoa000341a.

3   This reference is a paraphrase of Beaubien's statement about the Newport Jazz Festival's decision not to go to Bophuthatswana: "Anti-apartheid activists in the U.S. were encouraged over the recent decision of [American jazz producer] George Wein not to take the Newport Jazz Festival to Bophuthatswana. George Wein said that he was 'sympathetic to the opponents of apartheid and supportive of the cultural boycott.'" While Thomas Shepard, an associate producer for Wein, added, "George had some initial confusion over Sun City and Bophuthatswana. He was told that it was an old

African kingdom," (Beaubien, "Cultural Boycott," 13). Michael C. Beaubien, "The Cultural Boycott of South Africa," *Africa Today*, Vol. 29, No. 4 (1982): 5–16: http://www.jstor.org/stable/4186110.

4   Michael Drewett, "The Cultural Boycott Against Apartheid South Africa: A Case of Defensible Censorship?", in Michael Drewitt and Martin Cloonan, eds., *Popular Music Censorship in South Africa* (Surrey: Ashgate, 2006), 33.

5   As a harbinger of the counterculture of kwaito that emerged with the end of apartheid, bubblegum music was both a mimicry of and a hankering after the cosmopolitan world that South African audiences and musicians were prevented from accessing by the cultural boycott. It combined local idiom with the high energy and electronic amplification made possible by synthesizers and mixing tables. It was a kind of James Brown meets the apartheid-sanctioned faux-traditionalism of leopard skins and Zulu "dances." The relationship between bubblegum music and its successor kwaito is aptly summarized by Martina Viljoen as being discursive rather than positivist: "bubblegum and kwaito are investigated as 'patterns of discourse' representative of social realities that not only create and maintain specific cultural identities, but also mediate an interactive exchange among multiple cultures" (Viljoen, "On the Margins," 53). Martina Viljoen, "On the Margins of Kwaito," *The World of Music*, Vol. 50, No. 2 (2008): 51–73: http://www.jstor.org/stable/41699827.

6   Bongani Madondo, *I'm Not Your Weekend Special: Portraits on the Life+Style & Politics of Brenda Fassie* (Johannesburg: Picador Africa, 2014).

7   This brief history of the band Joy is from Madondo, *I'm Not Your Weekend Special*, 215–216.

8   Gwen Ansell, *Soweto Blues: Jazz, Popular Music, and Politics in South Africa* (New York: Continuum, 2005), 168.

9   Viljoen, "On the Margins of Kwaito," 60. The song is referenced in the title of Madondo's biography, *I'm Not Your Weekend Special*.

10   Charles Hamm, "Graceland Revisited," *Popular Music*, Vol. 8, No. 3, African Music, Oct. 1989, 303: http://www.jstor.org/stable/931279.

11   Madondo, xiv.

12   Hamm, 302.

13   Ibid., 303.

Incognegro: A Memoir of Exile and Apartheid (excerpt)

1   This is an excerpt of Frank B. Wilderson III, *Incognegro: A Memoir of Exile and Apartheid* (Durham, NC: Duke University Press, 2015), 102–113. It is reprinted here with the kind permission of the author and the publisher.

II. BDS and the Cultural Boycott of Israel
"We," Palestinians and Jewish Israelis: The Right Not to Be a Perpetrator

1   This essay was previously published as Ariella Azoulay, "'We,' Palestinians and Jewish Israelis: The Right Not to Be a Perpetrator," *South Atlantic Quarterly* 114:3, July 2015. It has been revised in collaboration with the author.

2   Hannah Arendt, *Eichmann in Jerusalem: A Report on the Banality of Evil* (New York: Penguin, 2006).

3   The problem, of course, is with the right itself, not with the fact that Jews were granted this right.

4   Arendt, *Eichmann in Jerusalem*, 287.

The Case for BDS and the Path to Co-Resistance

1   B'tselem, *Statistics on Settlements and Settler Population*, http://www.btselem.org/settlements/statistics.

2   Palestine Central Bureau of Statistics, *Special Statistical Bulletin on the 63rd Anniversary of the Nakba*, May 2011: http://www.pcbs.gov.ps/Portals/_pcbs/PressRelease/Nakba_E63.pdf.

3   Mya Guarnieri, "Is Israeli Annexation of Area C Imminent?", +972, July 26, 2012: http://972mag.com/is-israeli-annexation-of-area-c-of-the-west-bank-imminent/51956/.

4   UN OCHA, *The Humanitarian Impact of Israeli-declared Firing Zones in the West Bank*, August 2012: http://www.ochaopt.org/documents/ocha_opt_firing_zone_factsheet_august_2012_english.pdf.

5   Al Haq, "Legal Analysis of Military Orders 1649 & 1650: Deportation and Forcible Transfer as International Crimes," Ref. 61/2010: http://www .alzaytouna.net/english/Docs/2010/Al-Haq-April2010-Legal-Analysis.pdf.

6   UN News Centre, "Gaza could be uninhabitable in less than five years due to ongoing 'de-development'—UN Report," September 1, 2015: http:// www.un.org/apps/news/story.asp?NewsID=51770#.VsdtCMuJnww.

7   Stephanie Nebehay, "U.N. rights investigator accuses Israel of 'ethnic cleansing'," Reuters, March 21, 2014: http://uk.reuters.com/ article/uk-palestinian-israel-un-idUKBREA2K1JM20140321.

8   B'tselem, "Revocation of Residency in East Jerusalem," January 1, 2011: http://www.btselem.org/jerusalem/revocation_of_residency.

9   Joel Beinin, "The Demise of the Oslo Peace Process," MERIP, March 26, 1999: http://www.merip.org/mero/mero032699.

10 Noura Erakat, "Review: The Burden of the Israeli-Palestinian Conflict 2010 Report," Adva Center, November 17, 2010: http://www.jadaliyya.com/ pages/index/331/review_the-burden-of-the-israeli-palestinian-conflict-2010-report-adva-center.

11 Jim Zanotti, "U.S. Security Assistance to the Palestinian Authority," Congressional Research Service, January 8, 2010: http://www.fas.org/sgp/ crs/mideast/R40664.pdf.

12 David Horovitz, "Netanyahu finally speaks his mind," *Times of Israel*, July 13, 2014: http://www.timesofisrael.com/netanyahu-finally-speaks-his-mind/.

13 See e.g., Noura Erakat, *Whiteness as Property in Israel: Revival, Rehabilitation, and Removal* 31, Harv. J. Racial & Ethnic Just. 69, (2015).

14 Noura Erakat, "Permission to Kill in Gaza," *Jadaliyya*, July 7, 2015: http://www.jadaliyya.com/pages/index/22093/permission-to-kill-in-gaza.

15 See e.g., Noura Erakat, Bianca Isaias, and Salmah Rizvi, *Operation Protective Edge & Legal Remedies*, Issam Fares Institute for Public Policy and International Affairs, American University in

Beirut, October 2014: http://www.aub.edu.lb/ifi/publications/
Documents/working_papers/20141009_noura_erakat.pdf.

16   Adam Horowitz, "AIPAC ED fears the growing movement to
      sanction Israel could fundamentally change US policy towards
      Israel. He's right," *Mondoweiss*, May 7, 2009: http://mondoweiss
      .net/2009/05/howard-kohr bds#sthash.19Vbdqjk.dpuf.

17   See e.g., Ilan Pappe, *The Ethnic Cleansing of Palestine*, (Oxford, One
      World: 2006). ("Only a state with at least 80% Jews is a viable and
      stable state." David Ben-Gurion, in a speech given on December
      3, 1947 in front of senior members of his Mapai party.)

18   On settler colonization as a "structure rather than an event," see
      Patrick Wolfe, "Settler colonialism and the elimination of the native,"
      Journal of Genocide Research 8:4 (2006): 390.

19   See e.g., Human Rights Watch, *Separate and Unequal: Israel's
      Discriminatory Treatment of Palestinians in the Occupied Palestinian
      Territories*, 2010: http://www.refworld.org/pdfid/4d1049e12.pdf.

20   Erakat, "Whiteness as Property," *supra* note 13.

21   Yonah Jeremy Bob, "How will the latest anti-boycott ruling affect BDS?",
      The Jerusalem Post, April 17, 2015: http://www.jpost.com/Arab-Israeli-
      Conflict/How-will-High-Courts-ruling-on-anti-boycott-law-affect-
      BDS-398401.

Boycott, Decolonization, Return: BDS and the Limits of Political Solidarity

1   This piece has its origins in a March 2015 article published on
     Jadaliyya, "Boycott, Sovereign Anxieties, and the Decolonizing
     Temporality of Return," which responded to the Vera List Center's
     February 2015 panel, "Considering Palestine/Israel: What Does
     the Boycott Mean?": http://www.jadaliyya.com/pages/index/21188/
     boycott-sovereign-anxieties-and-the-decolonizing-t.

2   See "Arguing the Boycott, Divestment, and Sanctions (BDS) Campaign
     with Norman Finkelstein," an interview with Frank Barat: https://
     vimeo.com/36854424. Finkelstein frames his position in an appeal to the

normativism of international law, but the crux of his rejection of BDS rests not on its formal character as a civic-legal campaign but on its demand for "[r]especting, protecting and promoting the rights of Palestinian refugees to return to their homes and properties as stipulated in UN resolution 194," which Finkelstein reads as barely concealed code for the "end of Israel."

3   Todd Gitlin, "BDS and the Politics of 'Radical' Gestures," *Tablet*, October 27, 2014.

4   M.J. Rosenberg, "The BDS Movement Is About Dismantling Israel, Not the '67 Occupation," *The Huffington Post*, March 26, 2014.

5   Dan Rabinowitz, "Why the BDS campaign can't tolerate Israeli moderates," *Ha'aretz*, November 3, 2015.

6   Nadia Abu el-Haj, "An Open Letter to Dan Rabinowitz: Let's get our facts straight about BDS," *Mondoweiss,* November 9, 2015.

7   See Salman Abu Sitta, "The Implementation of the Right of Return," *Palestine-Israel Journal* Vol. 15–16 No. 3, 2008.

8   Adi Ophir, "The Challenge of the BDS," *South Atlantic Quarterly* 114:3 July 2015, 651–661.

9   Ibid., 659.

10   Ibid., 653.

11   Ibid., 658.

12   Quite the contrary, Palestinian national politics in its most formative and effective phase, and in stark contrast to Zionism, wagered its claim to a future around the inclusive vision of "a secular, democratic state" for all its citizens, Jews, Muslims, and Christians alike. This, more than anything else, was the source of both its revolutionary novelty and its total unacceptability to the political order. The omission of this central aspect of Palestinian political history seems to be one of the necessary steps in the characterization of the colonial encounter in Palestine as a 'tragic conflict' between two fundamentally incompatible sets of national claims, and in turn a zero-sum game in which Palestinian liberationist politics could, by definition, never have anything to offer Jewish-Israelis.

13   Raef Zreik, "When Does a Settler Become a Native? (With Apologies to Mamdani)," *Constellations* Vol. 23 No. 3 (2016): 355.

14   Ariella Azoulay, "'We,' Palestinians and Jewish Israelis: The Right Not to Be a Perpetrator," *South Atlantic Quarterly* 114:3, July 2015. A revised version of this essay is reprinted in the present volume.

15   Ibid., 689.

16   Todd Gitlin, "BDS' Biggest Victory is the Triumph of Zimbolism," *Tablet,* November 25, 2015.

17   Bruce Robbins, "The Logic of the Beneficiary," *n+1*, Issue 24: Winter 2016.

18   Ibid.

19   Gitlin, "BDS and the Politics of 'Radical' Gestures."

20   Joseph Massad, "The Cultural Work of Recovering Palestine," *boundary 2*, 42:4 (2015).

21   Gabriel Piterberg, "Erasures," *New Left Review* No. 10 (July–August 2001): 36.

Neoliberal Politics, Protective Edge, and BDS

1   This essay was written in direct response to the summer 2014 massacre in Gaza and the hopelessness it brought. The Israeli attack was vast and disproportionate, without as much as the promise of, or pretext for, a resolution. The extreme means used by Israel's military seemed to have no achievable aim; the Israeli government simply disposed of its usual reasoning for why these cycles of extreme violence are necessary for the greater good for Israelis. At the same time, it brought forth a perverse logic by which inflicting extreme violent measures on Palestinians is proof of Israelis being the ultimate victims.

2   See: Jonathan Nitzan and Shimshon Bichler, *The Global Political Economy of Israel: From War Profits to Peace Dividends* (London: Pluto Press, 2002). Another book that introduces a specific critique of Zionism's economic logic as colonial is Tamar Gozansky's *The Development of Capitalism in Palestine* (UPP, 1988) [in Hebrew].

3   See: Dan Senor and Saul Singer, *Start-up Nation: The Story of Israel's Economic Miracle* (New York: Hachette Book Group, 2009).

4   See: Eyal Weizman, *Hollow Land: Israel's Architecture of Occupation* (London: Verso Books, 2007).

5   See: Jeff Halper, "Matrix of Control," 2001: http://www.mediamonitors. net/halper1.html. Blockade, containment, quarantine, paralysis, control, and immobilization are some of the terms used to describe the current stage of the occupation.

6   For now, the most extensive report by the United Nations Office for the Coordination of Humanitarian Affairs (OCHA) presents these numbers: 2,189 killed, of whom 1,486 are believed to be civilians, including 513 children (323 boys and 190 girls, 70 percent under age twelve) and 269 women; 557 have been identified as militants, and 146 are of unknown status.

7   For various reasons, the Israeli government decided not to recognize these 51 days of fighting (July 7–August 26, 2014) as a war. A major reason is to avoid responsibility for reparations for Palestinians as well as for Israelis. See: Anat Kurz and Shlomo Brom, eds., *The Lessons of Operation Protective Edge*, The Institute for National Security Studies, Israel, 2014: http:// www.inss.org.il/uploadImages/systemFiles/ZukEtanENG_final.pdf. In November 2014, Israel's credit rating was lowered by Fitch Group from Positive to Stable. See announcement by Fitch Ratings, November 21, 2014: https://www.fitchratings.com/site/pr/931755.

8   See: Naomi Klein, *The Shock Doctrine: The Rise of Disaster Capitalism* (London: Picador, 2008); and Wendy Brown, *Undoing the Demos: Neoliberalism's Stealth Revolution* (New York: Zone Books, 2015). Both analyses can be applied very well to Israel. Indeed Klein's book deals with Israel directly, while Brown's basic proposition—that with neoliberalism, market competition defines every part of social life, including democracy—underlines the analysis I propose here.

9   In a series of lectures on the neoliberal condition that he gave at Goldsmiths College in London between 2013 and 2015, philosopher

Michel Feher portrayed a model of sovereignty that operates in
accordance with the logic of the corporation. The space of bargaining
shifts from the workers/management to management/shareholders.
This is applied to the neoliberal state as the space of politics shifts
from tax-paying citizen/government to government/bondholders.
See: http://www.gold.ac.uk/visual-cultures/life/guest-lectures/.

10   See: Adam Hanieh, "The Oslo Illusion," *Jacobin* 10, Spring 2013, 68–74.

11   See: Mezna Qato and Kareem Rabie, "Against the Law," *Jacobin* 10,
Spring 2013, 75–78.

The Utopian Conflict

1   This essay first appeared in *Tidal Magazine*, a journal for radical theory that
is available online at: http://www.tidalmag.org/. It is reprinted here with
the kind permission of *Tidal* editors Nitasha Dhillon and Amin Husain.

III. Who Speaks? Who Is Silenced?

The Shifting Grounds of Censorship and Freedom of Expression

1   *Tatlin's Whisper # 6* was held in the Wifredo Lam Center, the institution
in charge of hosting the Havana Biennials. Audience members were
provided with disposable cameras to document the performance and told
that they could freely express their thoughts for a minute from the podium.
Each person who took the podium was guarded by a woman and a man
in military uniform who placed a white dove on the speaker's shoulder,
an allusion to the emblematic image of Fidel Castro delivering his first
speech in Havana after the Triumph of the Revolution, on January 8, 1959.
In *Tatlin's Whisper # 6* there is no censorship for the one minute during
which a member of the audience is at the microphone. When the time
assigned for freedom of expression ends, the man and woman in military
uniform who until then had been on either side of the speaker—to defend
her/his right to talk or to control it—removed the dove from the speaker's
shoulder and made her/him return to the audience. This action was
repeated with each speaker. A total of 39 people made use of the mike to

express their affinity with the Cuban political system or criticize it, after which I stood at the podium to thank the Cubans for their courage and their exercise of freedom of expression. The piece was made possible thanks to Guillermo Gómez Peña, who invited me to join him at the biennial, and the production of Galería Saro León and Orlando Brito Jinorio.

2   The artist Angel Delgado was imprisoned for a year because of this piece.

The Loneliness of the Long-Distance Campaign

1   This essay was co-commissioned by the Walker Art Center for its Artist Op-Ed series and benefited from comments by Paul Schmelzer.

2   Hrag Vartanian, "Guggenheim Breaks Off Negotiations with Gulf Labor Over Migrant Rights," *Hyperallergic,* April 27, 2016: http://www .hyperallergic.com/291594/guggenheim-breaks-off-negotiations-with-gulf-labor-over-migrant-rights/.

3   Human Rights Watch. *The Island of Happiness: Exploitation of Migrant Workers on Saadiyat Island, Abu Dhabi* (New York: Human Rights Watch, 2009).

4   See the TDIC's page on worker welfare, which includes PwC's annual reports on TDIC's EPP: http://www.tdic.ae/TDIC/ourapproach/Pages/worker.aspx.

5   See GLC's April 2016 response to the 2015 PwC report: http://www .gulflabor.org/wp-content/uploads/2016/04/GLC-PWC-Report-Analysis-Version-2.pdf.

6   Hrag Vartanian, "Protest Action Erupts Inside Guggenheim Museum," *Hyperallergic*, February 23, 2014; Vartanian, "Protesters Stage Intervention at Guggenheim's Futurist Exhibition," *Hyperallergic*, May 25, 2014; Mostafa Heddaya, "Activists Picket Guggenheim Gala over Labor Abuses," *Hyperallergic*, November 7, 2014.

7   Andrew Ross, ed., *The Gulf: High Culture/Hard Labor* (New York/London: OR Books, 2015).

8   Reddy is an activist in South Asian New York circles, and author of *Nursing and Empire: Gendered Labor and Migration from India to the United States* (Chapel Hill, NC: University of North Carolina Press, 2015).

9   BP no longer sponsors the Tate, which Liberate Tate sees as a victory. However, neither the museum nor the company has attributed this decision to the protests.

10   GLC's comment on Guggenheim's silence since cancellation of talks: http://www.gulflabor.org/2016/guggenheim-silence/.

11   Ruchir Joshi, "A new satyagraha: In search of principles for contemporary non-violent struggles," *The Telegraph*, May 31, 2016: http://www .telegraphindia.com/1160531/jsp/opinion/story_88438.jsp# .WEWixKIrKi4.

12   Tony Chakar's Facebook feed.

13   Martha Rosler, "Why Are People Being So Nice?", *e-flux journal*, Journal #77, November 2016: http://www.e-flux.com/journal/77/ 76185/why-are-people-being-so-nice/.

Structures of Power and the Ethical Limits of Speech

1   Whether *Charlie Hebdo*'s humor was in fact offensive to Muslims living in France is a different discussion beyond the scope of this essay.

2   The focus of the article is the United States, though a similar situation can be identified in other developed liberal democracies. More repressive regimes present an entirely different picture.

3   The Catholic League often complains about art being "hate speech" against Catholics, as they did in 2010 with regard to *A Fire in My Belly*, a 1987 video by David Wojnarowicz, exhibited at the National Portrait Gallery; police officials claim that Black Lives Matter is spreading "hate speech" against police; anti-porn feminists argue that pornography constitutes "hate speech" against women; and so on.

4   "Decolonize Our Museums": http://www.decolonizeourmuseums .tumblr.com/.

5   Levi Rickert, "Students Playing Indian at Santa Barbara City College Causes Disgust," *Native News Online*, March 8, 2015: http://www .nativenewsonline.net/currents/students-playing-indian-at-santa- barbara-city-college-causes-disgust/.

6   See the comments to the SBCC Facebook page about the project: http://
     www.facebook.com/SantaBarbaraCityCollege/photos/a.1045851155
     89.126601.30620025589/10153064362265590/?type=1&theater.

7   See comments on Rickert, "Students Playing Indian at Santa Barbara
     City College Causes Disgust."

8   The hour-long conversation featured six speakers covering the
     appropriation of the cultures of specific groups. Some of them did
     reportedly mention free speech issues, but these were never the focus.

9   As evidenced by the profile and cover photo of the Twitter account—an
     image of Hattie McDaniel in her Oscar-winning role as Mammy in *Gone
     With the Wind* and a stereotypical black mammy image from the sheet
     music for the minstrel song "Jemima's Wedding Day," respectively—the
     project was unquestionably meant to be provocative, though in a much more
     complicated way than its detractors cared to acknowledge. Vanessa Place's
     statement of intent can be found here: http://www.genius.com/Vanessa-
     place-artists-statement-gone-with-the-wind-vanessaplace-annotated.

10   Evgeny Morozov, *The Net Delusion: The Dark Side of Internet
     Freedom* (New York: Public Affairs, 2011), 247.

11   Most attacks on artistic expression during the 1990s "culture
     wars" came from the religious right and targeted depictions of
     religious figures or of homosexuality, both of which were seen
     as offending religious beliefs. Most of the art world vigorously
     and vocally resisted those attempts at censorship.

12   2015–2016 has brought a number of cases in which historical murals
     and paintings, many of them commissioned by the Works Progress
     Administration (WPA) in the 1930s, were covered up, relocated, or
     entirely removed from college campuses and government buildings
     because of complaints about the pain and discomfort caused to Native
     Americans or African Americans by such reminders of their historical
     oppression. Some of the locations involved recently: Norwalk City
     Hall, CT; the Minnesota State Capitol; the University of Idaho; the
     University of Kentucky; and the University of Wisconsin-Stout.

By Colonial Design: Or, Why We Say We Don't Know Enough

1   Noam Chomsky, interview by Amy Goodman, *Democracy Now!*,
August 11, 2014: http://www.democracynow.org/2014/8/11/noam
_chomsky_on_bds_and_how. —Eds.

2   Elizabeth Redden, "BDS Movement Survives Challenge," *Inside Higher
Ed*, December 8, 2014: http://www.insidehighered.com/news/2014/12/08/
anthropologists-reject-resolution-opposing-academic-boycott-israel

3   Anthropologists for the Boycott of Israeli Institutions, "100 Days of Silence:
Why the Academic Boycott Is Still the Best Way for Anthropologists to
Support Justice in Palestine," October 2, 2016: https://anthroboycott
.wordpress.com/2016/10/02/100-days-of-silence-why-the-academic-boycott-
is-still-the-best-way-for-anthropologists-to-support-justice-in-palestine/

IV. Dis/engagement From Afar

The Distant Image

1   The full letter by Tan and Vidokle is published in Mostafa Heddaya,
"Istanbul Biennial Artists Plan 15-Minute 'Disruption,'" Artinfo.com,
September 1, 2015.

2   See Kaelen Wilson-Goldie, "Breaking the Waves,"
Artforum.com, September 7, 2015.

3   The artist-led protests during the Sydney Biennale led to the resignation
of Luca Belgiorno-Nettis, managing director of Transfield Holdings,
from the organization's board. The biennale also pledged to cut all
financial ties with the company. See "Sydney Biennale chairman
quits over company's links to detention centres," *The Guardian*,
March 7, 2014: http://www.theguardian.com/artanddesign/2014/
mar/07/sydney-biennale-chairman-quits-transfield-detention.

4   In an interview with Ben Davis, the collective stated they were subject
to multiple acts of "micro-aggression" by the institution, and particularly
curator Michelle Grabner, including failing to put up wall labels, not
including individual names in the collective in the exhibition catalogue,
moving screening times without notifying the artists, and failing to

respond to emails. See Ben Davis, "The Yams, On the Whitney and
White Supremacy," artnet news, May 30, 2014: https://news.artnet.com/
art-world/the-yams-on-the-whitney-and-white-supremacy-30364.

5   While the Whitney touted the 2014 biennial as "one of the broadest
and most diverse takes on art in the United States that the Whitney has
offered in many years," 77 percent of the exhibiting artists were white.
See Priscilla Frank, "What Does Diversity in the Art World Look
Like?", *Huffington Post*, November 18, 2013: http://www.huffingtonpost
.com/2013/11/16/whitney-biennial-2014_n_4283531.html.

6   Hailey Cunningham, "Backlash As Bronx Art Exhibition Sparks
Gentrification Fears," *New York Observer*, July 14, 2015.

7   Ben Davis, "Activism Pays Off, as Brooklyn Museum Embraces
Anti-Gentrification Forum," artnet.com, July 7, 2016.

8   For a summary of artistic activism and protest movements from
1965–1989, and an analysis of artists' political agency in the
contemporary global art world, see Gregory Sholette, "Art Out of
Joint: Artists' Activism Before and After the Cultural Turn," in
Andrew Ross, ed., *The Gulf: High Culture/Hard Labor* (New York/
London: OR Books, 2015), 64–85.

9   One notable exception is the curators of the 2014 São Paulo Biennial,
who publicly supported the artists' right to boycott sponsorship from
the Israeli consulate.

10   "Challenging Double Standards: A Call Against the Boycott of Israeli
Art and Society": http://www.cds-call.tumblr.com/.

11   Herbert Marcuse, *The Aesthetic Dimension: A Critique of Marxist Aesthetics*
(Boston: Beacon Press, 1978), xii.

12   Theodor Adorno, letter to Herbert Marcuse, June 19, 1969.

13   The recent warm reception of object-oriented ontology (or speculative
realism) in the art world points to a different, but just as activism-
averse, understanding of art: the idea that art has autonomous power
beyond its relationship to other objects, including humans. For an
introduction, see Graham Harman, "Art Without Relations," *ArtReview*,

September 2014. For a rebuttal of Harman's philosophy, see Andrew Cole, "Those Obscure Objects of Desire," *Artforum*, June 2015.

14 A more longstanding example may be the state of Israel's longstanding public relations strategy (*hasbara*).

15 Detailed accounts of the human rights violations and ongoing negotiations for better working conditions and compensation are available on Gulf Labor's website: gulflabor.org/.

16 Gulf Labor Artists Association Petition, March 16, 2011. Available on Gulf Labor's website: gulflabor.org/sign-the-petition/.

17 Richard Armstrong and Nancy Spector, "Guggenheim Responds to Proposed Artist Boycott," March 23, 2011: http://www.guggenheim .org/new-york/press-room/news/3971?utm_source=hootsuite&utm _medium=sm&utm_campaign=twitter.

18 "We believe that the Guggenheim Abu Dhabi will be a beacon for artistic free expression, which is critical to the work of all artists." Quoted in "Guggenheim's Richard Armstrong Responds to 'When Artspeak Masks Oppression'": http://www.hyperallergic.com, March 12, 2013.

19 Richard Armstrong, "Defending Plans for a Guggenheim Museum in Abu Dhabi," *New York Times*, June 4, 2015.

20 Quoted in Carol Vogel, "A New Art Capital, Finding Its Own Voice," *New York Times*, December 4, 2014.

21 Rosalind Krauss, "The Cultural Logic of the Late Capitalist Museum," *October* (Fall 1990): 13–17.

22 I am grateful to Benjamin Young for his insights in this paragraph.

23 Quoted in Mostafa Heddaya, "When Artspeak Masks Oppression": http://www.hyperallergic.com, March 6, 2013.

24 Ibid.

25 Quoted in "Richard Armstrong interview: Guggenheim's director on its projects in Helsinki, Abu Dhabi and back home in New York," *The Art Newspaper*, June 14, 2015: http://www.theartnewspaper.com/ news/museums/156208/.

26   This is the kind of thinking that led an *Artnews* critic, Walter
     Robinson, to describe the emergence of Gulf Labor as a "sudden and
     rather strange concern for low-paid workers in the Middle East."
     Walter Robinson, "Guggenheim: Protest Jeopardizes Abu Dhabi
     Project," March 24, 2011: http://www.artnet.com/magazineus/
     news/artnetnews/guggenheim-abu-dhabi-protest-3-24-11.asp.

27   Azoulay uses the phrase "the right not to be a perpetrator" to imagine an
     alternative political discourse for Israeli-Palestinian relations. See Ariella
     Azoulay, "Palestine as Symptom, Palestine as Hope: Revising Human
     Rights Discourse," *Critical Inquiry*, vol. 40, no. 4 (Summer 2014): 285–297.

28   Ibid.

52 Weeks, and Engaging by Disengaging

1   The following text was written in spring 2015 and first published in Andrew
     Ross, ed., *The Gulf: High Culture/Hard Labor* (New York/London: OR
     Books, 2015): 178–187. Reprinted by kind permission of the publisher.

Loose Connections

1   James C. Scott, *Weapons of the Weak: Everyday Forms of Peasant
     Resistance* (New Haven: Yale University Press, 1985).

2   McKenzie Wark, *Virtual Geography: Living with Global Media
     Events* (Bloomington: Indiana University Press, 1994). See also
     Wark's more recent book, *Telesthesia: Communication, Culture
     and Class* (Cambridge: Polity Press, 2012), in which he defines
     telesthesia by its capacity "to make what is distant a site of action."

3   Benedict Anderson, *Long-Distance Nationalism: World Capitalism and the
     Rise of Identity Politics* (Amsterdam: Centre for Asian Studies, 1992).

4   I owe this insight to Laura Liu, who astutely suggested that
     the appeal of "engagement" might lie in the way in which it
     calibrates the level of touch—neither too much nor too little.

5   Cindi Katz, "On the Grounds of Globalization: A Topography for
     Feminist Political Engagement," *Signs*, Vol. 26, No. 4 (2001): 1213–1234.

EDITOR BIOGRAPHIES

Kareem Estefan is an art critic, writer, editor, and PhD student in Brown University's Modern Culture and Media department, where he researches contemporary visual culture and the intersections of art, media, and politics, with a focus on the Middle East. His writing on contemporary art and cultural activism has appeared in publications including *Art in America*, *Art-Agenda*, *BOMB*, *The Brooklyn Rail*, *Frieze*, *Ibraaz*, the *Movement Research Performance Journal*, and *The New Inquiry*. From 2012–2015 Estefan was associate editor of *Creative Time Reports*, an online magazine of the New York–based public art nonprofit Creative Time that featured artists' perspectives on pressing political issues. Previously he worked as an editorial assistant at National Public Radio and the Creative Capital | Andy Warhol Foundation Arts Writers Grant Program. Estefan holds an MFA in Art Criticism and Writing from the School of Visual Arts and a BA in Comparative Literature from New York University.

Carin Kuoni is a curator and editor whose work examines how contemporary artistic practices reflect and inform social, political, and cultural conditions. She is the director and curator of The New School's Vera List Center for Art and Politics. Prior to joining The New School where she also teaches, she was director of exhibitions at Independent Curators International and director of The Swiss Institute, New York. A founding member of the artists' collective REPOhistory, Kuoni has curated and co-curated numerous transdisciplinary exhibitions, and edited and co-edited several books, among them *Energy Plan for the Western Man: Joseph Beuys in America*; *Words of Wisdom: A Curator's Vademecum*; and *Speculation, Now*; *Entry Points: The Vera List Center Field Guide on Art and Social Justice*. She is the recipient of a 2014 Andy Warhol Foundation Curatorial Fellowship, directed SITAC XII: *Arte, justamente* in Mexico City in 2015, and is a Travel Companion for the 57th Carnegie International in 2018.

Laura Raicovich is president and executive director of the Queens Museum. She is a champion of socially engaged art practices that address the most pressing social, political, and ecological issues of our times, and has defined her career with artist-driven projects and programs. Recent projects at the Queens Museum include *Mierle Laderman Ukeles: Maintenance Art*; *William Gropper: Bearing Witness*; *Mickalene Thomas: Untitled*; *Mariam Ghani: Garden of Forked Tongues*; *Duke Riley: That's What She Said*; *Hey! Ho! Let's Go: Ramones and the Birth of Punk*; as well as a series of programs designed with Rebecca Solnit and Joshua Jelly-Shapiro to launch their *Nonstop Metropolis: A New York City Atlas*. Prior to the Queens Museum, Raicovich launched Creative Time's Global Initiatives, expanding the institution's international reach. Raicovich came to Creative Time following a decade at Dia Art Foundation, where she served as deputy director. Previously she worked at the Solomon R. Guggenheim Museum, Public Art Fund, and New York City's Parks Department. She graduated from Swarthmore College and holds a Master's Degree in Liberal Studies from the Graduate Center at the City University of New York. She lectures internationally, has contributed regularly to *The Brooklyn Rail*, and is the author of *A Diary of Mysterious Difficulties* (Publication Studio, 2014) and *At the Lightning Field* (Coffee House Press, 2017).

VERA LIST CENTER FOR ART AND POLITICS

Assuming Boycott: Resistance, Agency, and Cultural Production was the title of a series of public research seminars, presented by the Vera List Center for Art and Politics at The New School in 2014 and 2015, curated by Carin Kuoni and Laura Raicovich. They were the incubator for this book, and several seminar participants are included herein.

Established at The New School in 1992 at the height of the culture wars, the Vera List Center for Art and Politics is a public forum for art, culture, and politics. A pioneer in the field, the center serves a critical mission: to foster a vibrant and diverse community of artists, scholars, and policy makers who take creative, intellectual, and political risks to bring about positive change.

The center champions the arts as expressions of the political moments from which they emerge, and considers the intersection between art and politics the space where new forms of civic engagement must be developed. It is the only university-based institution committed exclusively to leading public research on this intersection. Through public programs and classes, prizes and fellowships, publications and exhibitions that probe some of the pressing issues of our time, we curate and support new roles for the arts and artists in advancing social justice.

The activities of the Vera List Center coalesce around a two-year curatorial focus theme. Called for its urgency and broad resonance, each theme informs timely and expansive investigations across a variety of initiatives. From 2013 to 2015, the center embarked on an extended investigation of Alignment, defined as the "proper or desirable relation of components." *Assuming Boycott: Resistance, Agency, and Cultural Production* was part of the Alignment cycle. Other themes were *Homeland* (2004–2005), acknowledging the profound paradigm shifts in a post-9/11 world; *Considering Forgiveness* (2005–2006), encompassing new transitional justice systems; *The Public Domain*, regarding the explosion of social media (2006–2007); followed by *Speculating on Change* (2009–2011), which responded to Obama's call for change; and *Thingness* (2011–2013) looked at the entanglement of living and non-living matter in the Anthropocene.

Assuming Boycott, Resistance, Agency, and Cultural Production is the Vera List Center's fourth book, following *Entry Points: The Vera List Center Field Guide on Art and Social Justice, No. 1* (Duke University Press, 2016), *Speculation, Now* (Duke University Press, 2014), and *Considering Forgiveness* (Vera List Center for Art and Politics, 2009). Each book is edited by a small collaborative team of scholars and artists that conceives of the format, structure, and content of the book, selects the contributors and, in turn, brings to the book their visual and academic expertise. This interdisciplinary approach acknowledges recent developments in artistic and cultural practices and reflects The New School's own commitment to merging theory and practice.

Assuming Boycott

The Vera List Center Advisory Committee

Assuming Boycott: Resistance, Agency and Cultural Production has benefitted from the council and support of the Vera List Center's Advisory Committee.

James-Keith Brown, chair
Carlos Basualdo
Sunny Bates
Frances Beatty
Michelle Coffey
Gabriella De Ferrari
Ronald Feldman
Andrew Francis
Marilyn Greene
Ken Grossinger and Micheline Klagsbrun
Elizabeth R. Hilpman
Nicole Klagsbrun
Norman L. Kleeblatt
Prem Krishnamurthy
Carin Kuoni, director/curator, Vera List Center for Art and Politics
Thomas J. Lax
Jane Lombard
Joshua Mack
Lydia Matthews
Susan Meiselas
Sina Najafi
Megan E. Noh
Mendi and Keith Obadike
Nancy Delman Portnoy
Martha Rosler
Ingrid Schaffner
Mary Watson, executive dean, The Schools of Public Engagement, The New School

INDEX

Index

Index

Index

Index

O/R C

AVAILABLE AT GOOD BOOKSTORES EVERYWHERE
FROM OR BOOKS/COUNTERPOINT PRESS

Beautiful Trouble
A Toolbox for Revolution
ASSEMBLED BY ANDREW BOYD
WITH DAVE OSWALD MITCHELL

Desperately Seeking Self-Improvement
A Year Inside the Optimization
Movement
CARL CEDERSTRÖM AND ANDRÉ
SPICER

Bowie
SIMON CRITCHLEY

Extinction
A Radical History
ASHLEY DAWSON

Black Ops Advertising
Native Ads, Content Marketing, and the
Covert World of the Digital Sell
MARA EINSTEIN

Assuming Boycott
Resistance, Agency, and Cultural
Production
EDITED BY KAREEM ESTEFAN, CARIN
KUONI, AND LAURA RAICOVICH

Folding the Red into the Black
or Developing a Viable Untopia for
Human Survival in the 21st Century
WALTER MOSLEY

Inferno
(A Poet's Novel)
EILEEN MYLES

With Ash on Their Faces
Yezidi Women and the Islamic State
CATHY OTTEN

Pocket Piketty
A Handy Guide to *Capital in the Twenty-first Century*
JESPER ROINE

Ours to Hack and to Own
The Rise of Platform Cooperativism, A
New Vision for the Future of Work and a
Fairer Internet
EDITED BY TREBOR SCHOLZ AND
NATHAN SCHNEIDER

What's Yours Is Mine
Against the Sharing Economy
TOM SLEE

Distributed to the trade by Publishers Group West